SAINTE-BEUVE'S PORTRAITS
OF MEN

1848

PORTRAITS OF MEN

BY CHARLES A. SAINTE-BEUVE

TRANSLATED BY

FORSYTH EDEVEAIN

WITH CRITICAL MEMOIR BY

WILLIAM SHARP

Essay Index Reprint Series

BOOKS FOR LIBRARIES PRESS
FREEPORT, NEW YORK

First Published 1891
Reprinted 1972

Library of Congress Cataloging in Publication Data

Sainte-Beuve, Charles Augustin, 1804-1869.
    Portraits of men.

    (Essay index reprint series)
    Reprint of the 1891 ed.
    CONTENTS: Goethe and Bettina, 1850.--Alfred de
Musset, 1857.--Letters of Lord Chesterfield to his son,
1850. [etc.]
    1. Authors--Biography.   I.   Title.
PN457.S213   1972   809   72-4650
ISBN 0-8369-2972-1·

CONTENTS.

———◆———

CRITICAL MEMOIR.

——o——

AMONG the innumerable apt sentences with one of which an essay upon Sainte - Beuve, the sovereign critic, might fittingly be introduced, I doubt if there be any better than this : " I have but one diversion, one pursuit : I analyze, I botanize, I am a naturalist of minds. What I would fain create is Literary Natural History." He was, and is, unquestionably the foremost " naturaliste des esprits : " in literary natural history he is at once the Buffon and Humboldt, the Linnæus and Cuvier, the Darwin even, of scientific criticism. It is conceivable that the future historian of our age will allot to Sainte-Beuve a place higher even than that which he holds by common consent of his cultured countrymen, even than that claimed for him by one or two of our own ablest critics, Matthew Arnold, in particular, and Mr. John Morley. He was not a great inventor, a new creative force, it is true ; but he was, so to say, one of the foremost practical engineers in literature, — he altered the course of the alien stream of criticism, compelled its waters to be tributary to the main river, and gave it a new impetus, an irresistible energy, a fresh and vital importance.

I.

During the ten or twelve years in which I have been a systematic reader of Sainte-Beuve, I have often wondered if his literary career would have been a very different one from what we know it, if he had been born ere the parental tides of life were already on the ebb. Students of physiology are

well aware of the fact that children born of parents beyond
the prime of life are, in the first degree, inferior in physique
to those born, say, to a father of thirty years of age and to
a mother five-and-twenty years old; and, in the second
degree, that the children of parents married after the prime
of life, are, as a rule, less emotional than those born of a
union in the more ardent and excitable years of youth. The
present writer admits that he is one of the seemingly very
few who regard the greatest of literary critics as also a true
poet,—not a great, not even an important, but at least a
genuine poet, whose radical shortcoming was the tendency
to produce beautiful verse rather than poetry, but the best
of whose metrical writings may confidently be compared
with those of any of the notable contemporary lesser poets
of France. And it is because in the "Life, Poems, and
Thoughts of Joseph Delorme," in "Les Consolations," in
the "Pensées d'Août," I for one find so much which is
praiseworthy, which is excellent even, that I have often
wondered if, his natal circumstances having been other
than they were, the author who has become so celebrated
for his inimitable *Causeries du Lundi* might have become
famous as a poet. That the keen subjectivity of emotion
which is at the base of the poetic nature was his may be
inferred from a hundred hints throughout his writings: he
was very far from being, what some one has called him,
a "mere bloodless critic, serenely impartial because of his
imperturbable pulse." To cite a single example: in one of
his "Notes et Remarques," printed in M. Pierrot's appendical volume (Tome xvime.) to the collected *Causeries
du Lundi*, he says, *a propos* of his novel "Volupte,"
"Why do I not write another novel? To write a romance
was for me but another, an indirect way of being in love, and
to say so." It was not "a mere bloodless critic" who penned
that remark. But, withal, in his poetry, in his essays, in
his critiques, in the episodes of his long and intellectually
active life, it is obvious to the discerning reader that
Sainte-Beuve rarely attained to the white-heat of emotion
for any length of time: that a cold wave of serene judg-

ment of *ennui* often enough, speedily dissipated the intoxication of spiritual ardour. But in those white-heat moment he touches so fine a note, reaches so high a level, that one realizes the poet within him is not buried so deep below his ordinary self as the common judgment would have us believe. Had Mlle. Augustine Coilliot not been past forty when she gave her hand to the cultivated, respected M. de Sainte-Beuve, Commissioner of Taxes at Boulogne-sur-mer, and had he, then in his fifty-second year, been more robust in health (he died à few months after his marriage), their child might have inherited just that impulse of passionate life, to the absence of which perhaps we owe the critic at the expense of the poet. But the century has been rich in poetic literature, while there have been few eminent critics,—till Sainte-Beuve no French critic, great by virtue of the art of criticism alone. It is only since the advent of Sainte-Beuve, indeed, that criticism has come to be accepted as an art, that is in France; for, among us, criticism, as distinct from conventional book-reviewing, can at most be said just to exist.

The Mlle. Augustine Coilliot referred to was the daughter of a Boulogne sailor who had married an Englishwoman, and the writers of biographical articles have been fond of tracing to this Anglo-Saxon strain the great critic's strong predilection for English poetry. It may, however, be doubted if the fact that his grandmother was English had much to do with Sainte-Beuve's love of Wordsworth, Coleridge, Southey, and Cowper. Earnestness, austerity even, always deeply appealed to him; he loved Pascal and Bossuet better than Villon or the Abbé Galiani; and this love would in any case have led him to the British poets who are pre-eminently the exponents of earnest reflection upon human life. Besides this, Sainte-Beuve the elder was a man of culture, of a serious bias of mind, an admirer of Shakespeare in the original, and probably, therefore, of other English authors; and again, Boulogne, even at the beginning of the century, was much frequented by visitors from the other side of the Channel, and its

schools contained many young Anglo-Saxons sent thither
to learn French.   Only once, so far as I can recollect, and
that incidentally, does he allude to the strain of English
blood in him, though with the non-existence of any service-
able index to his voluminous writings it is impossible to
make any such assertion with assurance.   The absence of
allusion would, with so scrupulous a literary analyst as
Sainte-Beuve, indicate that he laid no stress whatever upon
the circumstance.

Mlle. Coilliot was of an old bourgeois family which,
though it held a reputable position in the lower town, was
accustomed to straits of poverty.   She had not even the
smallest dowry to bring to the man who married her,
and this was one reason why M. Sainte-Beuve (*de Sainte-
Beuve*, he maintained, though his son discarded the aristocratic prefix, partly from a conviction that the family had
no right to it, partly from republican scruple) postponed
marriage for a goodly space of time after he had won
the already middle-aged Augustine's consent to a betrothal.
He himself was also a native of Picardy, having been born
at Moreuil : a person, indubitably, of exceptional culture,
genial, sympathetic, a student, a man of the world.   Sainte-
Beuve was convinced that he owed his most distinctive
traits not to his mother but to his father, though, as a
posthumous child, the sole intellectual communion with
the latter which he enjoyed was through the discriminative
and suggestive annotations which the " Commissioner " was
wont to make upon the margins of many of the books in
his well-selected library.   A few months (not a few weeks,
as sometimes affirmed) after his marriage, M. Sainte-
Beuve died suddenly ; and within three months from that
event, that is on December 23rd, 1804, his wife gave birth
to a son, who, in remembrance of both his parents, was
christened Charles Augustin.   In the invaluable autobiographical fragment which was found among his papers
on the morrow of his death, Sainte-Beuve states that he
was brought up by his widowed mother, who had been left
with sadly straitened means yet not in extreme poverty,

and by a sister of his father, who united her slender income
to that of Mme. Sainte-Beuve, and so enabled the small
family of three to live in comparative comfort. The boy
was carefully educated at the lay school of a M. Blériot,
and was particularly well grounded in Latin. His intellectual development was rapid. He had scarcely entered
upon his teens before he had become a student, and his
mother, sympathetic and intelligent if not actively intellectual, gave him every encouragement. It was at this
time that he read many of the books which bore his
father's marginalia ; and no doubt the mere circumstance
of annotation impressed him with the importance of the
subject-matter. Some ten years or so later he alluded, in
one of his poems, to his father and his indirect influence
upon him :—

> " Mon père ainsi sentait. Si, né dans sa mort même,
> Ma mémoire n'eut pas son image suprême,
> Il m'a laissé du moins son âme et son esprit,
> Et son goût tout entier à chaque marge écrit."

What is even more noteworthy is his consciousness of his
educational shortcomings when, in his fourteenth year, he
realised that he was not likely to learn anything more at
M. Blériot's school. "I felt strongly how much I lacked :"
and in this persuasion he urged his mother to take, or send,
him to Paris. It was not an easy thing for the widow to
do, but she managed to send him to the capital (September
1818), and to arrange for his board with a M. Landry, a
man of some note, who had formerly been a professor at
the College of Louis-le-Grand, and was a mathematician
and philosopher. At the house in the Rue de la Cerisail
of this *esprit libre*, this free-thinker, as Sainte-Beuve calls
him, the young scholar met several men of high standing
in the world of letters, among them certain eminent
students of science. He seems to have been noticed by
them, though he did not quite relish being treated as a
hobbledehoy, "as a big boy, as a little man." He was an
instinctive student : to learn was as natural to him as to play
is easy for most boys, and yet he does not seem to have been

devoid of the gaiety and even *abandon* of youth. At the College of Charlemagne, at the end of the first year of his attendance, he took part in the general competition, and succeeded in carrying off the highest prize for history; and in the following year, at the Bourbon College, he gained the prize for Latin verse, and had the further distinction of a Governmental award, in the form of a medal, as a special recognition of his scholarly achievements. One of his school friends, Charles Potier, the son of the eminent actor, and himself afterwards successful on the stage, has put on record his recollection of how he and Sainte-Beuve acted the familiar old parts of the clever and the stupid boy; — how while he dug or hoed the garden-plot which had been allotted to them, the other Charles sat idly by, obliviously engaged in some book or indolently abstracted; and how, in return, he was helped by his friend in the uncongenial task of class-exercises. Sainte-Beuve was free to spend his evenings as he chose, and he voluntarily studied medical science, at first with the full intention of becoming a physician, later with the idea of making the philosophical study of physiology and chemistry his speci- alities, and, finally, simply for the value of the training and its bearing upon that new science of literature which he was one of the earliest to apprehend as a complex unity. The lectures of Messieurs Magendie, Robiquet, and Blain- ville, respectively upon physiology, chemistry, and natural history, interested him profoundly. "I went every evening to these lectures at the *Athénée*, off the Palais Royal, from seven to ten o'clock," he says in his autobiographical fragment, "and also to some literary lectures." It was natural that this preoccupation with strictly scientific study should bias his mind to the materialistic school of thought; and one is not surprised to learn, on the authority of D'Haussonville, his biographer, that in his own judgment he had reached his true ground, "mon fonds véritable," in the most pronounced eighteenth-century materialism. It is, however, interesting and suggestive to note that even at that time Sainte-Beuve was dominated by his exceptional

mental receptivity ; that he was swayed this way and that by
the intellectual duality which has puzzled so many of his
readers. Daunou and Lamarck were his prophets ; by them
he swore, their words contained the authentic gospel; but
the same week, perhaps, as that in which he proclaimed his
enfranchisement from the most abstract Deism, he would
announce his conviction that a Supreme Power controlled
the tides of life,—as when he wrote to his friend, afterwards
the Abbé Barbe, distinctly asserting his recognition of God
as "the source of all things." The mystic in him was always
side by side with the physiologist, the unflinching analyst,
just as the poet was ever comrade to the critic. It is to
this, indeed, that Sainte-Beuve owes his pre-eminence, to
this that is to be traced the fundamental secret of his spell.
In later life he was fully conscious of his indebtedness to
those early medical and scientific studies ; and many will
call to mind his famous defence of the Faculty, in the
Senate of the Second Empire, when an attempt was made
to limit the medical professors in Governmental institutions in the free expression of their views. The very
least he could do, he declared, was to give his testimony
in favour of that Faculty to which he owed the philosophical spirit, the love of exactitude and of physiological reality, and "such good method as may have
entered into my writings." As a matter of fact, his early
scientific training was of the highest value. It is possible
that, with his strong religious bias, if he had been educated
at an ecclesiastical seminary he would have become one of
the great company led by Pascal and Bossuet, a spiritual
comrade of his contemporaries Lamennais and Lacordaire ;
that, but for his liaison with radical materialism, the Art,
the Science of Criticism, would have remained half-formless
and indeterminate, and waited long for its first great master.

His several scientific excursions led to his following
the regular course in the study of medicine ; and, with the
goal of a medical career in view, he was an assiduous
student till 1827, when he was in his twenty-third year.
At that date an event occurred which determined his

particular line of energy.   But before this he had already
begun to write.   These tentative efforts, in verse and prose,
conventional though they were, encouraged him to believe
that he had the literary faculty, though even then his sense
of style was so developed that he realized how wide was the
gulf between mere facility and a vital dominating impulse.
His mother, who had come from Boulogne to watch over
her son, saw these literary indications with an annoyance
which grew into alarm ; for at that time the literary career
was rarely a remunerative one, and, moreover, her heart
was set upon her son's success as a physician or collegiate
professor of medicine.   It was not, as a matter of fact, till
his election to the Academy, that she admitted the wisdom
of his early decision ; and even then she complained, and
not without justice, of the terrible wear and tear of an
unceasingly active literary life.   Mme. Sainte-Beuve, who
lived with her son till her death at the goodly age of eighty-
six, seems to have been an intelligent and sympathetic
rather than an intellectually clever woman ; and though her
always affectionate Charles loved and admired her, it would
not appear that he enjoyed with her any rare mental communion.

The youth who at the College of Charlemagne had gained
the History prize attracted the particular attention of his
professor, M. Dubois.   A friendship, as intimate as practicable in the circumstances, ensued ; and when, in 1824, M.
Dubois founded the *Globe*, the journal which ere long became
so famous and so influential both in politics and literature,
he asked Sainte - Beuve to join the staff as an occasional
contributor.   This was a remarkable compliment, for the
young student was quite unknown, and had done nothing
to warrant such an honour ; so it is clear that M. Dubois
must have had a strong opinion as to the young man's
capabilities.   Sainte - Beuve was all the more gratified
because the staff of writers who had promised their practical
support comprised men so famous as Guizot and Victor
Cousin, Jouffroy, Ampère, Mérimée, De Broglie, and Villemain.   It was not long before the *Globe* became a power in

Paris, and thereafter throughout France and northern Europe : even the great Goethe read it regularly, and alluded to it in terms of cordial praise. It was regarded as the organ of the principal exponents of that earlier Romantic movement which made the latter years of the Restoration so brilliant, and worked like powerful yeast through contemporary thought and literature. Politically, it was the mouthpiece of those who were characterised as *les Doctrinaires.* Naturally the young medical student, who had scarce unsheathed his virginal literary sword, was not among the first contributors. When M. Dubois did entrust to him several short reviews, he did not allow these to appear without, on his own part, scrupulous revision. They did not attract any particular notice : few were curious as to the personality of the critic whose articles appeared above the initials "S.B." But the editor soon discovered that his youngest contributor was quite able to stand alone so far as literary craftsmanship was concerned. One day he delighted the novice by saying to him, "*Now* you know how to write ; henceforth you can go alone." Confidence helped style, and Parisian men of letters read with appreciative interest the new recruit's articles on Thiers' "Histoire de la Révolution" and Mignet's "Tableau" of the same epoch. He may be said to have definitively gained his place as a recognised literary critic by the time that he had published his able and scholarly review of Alfred de Vigny's "Cinq Mars." It was still before he had finally given up a medical career that, by means of a review, he formed a new acquaintanceship which was to prove of great importance to him, and not only as a man of letters. One morning, late in 1826, he chanced to call upon M. Dubois, who was engaged in turning over the pages of two volumes of "Odes and Ballads," which he had just received. The editor of the *Globe* asked Sainte-Beuve to review them, having first explained that they were by an acquaintance of his, "a young barbarian of talent," interesting on account of his forceful character and the incidents of his life—Victor Hugo. The volumes were duly

carried off, read, re-read, and reviewed. When the critic
took his MS. to his editor he told the latter that this
Victor Hugo was not such a barbarian after all, but a man
of genius. The review appeared in the issue of the *Globe*
for the 2nd of January 1827 ; and it is interesting to know
that among the earliest foreign readers of it was Goethe,
who on the 4th expressed to Eckermann his appreciation of
Hugo, and his belief that the young poet's fortunes were
assured since he had the *Globe* on his side. And of course
the author of " Odes et Ballades " was delighted. He called
upon M. Dubois, enthusiastically expressed his gratification,
maugre the few strictures upon his poetic and metrical
extravagances which the article contained, and begged for
the address of the writer, which to his surprise he ascertained to be in the same street as that wherein he and
his beautiful wife Adèle had their apartments. The latter
were at No. 11 Rue Notre Dame des Champs, while Sainte-
Beuve and his mother resided in simpler and much smaller
rooms on the fourth floor at No. 19. The critic was out
when the poet called, but a return visit was speedily made.
No doubt Sainte-Beuve was not the man to regret any useful experience, and yet one may question, from knowledge
of the man in his later years, if, could he have relived and
at the same time refashioned the drift of his life, he would
have made that eventful call. From it, indirectly, arose
his "one critical crime," that of wilful blindness to shortcomings because of the influence of a personal charm ; and
to it, also, was due the "romantic" prose and poetry of the
morbid and supersensitive Joseph Delorme. Poetically, in
a word, he would not have had what he calls somewhere
his " liaison avec l'école poétique de Victor Hugo." On the
other hand, he owed much to his intimacy with the Hugos
and their circle, which at that time comprised Alfred de
Vigny, Lamartine, Musset, and other ardent representatives
of *Jeune France.* The recollection of his critical reception
of Alfred de Musset was always, in late years, one of Sainte-
Beuve's thorns in the flesh. But the accusation which has
been made, that he was chagrined by the poet's manner to

him when they first met, and that the critic allowed his personal resentment to bias his judgment, is ridiculous. I was surprised to see something to this effect in some recent critical volume. Surely the writer must, for one thing, have forgotten that passage in "Ma Biographie" (*Nouveaux Lundis*, Tome xiii,) where the author expressly recounts the circumstances.*

Sainte-Beuve was impressed by Victor Hugo's genius and captivated by his personal charm; and, at the same time, he was fascinated by Madame Hugo. He became an intimate friend; visited No. 11 whensoever he willed; saw the poet at least twice daily; praised, admired, wrote about the beautiful Adele—and, indeed, became so enthusiastically friendly that the brilliant group which formed *Le Cenacle* (the Guest-Chamber), a club of kindred spirits in the several arts, must have thought that their latest recruit was qualifying to be the prophet of woman's supremacy in all things. As a matter of fact, the Hugo circle was not fettered by severe social conventionalities; yet even the self-confident Victor made objections when he found his numerous friends, from the polished Alfred de Vigny and the sentimental Lamartine to "Musset l'Ennuyé" and the brilliant light-hearted essayist, whom Monselet

* "Quelques biographes veulent bien ajouter que c'est alors que je fus *présenté* à Alfred de Musset. Ces messieurs n'ont aucune idée des dates. Musset avait alors à peine dix-huit ans. Je le rencontrai un soir chez Hugo, car les familles se connaissaient; mais on ignorait chez Hugo que Musset fit des vers. C'est ce lendemain matin, après cette soirée, que Musset vint frapper à ma porte. Il me dit en entrant: vous avez hier récité des vers; eh bien, j'en fais et je viens vous les lire. Il m'en récita de charmants, un peu dans le goût d'André Chénier. Je m'empressai de faire part à Hugo de cette heureuse recrue poétique. On lui demanda désormais des vers à lui-même, et c'est alors que nous lui vîmes faire ses charmantes pièces de *l'Andalouse* et du Départ pour la chasse (*le Lever*)." After this explicit statement that at the Hugo's no one knew that the youthful Musset wrote verse; that the latter sought out the critic, read him some of his poems, which his courteous auditor found charming; and that Sainte-Beuve made haste to announce to Hugo that a promising poetic recruit had come to the fore;—after this, it is absurd to allude to Sainte-Beuve as prejudiced against Musset from the first on account of pique.

afterwards with so much justice called "the smiling critic" (*le critique souriant*), addressing his wife as Adèle, as freely as they called each other Alfred or Victor or Charles, as frequently as they applied one to the other the term "master." In France every writer is called *cher maître* by some other author. As for Sainte-Beuve, his complaint was so severe that, though he laughed at it afterwards as a flirtation with Romanticism, it might best be called *Adelaïsme*. This one-sided passion was no doubt the mainspring of the sufferings, thoughts, and poesies of the melancholy Joseph Delorme, that Gallic counterpart of the much more unendurable Werther. True, something of Sainte-Beuve's deeper melancholy of "seriousness" may have been due to his remote English strain, and his splenetic temperament to the fact that his mother passed several dolorous months between his birth and the death of her husband. It seems strange that so acute a critic of literary physiology should not have seen that his "spleen" was due more to want of outdoor life and to incessant mental preoccupation, and (in the "Joseph Delorme" period) to what I have in persiflage called *Adelaïsme*, than to the circumstance of his mother having borne him during months of widowhood, or to that of his grandmother having been an Englishwoman. Although he was never married, Sainte-Beuve was of a susceptible nature. There is absolutely no warrant for the belief that he was so deeply in love with Adèle Hugo that his whole life was affected by the blight of unrequited affection. On the contrary, if he was the *critique souriant* in the world of literature, he was the *critique gai* in the affairs of life.

For a time everything prospered with *Le Cénacle*. Then one member and then another grew lukewarm or directly seceded. Sainte-Beuve slowly diverged from the views he had allowed himself to expound, overborne as he had been by the charm of Victor and the fascination of Madame Hugo. The already famous poet does not seem to have had any particularly high appreciation of his critical friend as a

man of letters ; indeed, Sainte-Beuve was commonly regarded as nothing more than, at most, a conscientious and
able critic, with genuine enough but mediocre original
powers. In the first flush of intimacy, however, Hugo was
as immoderate in his praise of his new acquaintance as
was his wont in the matter of superlatives.* But when the
"eagle," the "royal meteor," ceased from the making of
critical honey, when, in giving a present of a book, he no
more inscribed above his signature on the flyleaf such
pleasant phrases as, "To the greatest lyrical inventor
French poetry has known since Ronsard"—but, instead,
uttered such words as "theatricality," "violence,"
"eccentricity," then there was a cooling of enthusiasm.

But about this time, and indirectly owing to the Hugo
connection, two important things happened. A journalistic, a literary career was opened to Sainte-Beuve. He at
once availed himself of the chance : so eager was he, indeed,
that he left his surgeon's case at St. Louis' Hospital, where
he had been a day-pupil, and it is said that he never went
back for it. His vocation was in the art of literature, not
in the science of medicine. As soon as he realised this,
and saw his way to a possibility of living by the pen, he
not only busied himself as a journalist, but prepared to
undertake an ambitious literary task, a work of real magnitude. Probably if it had not been for Victor Hugo and
Sainte-Beuve's ardent if transient romanticism, the admirable studies on "The French Poetry of the Sixteenth
Century" would not have been written—then, at any rate,

* In Mr. Frank T. Marzials' admirable "Life of Victor Hugo"
there is the following allusion to Sainte-Beuve : "There is one of
[Hugo's] odes, written in December 1827, and inscribed 'To my friend,
S.B.,' in which he addresses that young gentleman as an 'eagle,' a
'giant,' a 'star,' and exhorts him to make the acquaintance of light-
ning, and to roll through the realms of thought like a 'royal meteor'
with trailing locks. We, who chiefly know a later Sainte-Beuve, can
scarcely recognise him in the character of a [poetic] comet ; and, even
then, he himself . . . must sometimes have smiled at these grandiose
epithets. Sitting somewhat apart in the shadow, and rhyming a
sonnet to a white cap, or an eye of jet—this is how he lives in Alfred
de Musset's reminiscences, and I take it the sketch is truer to nature."

and in the form in which we know them. The critic had
been impressed by the enthusiasm of Hugo and his circle
for the early poets. He read, studied, and came to the
conclusion that these were unworthily neglected. He discerned in them, moreover, the poetic ancestors of the
enthusiastic members of *Le Cénacle:* both were uncon-
ventional, individual, comparatively simple. The series of
studies which, as the result, appeared in the *Globe,*
delighted the writer's friends and attracted no little share
of literary attention ; but it was not till the publication
of them collectively in book form that Sainte-Beuve's name
became widely known as that of a scholarly and above
all an independent critic. It was the prevalent literary
vogue to decry the pre-classicists, or, at least, to affirm that
there was little of abiding worth prior to Molière, Racine,
and Corneille. By insight, critical acumen, felicitous
quotation, and a light and graceful while incisive style
(not, however, characterised by the limpid delicacy and
suppleness of his best manner, as in the *Causeries du
Lundi*), he won many admirers and did good service to
literature, and particularly to literary criticism.

From this time forward Sainte-Beuve's career was a
prosperous one, chequered now and again indeed, but in
the main happy and marvellously fruitful. For some years
he dreamed of poetic fame ; gradually he realized that his
well-loved "Life, Poetry, and Thoughts of Joseph Delorme,"
his "Consolations," and his "August Thoughts" would
never appeal to a public outside the literary world of Paris,
and even there that they were assured of mere respect at
most ; and finally, he became convinced that it was neither
as poet nor as novelist, but as critic, that he was to win the
laurels of fame. To the last, however, he had a tender
feeling for his poetic performances, and there was no surer
way to his good graces than admiration of his poems. The
most unsympathetic critic cannot regret Sainte - Beuve's
having devoted so much time and so many hopes to those
springtide blossoms of a summer that never came. At the
least, they helped their author to a wide sympathy, to a

deep insight, to that catholicity of taste which enabled him
not only to enjoy for himself, but to interpret for others, the
essential merits of a great number of poets,—writers so
absolutely distinct as Virgil and Victor Hugo, Villon and
William Cowper, Dante and Firdausi, Theocritus and
Molière, Ronsard and Racine, and so forth.

When Dr. Véron founded in 1829 the *Revue de Paris*,
the predecessor of the more famous *Revue des Deux
Mondes*, he made haste to enrol Sainte-Beuve among his
contributors. He thought it possible that the poet might
make a great name, but he was quite convinced that the
critic would become a prince of his tribe. The result of his
trust was more than satisfactory. Although Sainte-Beuve
was only five or six and twenty when he wrote his articles
on Boileau, Racine, La Fontaine, Rousseau, André Chenier,
and others, how admirable they are, and how well worth
perusal even at the present date. In style, it is true,
they are graceful and scholarly rather than winsome with
individual charm, for the latter does not become a
characteristic of his work till he has reached the noon of
his maturity ; but, even with this qualification, they are
unquestionably delightful reading.

In the summer of 1830 Sainte-Beuve was in Normandy,
at Honfleur, on a visit to his friend Ulric Guttinguer, when
the July Revolution overthrew many institutions besides
that of the old monarchy. With the advent of Louis
Philippe arose schism among the brilliant staff of the
Globe. Some maintained that the hour had come in
which to cry "Halt" to further innovations ; one or two
wavered and talked of compromise ; the more strenuous
affirmed that there was as pressing need of progress as ever.
Among the progressists was Sainte-Beuve, who had hurried
back to Paris. The *Globe* became the organ of the Saint-
Simonians ; and though Sainte-Beuve never identified himself with the school of Saint-Simon, he fought valiantly as
a free-lance by the side of its exponents. But, before this
change in the destiny of the paper (for, after the split, it
abruptly lost its place in the van of Parisian journals, and

was sold at a loss to a sanguine experimentalist, who in turn speedily disposed of it to the Saint-Simonians), a tragi-comedy, in which Sainte-Beuve and his former good friend M. Dubois were the chief actors, occurred. The clash of opinions at the editorial office begat heated discussions, reproaches, taunts even. Dubois reminded Sainte-Beuve, in not very complimentary terms, of how he had given him a lift into the literary world : the critic made a scathing reply. The blood of all the Dubois boiled in the veins of the worthy editor, and he challenged Sainte-Beuve to mortal combat. So high did feeling run that the matter was really a serious one ; though we may hesitate to accept the great critic's after-statement, that he went to the duel with the full intention of killing his adversary. It was the Joseph Delorme lying latent in Charles Augustin Sainte-Beuve who made this affirmation. The preliminaries of the duel were arranged with all circumspection ; both antagonists made their wills and felt alternately heroic and despondent; and at last the hour came. It was a chill and wretched morning, for the rain came down in a steady pour. What was the astonishment of M. Dubois and the seconds of both principals to see Sainte-Beuve take up his position with his pistol in his right hand and his unfolded umbrella upheld by his left. To the remonstrances of the seconds, he protested that he was willing to be shot, if need be— but to be drenched, no ! (*Je veux bien être tué ; mais mouillé, non.*) Four shots were exchanged, and editor and critic remained unhurt. Neither their ill-success nor the rain damped their bloodthirstiness, however, and if it had not been for the firm remonstrances of the seconds, who declared that the demands of honour had been amply satisfied, one or other of the combatants would have suffered for his folly. Happily, this was Sainte-Beuve's sole martial experience. As one of his detractors long afterwards maliciously remarked, thenceforth he confined himself to stabbing with the pen, and to destroying literary reputations by a *causerie*.

Sainte-Beuve's renewed connection with the *Globe* was not

of long duration, however. He had no interest but one of curiosity in the doctrines of the St. Simonians : neither more nor less than he, pre-eminently the hedonist of modern literature, felt in those of the enthusiasts who were bent upon reconciling democratic and radical politics with the most conservative Roman Catholicism. Although he knew and admired Lacordaire, Lamennais, and Montalembert, he refused to co-operate with them in the writing of articles for their journalistic organ, *L'Avenir.* These eminent men were not alone in their inability to understand Sainte-Beuve's mental temperament. They thought that because he seemed profoundly interested he was therefore a disciple. But the foremost critic of the day was a man of a passionate intellectual curiosity : his sovereign need was for new mental intellectual impressions. It was his insatiable curiosity into all manifestations of mental activity, as much as his exceptional receptivity, elasticity of sympathy, searching insight, and extraordinary synthetic faculty, that enabled him to become the master-critic. His catholicity of taste was his strength as, with others, it is often a source of weakness. It was not through inability to find anchorage in the sea of truth that his was a restless barque, with sails trimmed for seafaring again as soon as a haven was entered : it was because he was a literary viking, consumed with a passion for mental voyaging and remote explorations — because he loved the deep sea, and found that even the profoundest inlets, the grandest bays, were too shallow for him to rest content therein.

"No one," he says, "ever went through more mental vicissitudes than I have done. I began my intellectual life as an uncompromising adherent of the most advanced form of eighteenth-century thought, as exemplified by Tracy, Daunou, Lamarck, and the physiologists : *là est mon fonds véritable.* Then I passed through the psychological and doctrinaire school as represented by my confrères on the *Globe,* but without giving it my unqualified adhesion. For a time thereafter I had my liaison with the school of Victor Hugo, and seemed to lose myself in poetical romanticism. Later, I fared by the margins of St. Simonism, and, soon thereafter, liberal-Catholicism as represented by Lamennais and his group. In 1837, when residing at Lausanne, I glided past Calvinism and Methodism . . . but in all these wanderings I never (save for a moment in the Hugo period, and when under the influence of a charm) forfeited my will or my judgment, never pawned my belief. On the other hand, I understood so well both the world of books and that of men that I gave dubious encouragement to those ardent spirits who wished to convert me to their convictions, and indeed claimed me as one of themselves. But it was all curiosity on my part, a desire to see everything, to examine closely, to analyse, along with the keen pleasure I felt in discovering the relative truth of each new idea and each system, which allured me to my long series of experiments, to me nothing else than a prolonged course of moral physiology."

The short space at my command prevents my enlarging upon the hint conveyed in the last phrase, except to say that it is directly indicative to Sainte-Beuve's fundamental critical principle. To him criticism was literary physiology. With him a series of critiques meant a series of studies of— (1) a writer as one of a group, as the product of the shaping spirit of the time ; (2) a writer as an individual, with all his inherited and acquired idiosyncrasies ; (3) a writer as seen in his writings, viewed in the light of all ascertainable *personalia ;* (4) the writings themselves, intrinsically and comparatively estimated. But, primarily, his essays were as much studies of character, of moral physiology, as of literary values.

After his withdrawal from the too sectarian *Globe,* Sainte-Beuve joined the staff of the *National.* With the ultra-Republican principles of that paper he had but a lukewarm sympathy, but his friend Armand Carrel, the editor, assured him that nothing would be expected from him save purely literary contributions. For about three years (1831-4) he remained on the staff of the *National,* and it was in the last year of the connection that he published his one novel, "Volupté." The book had a gratifying reception so far as wide notice was concerned ; but it was generally adjudged to be unwholesome in tone and somewhat too self-conscious in style—though so beautiful a nature and so refined a critic as Eugénie de Guérin affirmed it to be a notable and even a noble book. That the prejudice against the author on account of it must have been strong, is evident from the fact that when it was suggested to Guizot, then Minister of Public Instruction, that he should confer upon Sainte - Beuve a professional post at the Normal School, just vacant through the resignation of Ampère, he refused to appoint a mar, howsoever brilliantly qualified, who had written such books as "Joseph Delorme" and "Volupte." Guizot was conscientiously scrupulous in this matter; and to show that he bore no personal ill-feeling, he appointed Sainte-Beuve to the secretaryship of an historical Commission, a post which the equally conscientious critic resigned in less than a year, on the ground that it was becoming or had become a mere sinecure. Another instance of his conscientiousness is his having declined, about the same date, the Cross of the Legion of Honour—a distinction he would have been proud to accept had he felt assured that it was offered in recognition of his literary merits, but upon which he looked suspiciously because it came when the Ministry of M. Molé and M. Salvandy, both personal friends of his, was in power. Three years after the publication of his novel, he issued the last of his purely imaginative productions, the "Pensées d'Août." In the same year (1837) he went to Switzerland, and having been invited by the Academy of Lausanne to deliver a course of lectures, he settled for a time in the pleasant Swiss town. There he delivered in all eighty-one lectures, the foundation of his famous and voluminous work on Port Royal (the story of the religious movement in the seventeenth century known as Jansenism), which occupied him intermittently for twenty years, is a monument of labour, research, and scrupulous historic fairness, and, though the least read, is one of his greatest achievements.

Both before and during his Swiss sojourn, and for about ten years thereafter, Sainte-Beuve was a regular contributor to the most famous magazine in Europe, the *Revue des Deux Mondes*, which had been founded in 1831, heir to the defunct *Revue de Paris*. The first number contains an article by him upon his friend George Farcy, a victim of the July Revolution; and thereafter appeared that long and delightful series of "Portraits Littéraires," studies of contemporary as well as of deceased writers, which not only gave him a European reputa†˙ ˳ as a leading critic, but ultimately won him his election to the French Academy. This signal good-fortune happened in 1845, on the occasion of the death of Casimir Delavigne ; and the irony of circumstances was obvious to many in the fact that the eulogium on the new "immortal" had to be pronounced by the reluctant Victor Hugo, his immediate predecessor. It was a memorable date, that 17th of February ; and if among the many "immortals" who have been raised to glory by the Academy there are relatively few whose fame will be imperishable, there are not many with juster claims to remembrance, though in widely different degrees, than the two authors who were then elected to the coveted honour, Prosper Merimée and Sainte-Beuve.

His periodical articles and his books (including five volumes of essays which he had contributed to the *Revue de Paris* and the *Revue des Deux Mondes*) brought him in a very moderate income ; and it was not till 1840 that his means were materially improved. In that year he was appointed one of the keepers of the Mazarin Library. The appointment meant not only an increase of income, but a change of residence, for it comprised a suite of residential apartments at the Institute. Up to this time Sainte-Beuve had been living in two small rooms on the fourth floor of a house in a remote street—living extremely moderately, and in a seclusion almost monastic ; indeed, he had even adopted the ruse of calling himself Joseph Delorme. In his new abode he was happy as well as comfortable, and thankfully embraced the opportunity of study and leisurely composition which his post afforded him. This pleasant state of affairs came to an end after the Revolution in 1848. A ridiculous charge of corruption was brought up against him by envious and inimical journalists and political adversaries ; the ultra-Republicans accused him of having accepted bribes, hush-money, from the late Government. In vain Sainte-Beuve protested, and vainly he demanded a searching inquiry. The hint was taken up : everywhere he was abused, condemned, scathingly ridiculed. Even when, at last, the truth was revealed, and the greedy public learned that the amount of Sainte-Beuve's indebtedness was £4, and that that sum had been expended upon the alteration of a smoking chimney in his department of the Library, and the charge inadvertently entered in the official books simply under the heading "Ste. Beuve,"—even then there were many ungenerous souls who kept up the parrot cry of contumely. It somewhat unfortunately happened that about this time Sainte-Beuve left Paris, and of course there was at once a shout of triumph from his enemies. The real reasons for his departure were primarily financial, though no doubt he was not at all sorry to leave a city which had for the time being become so disagreeable to him —moreover, his distaste for the political issues then in full development was very strong. But after his resignation of his post at the Mazarin Library, which he had given in the heat of his indignation during the bribery controversy, he found that he would have to do something at once for a living. The political turmoil of 1848 was unfavourable for the pursuit of pure literature ; and despite his high reputation, the editors whom he knew could not promise him a sufficiency of remunerative work until the times changed for the better. Accordingly, he very willingly accepted the Professorship of French Literature at the University of Liège, offered to him by M. Rogier, the Belgian Minister of the Interior. Liège he found mono-tonous and provincial, but he stayed there for some time, and attracted more than local, more even than national attention by his preliminary course of lectures on the chronological history of French literature. There, also, he delivered the famous series on Chateaubriand and his Contemporaries, which amply demonstrated his independ-ence as a critic, though many of his judgments and reserva-tions brought a veritable storm of reproaches and angry recriminations about his ears. For a long time he was called an ingrate, a hypocrite, a resentful critic inspired by pique ; but ultimately it was acknowledged that he had written the ablest and justest critique of the celebrated egotist and *poseur.* The fundamental reason of the attacks upon Sainte-Beuve was on account of his so-called inconsistency. True, among his early "Literary Portraits" was a flattering essay on Chateaubriand, but he was then under the magic charm of Madame Recamier, at whose house, Abbaye-aux-Bois, he heard read aloud in solemn state numerous extracts from the famous writer's unpublished "Memoirs." Moreover, Chateaubriand had inspired him with a temporary enthusiasm. When, with fuller knowledge of the man and his writings and with the "Correspondence" to boot, he found that he had been mistaken, he said so. The commonplace mind detests inconsistency with an almost rancorous hatred, oblivious of the fact that, as Emerson has said, only fools never change their views.

"Chateaubriand and his Literary Group under the Empire" is the work which marks the turning-point in Sainte-Beuve's genius. Thenceforth he was, in truth, the foremost critic of his time. In style as well as in matter, his productions from this time are masterpieces ; and though there are some essays which could now be dispensed with, either because of the fuller light cast upon their subjects by later students, or on account of certain shortcomings in the matter of prejudiced judgment, seven-tenths of them may be read to-day with much the same pleasure as they were perused two, three, or four decades ago.

Late in 1849 Sainte-Beuve, much to the chagrin of his Belgian friends and admirers, left Liège and returned to Paris. He was still hesitating how best to employ his pen, when he received a flattering but to him somewhat startling offer from his friend, Dr. de Véron, editor of *Le Constitutionnel.* This was to the effect that he should write a literary article for that paper every week. The reason of his perturbation was that hitherto he had always composed in leisurely fashion, and for papers or magazines whose readers were cultivated people, much more interested in literature than in politics and local news. Fortunately, M. de Véron overruled his scruples, and so there began that delightful and now famous series of literary critiques which the writer himself entitled *Causeries du Lundi.* He called them "Monday Chats," because each appeared on a Monday. For five days every week he "sported his oak," and occupied himself for twelve hours daily with the study of his subject and the writing of his article; on the sixth he finally revised it; Sunday was his sole holiday from his task. By next morning he was deep in the subject of the *Causerie* for the following week. It was the need to be concise and simple that did so much good to Sainte-Beuve's style. The charm of these *Causeries* can be appreciated alike by the most cultivated and the most casual reader. As two of his most eminent friends said of them, they were all the better insomuch as he had not had time to spoil them. From the end of 1849 to almost exactly twenty years later he wrote weekly, in the *Constitutionnel* or the *Moniteur*, with a single considerable interval, one of those brilliant, scholarly, fascinating articles,—collectively, a mass of extraordinarily varied work now embodied in fifteen goodly volumes.

When the *coup d'état* occurred, Sainte-Beuve gave his approval to the Empire. Thereby he won for himself no little unpopularity. His first materially disagreeable experience of this was when he proceeded to lecture at the Collège de France, to the Professorship of Latin Poetry at which he had been appointed. The students would have none of him. He was an Imperialist, a Government payee, he wrote in the official organ, *Le Moniteur.* He was literally hissed from the lecture-room, whence he retired in high dudgeon. Ultimately the lecture he had tried to deliver, and those which were to have followed, were published in a volume entitled "A Study on Virgil." The single intermission to his regular literary work, already alluded to, was during the four years when he held the post of Maître des Conférences at the Ecole Normale, at a salary of about £240. When he again took up literary journalism, after his resignation of his professional post, it was once more as a contributor to the *Constitutionnel.* He now made a fair income, for his weekly contributions to that journal brought him in, by special arrangement, an annual salary of £624. The *Causeries* were now called *Nouveaux Lundis,* "New Monday-Chats." In the main this series (begun in 1861) is equal to the *Causeries du Lundi,* though there are signs ever and again of lassitude. This might well be. The work was a steady and serious strain, and the great critic's health gradually became undermined. In 1865, when he was in his sixty-first year, he wrote : "I am of the age at which died Horace, Montaigne, and Bayle, my masters : so I am content to die." It was in this very year that good fortune came to him, and greatly relieved the mental strain under which his strength was waning. He was appointed to a Senator-ship of the Second Empire, a position which secured him an annual income of £1200. His senatorial career was a dignified though not a brilliant one. He was ever on the side of true freedom, and was so independent in his atti-tude that he gave offence to those of his fellow-senators who were Imperialists and resented his championship of religious liberty. This muzzled wrath broke into clamorous fury at an incident concerning which an absurd fuss has been made. Sainte-Beuve had arranged to give a dinner to some of his friends, on the occasion of Prince Napoleon's departure from Paris, and, to suit that gentleman, had appointed Friday (which chanced to be Good Friday) as the night. The Prince, Edmond About, Gustave Flaubert, Rénan, Robin, and Taine duly joined their host and spent a pleasant evening. But the jackals were on the trail. A howl arose about a conspiracy to undermine the religious welfare of the nation ; the diners were arraigned as impious debauchees ; and Sainte-Beuve in particular was upbraided for his "scandalous orgy."

One other and much more serious annoyance troubled the latter years of Sainte-Beuve. This arose from his writing for *Le Temps* (whither he had transferred his

Causeries, on account of a servile attempt to muzzle him
on the part of the temeritous directorate of the *Moniteur*) ;
and as *Le Temps* was hostile to the Government, M.
Rouher and his confrères in the Ministry, as well as the
whole Senate, thought it shameful that the critic should
write for that journal, and did all in their power to force
him into conformity with their views. But Sainte-Beuve
was firmly independent, and emerged triumphantly from
the ordeal.

For some years Sainte-Beuve had been in indifferent
health. At last he became ill indeed, and his malady
(the stone) caused him such extreme pain that he could
only stand or lie when he had writing to do, as to sit was
impossible. By the late summer of 1869 his case was
desperate. Ultimately a perilous operation was made, but
the patient sank under its effects. He died in his house
in the Rue Mont Parnasse, on the 13th of October, at the
age of sixty-four. Along with the biographical fragment
found on his desk on the morrow of his death, which
concluded with the celebrated words, " Voué et adonné a
mon métier de critique, j'ai tâché d'être de plus en plus un
bon et, s'il se peut, habile ouvrier "—" Devoted with all my
heart to my profession as critic, I have done my utmost
to be more and more a good and, if possible, an able
workman ; "—along with " Ma Biographie " were found
written instructions as to his funeral. He directed that
he should be buried in the Cemetery of Mont Parnasse
beside his mother ; that the ceremony should be as simple
as practicable, and without religious rites or even a friendly
oration. All due respect was paid to his wishes, and yet
seldom has a funeral been attended with greater honour.
It was not the Senator of the Second Empire who was
carried to the grave, but the greatest of French critics,
a writer of European renown. In the immense crowd
which formed the voluntary procession—estimated at ten
thousand—all political differences were forgotten : uncompromising Imperialists and equally uncompromising Re-
publicans walked in union for once, in company with nearly

all who were distinguished in letters, science, or art. The only words uttered above his grave were more eloquent in their poignant simplicity than the most glowing exordium : " Farewell, Sainte-Beuve ; farewell, our friend."

II.

Sainte-Beuve's literary career may be studied in three main phases. The novelist least claims our attention ; the poet demands it ; while as a critic he appears as of supreme importance.

"Volupte," so far, but, to a much greater extent, the " Vie, Poésies, et Pensées de Joseph Delorme," may be taken as embodying some of the positive and many of the spiritual experiences of Sainte-Beuve's life. We have his own testimony to the fact that "Joseph Delorme" was "a pretty faithful representation of himself morally, but not in the biographical details." This alone would give a permanent interest to the book, as it is admittedly in some degree the autopsychical record of the most complex, brilliant, protean spirit of our time. No one indeed has yet limned Sainte-Beuve for us as he, for instance, has revealed the heart, mind, and soul of Pascal. Neither D'Haussonville, his biographer, nor any of his critics, French and English, has done more than introduce us to the author of so many inimitable *Causeries ;* none of then has made us intimate with Sainte-Beuve himself, notwithstanding the array of authentic facts and suggestive hints which can now be marshalled. He is easiest to be discerned in his writings : not in this essay nor in that series of essays, not in the grave pages of "Port Royal " nor in the alluring byways of the " Lundis," neither in the sensitive poet of " The Consolations " nor in the austere pages of " Pensees d'Août," not in that Gallic Werther, Amaury, the hero of " Volupte," not even in Joseph Delorme, but in all collectively. One is always being surprised in him. There is one man in Amaury, another in Joseph Delorme, a very different one in "Pensées d'Août," a still more distinct one in the "Nouveaux Landis," and in his single short tale, the charming "Christel," there are hints of a personality whose ᵦ ₐ₁₀wy features rarely, if ever, haunt the corridors of the "Causeries." As a matter of fact, Sainte-Beuve became more and more reserved as he found himself deceived by the glowing perspectives of youth.   Often he was consumed with a nostalgia for a country whence he was half-voluntarily, half-perforce an exile, the country of the Poetic Land where once he spent "six fleeting celestial months,"* as a native of which he would fain be regarded even in the remote days when he found himself an alien among those whom he yearned to claim as brothers. Thenceforth the man shrank more and more behind the writer.   The real Sainte-Beuve was no doubt less recluse in the days when he was a member of *Le Cénacle,* when he was one of the sprightliest in the Hugo circle, and laughed with de Vigny and sighed with Lamartine, debated with Hugo, and flirted with Adèle.   But even then his nature could not have been transparent to all, otherwise Alfred de Musset would not have drawn his picture of him as sitting somewhat apart in the shadow, rhyming a sonnet to a demoiselle's cap, or a lyric to his mistress's eyebrow.   Truly, as he himself says, in the preface to his "Poésies Complètes," almost all of us have within ourselves a second self ("nous avons presque tous en nous un homme double ").

The " Vie, Poésies, et Pensées de Joseph Delorme" has been put forward as an effort on the part of Sainte-Beuve to introduce into France a poetic literature as simple, fresh, and spontaneous as that of the naturalistic poets of England, and of Cowper and Wordsworth in particular. Readers of that notable book will find it difficult to perceive any direct Wordsworthian influence, though the author makes clear his great admiration for the English poet and his school.   Joseph Delorme, in fact, is a cousin-

* *Causeries du Lundi,* Tome xvi.

german to Don Juan, closely akin to Chateaubriand's René, the French half-brother to Goethe's Werther. He is the most literary of the family, but while he is as sentimental as René, and as melancholy as Werther, he has not the frank debonnaire licentiousness of Don Juan. He is morbid in his thoughts and in his desires. The fellowship of a Tom Jones would have done him good, the laughing Juan, even, would have acted as a tonic. "The road of excess leads to the palace of wisdom," says Blake; but the poet-visionary did not mean the kind of excess in which the too introspective Joseph indulged. He said one good thing, however, for which he will be remembered—when he spoke of his dread of marriage because of its restrictions upon his "rather rude philanthropy" (a euphemism for "free morals"), and defined it as *une egoisme à deux personnes.*

Rousseau and Goethe were the literary godfathers of Joseph Delorme, who was born when the author of his being was only five-and-twenty. The nature of the book is indicated by a passage from Senancour's "Obermann," which exactly strikes the key-note: "I have seen him, I have pitied him; I respected him; he was unhappy and virtuous. He had no transcendent misfortunes; but, on entering life, he found himself in a mesh of distastes and satieties ('il s'est trouvé sur une longue trace de dégoûts et d'ennuis'): there he is still, there he has dwelt, there he has grown old ere age has come upon him, there he has literally buried himself." The Adolphe of "Obermann," indeed, is but a more melancholy and a more austere "double" of Joseph.

The following lines are fairly representative of the dominant sentiment of the book.

VŒU.

" *Tout le jour du loisir ; rêver avec des larmes ;*
  Vers midi, me coucher à l'ombre des grands charmes ;
  Voir la vigne courir sur mon toit ardoisé,
  Et mon vallon riant sous le coteau boisé ;

Chaque soir m'endormir en ma douce folie,
Comme l'heureux ruisseau qui dans mon pré s'oublie;
Ne rien vouloir de plus, ne pas me souvenir,
Vivre à me sentir vivre! . . . Et la mort peut venir." *

But a healthier note is often struck, as in the blithe strain wedded to a pathetic thought, "Ce ciel restera bleu Quand nous ne serons plus;" often, too, one fresh and haunting, as in

" Et dans ses blonds cheveux, ses blanches mains errantes—
Tels deux cygnes nageant dans les eaux transparentes." . . . †

The " Life, Poetry, and Thoughts " are worth reading ; the book contains much that is interesting, no little that is suggestive, not infrequently thoughts, lines, and passages of genuine beauty. But it can enthral only those who are enjoying the exquisite sentimentalism of adolescence ; ere long it will interest only the student of a certain literary epoch, the epoch begun by Rousseau, that finds its acme in Byron, which knows its autumn in Werther, that has its grave in the René of Chateaubriand, its brief phantasmal second life in Joseph Delorme. The poetry in it is often sterile, and is frequently forced, self - conscious, obtrusively sedate in imagery, occasionally even is markedly derivative. We find Sainte - Beuve the poet much better worth listening to in " Les Consolations." In point of style there is not very much difference, though a greater dexterity is manifest, a more delicate metrical tact, perhaps also a more unmistakably natural note. But there is no more kinship between the author of "Les Consolations" and

* A WISH.

. . . .
" Leisure all the livelong day ; to dream, with tears ; towards noon, to rest in the shade of great elms ; to see the vine-branches trail over my slated roof, and my own little valley smiling under its wooded slope : to fall asleep each evening rapt in my sweet folly, as the happy brook which loses itself in my meadow : to wish for nothing more, to remember nought, in a word, to live as I would fain live ! . . . Then death may come ! "

† " Through her fair hair her white hands wandering,
   Like two swans swimming in transparent waters." . . .

Joseph Delorme than between Don Juan and Manfred.
The volume was the product of the religious mysticism
which underlay Sainte-Beuve's mental robustness—a trait
which allured him often by dangerous pitfalls, but also
enabled him to understand so well the great religious
writers of whom he still remains the most sympathetic as
well as the most brilliant exponent. It seemed ultra-
saintly to some of those who read it on its appearance.
Béranger annoyed the author by some sly disparagement ;
Prosper Merimée cynically smiled at what he took to be
a literary ruse ; Gustave Planche and others gleefully
whetted their vivisectionary knives. On the other hand,
it was for the most part well received by the critics,
and no cruel witticism like that of Guizot on its predecessor
(that Joseph Delorme was "a Werther turned Jacobin
and sawbones") went echoing through Paris. The public
remained indifferent, but the poet was gratified when
Chateaubriand wrote him a letter of praise, with a characteristic "Écoutez votre génie, Monsieur ; " when Hugo and
Alfred de Vigny waxed enthusiastic ; when Béranger sent
an epistle of kindly criticism ; and when Lamartine un-
bosomed himself as follows :—"Yesterday I re-read the
'Consolations' . . . they are ravishing. I say it and I
repeat it : it is this that I care for in French poetry of this
order. What truth, what soul, what grace and poetry !
I have wept, I who never weep." (This must have amused
Sainte-Beuve, if not then, later. The sentimental Lamartine was always weeping over one thing or another, and the
"J'en ai pleure, moi qui oneques ne pleure," is as little
apt as though Mr. Pickwick were to say "I have smiled,
who never smile.") . . . . It was at this time, the period
wherein "The Consolations" were produced, that Sainte-
Beuve dreamed upon Latmos and believed that the goddess
whom he loved was going to reward his passion. The
"celestial months" passed, but they were ever an oasis
to which he delighted to return in memory. He even
wished, in later years, that those who desired to know him
should seek and find him, a happy Dryad flitting through

the shadowy vales and sunlit glades of the woodlands of
song. No doubt the real Sainte-Beuve is as much in this
book of verse as in any other of his library of volumes,
but it is the Sainte - Beuve of a certain period, and even
then only one of two selves. "The Consolations" always
remained his favourite volume. It contains a great deal
of gracious and even beautiful verse, in style often clear as
a trout-stream, fresh and fragrant as a May-meadow, though
even here, as certainly with his other "poésies," one is
inclined to say of him, in the words of his own Joseph,
Delorme, that he had not sufficiently "the ingenuousness
of deep faith, the instinctive and spontaneous cry of
passionate emotion." Some of the "Consolations" are
extremely Wordsworthian—how closely, indeed, he could
enter into the spirit of the great English poet is evident
in the following free translation of that most lovely sonnet
beginning, "It is a beauteous Evening, calm and free":—

> " *C'est un beau soir, un soir paisible et solennel ;*
> *A la fin du saint jour, la Nature en prière*
> *Se tait, comme Marie à genoux sur la pierre,*
> *Qui tremblante et muette écoutait Gabriel :*
>
> *La mer dort ; le soleil descend en paix du ciel ;*
> *Mais dans ce grand silence, au-dessus et derrière,*
> *On entend l'hymne heureux du triple sanctuaire,*
> *Et l'orgue immense où gronde un tonnerre éternel.*
>
> *O blonde jeune fille, à la tête baissée,*
> *Qui marches près de moi, si ta sainte pensée,*
> *Semble moins qui la mienne adorer ce moment,*
> *C'est qu'au sein d'Abraham vivant toute l'année,*
> *Ton ame est de prière, à chaque heure, baignée ;*
> *C'est que ton cœur recite un divin firmament.*"

This, of course, is but indifferent verse after the superb
original, but it shows both how Sainte-Beuve was inspired
by Wordsworth, and how ably he too could write, albeit
as a translator, in simple and unaffected strains. Although
the second, third, and fourth lines bear no resemblance to

> " The holy time is quite as a Nun
> Breathless with adoration, ..."

and the rest of the version is only in a lesser degree un-
literal, it must be borne in mind that the full beauty of
the original is untranslatable, and that the French poet
strove to convey to the French reader the same impression as an English reader would gain from the English
sonnet. However, the importance of this and other experiments is not to be overlooked. Many of the younger poets
owe much, directly or indirectly, to the lesson taught by
Sainte-Beuve in what a hostile critic has called his
" Anglo-French metrical essays."

Yet, while it is true that the man is perhaps to be seen
most clearly in his poetry,—" it is in following the poet
that we find the man," as M. Anatole France says,—
even here he is an evasive, an uncertain personality. The
strange mixture of a sensuousness that is at times almost
sensual, a mysticism which would suit a religious enthusiast,
a clarity of thought and an exquisite sense of the beauty of
precision and artistic form, a frequent remoteness of shaping
emotion, coupled with keen perception of the sovereign value
of that resistless formative power which makes the creatures
of the imagination more real than the actual beings about
us,*—all this, along with his complex style, which now is
simple, now is heated with fires unlit of the sun, and again
is involved, obscure almost, wrought to an excessive finish,
tourmenté, makes Sainte - Beuve the poet a profoundly
puzzling as well as interesting study. In his last volume
of verse, particularly, he is, as one of his critics has said,
" tourmenté à l'excès, souvent d'une étrangeté qui décon-
certe." But it is quite wrong to assert, as has been affirmed
more than once, that Sainte-Beuve's poetic melancholy, the
undertone of each of his three books, is assumed. One
writer in *Le Temps* (or *Le Figaro*) recently found a proof
of this literary insincerity in some remarks made by the
critic in his old age, remarks treating lightly his former
mysticism, with an avowal that " his odours of the sacristy

---

* In his own words he sought to arrive " at that particularity and
at that precision which causes the creations of our mind to become
altogether ours and to be recognised as ours."

were really meant for the ladies." " I have been guilty of
a little Christian mythology in my time," he admitted,
" but it all evaporated long ago. It was for me, as the
swan to Leda's wooer, merely a means to reach fair readers
and to win their tender regard." But this, quite obviously,
is mere badinage.   If there be any truth in it at all, it
is one of those remote filaments of fact which go to the
weaving of the web of truth ; nothing more.   His melancholy was a genuine sentiment, which found expression
differently at divers times.   Even in his latest essays,
when his natural geniality is allowed free play, it is trace-
able in those occasional bitternesses and abrupt dislikes,
those half-weary and yet mordant "asides," which show
that the man was by no means wholly absorbed in the
critic.   He himself, as we have seen, attributed this fundamental strain of sadness in his nature to his mother's
early widowhood. " My mother bore me in mourning and
grief," he says ; " I have been as it were soaked in sorrow
and bathed in tears—and, well, I have often attributed
to this maternal grief the melancholy of my young years,
and my disposition to weariness of mind and spirit." *

---

* *Vide* " Correspondance de Sainte-Beuve :" Lettre à M. de Frabière,
25th June 1862.

The " melancholy of my young years " must not be taken too literally
Sainte - Beuve's boyhood seems to have been a happy one. He had
love affairs when he was a small child, moreover, if we may take his
own word for it.   In one of his poems he has the following Boulogne
reminiscences :—

> " N'eus-je pas ma Camille,
> Douce blonde au front pur, paisible jeune fille,
> Qu'au jardin je suivais, la dévorant des yeux?
> N'eus-je pas Mathilde, au parler sérieux,
> Qui remplaça Camille, et plus d'une autre encore?"

" Had I not my Camille, sweet white-browed fair maid, calm damsel,
whom I followed to the garden, devouring her with my eyes? Had I
not Mathilde, who replaced Camille, and many others beside?"
" Oh, these nursemaids, these nursemaids !" the precocious young *roué*
may have thought, shaking his curly head, ere he went to play on the
sands or upon the old ramparts.

But, as M. France has well said, it was another mother,
the Revolution, who inoculated him with the malady of
the age — that malady of which M. Taine, the most
brilliant of the disciples of Sainte-Beuve, has alluded to so
eloquently : "It was then that the malady of the age
appeared, the spiritual inquietude typified by Werther and
Faust, almost identical with that which, in a somewhat
similar time, agitated men at the beginning of the century.
I would call it the discontent with present horizons, the
vague desire after a higher beauty and an ideal happiness,
a pathetically sad aspiration towards the infinite. Man
suffers in doubting and yet he doubts : he tries to recapture
his lost beliefs, they are really in his hand." (*Hist. de la
Lit. Anglaise,* Tome iii.) This melancholy nature, induced
by the spirit of the age, derived now from this source and
now from that, and occasionally insincere, is most marked
in its least genuine aspects in the "Pensées d'Août." There
is nothing in it so fine, in the poetry of melancholy, as the
"Lines" in the "Consolations" (inscribed to Mme. V. H.; no
other, of course, than the immaculate Adéle Hugo) beginning

"Plus fraîche que la vigne au bord d'un antre frais."

The chief poem in the collection, entitled "Monsieur
Jean," is an ill-considered attempt at a didactic novelette in
verse. The author did not so regard it: he believed that
he had wooed and won *Musa Pedestris,* and had given his
poetry the tone of serene wisdom. Jean is a natural son of
Jean Jacques Rousseau, and is a simple, gentle creature,
eager to expiate in his remote village, by piety and endless
good deeds, what he cannot but regard as the disastrous
glory of his father. But the poet's failure is a signal
instance of the folly of metrical didactics. "Jean" bored the
reading public, who combined in awarding the "Pensées
d'Août" what its author called a really savage reception.
In this book, more than anywhere else in his poetical
writings, is true what Matthew Arnold said of him, that he
lacked something of flame, of breath, of pinion : here, more
than elsewhere, his poems *côtoient la prose*—coasted peril-

ously near the land of prose. As a matter of fact, the book was a complete failure : it caused the pendulum of his poetic repute to swing back, and to be caught up and never let go again. Moreover, its reception stifled the poet in Sainte-Beuve. It is a poignant personal note that underlies his famous remark, "Every one contains a dead poet in his soul."

But, after all, even the most reluctant reader of Sainte-Beuve as a poet cannot, if he be minded to criticism, afford to overlook this important section of the life-work of the great critic. It is necessary, indeed, not only to an understanding of the man but of the writer. For in these *Poésies Complètes*, to quote the words of a sympathetic critic, "Se peint l'âme la plus curieux, la plus sagace, et la plus compliquée qu'une vieille civilisation ait jamais produite"—"is revealed the most inquiring, the most sagacious, the most complex spirit" to whom the age has given birth.

It is not feasible here, in the limited space at my command, to attempt any analysis of "Volupté," Sainte-Beuve's sole effort in fiction save the short tale "Christel." Some day when a critical historian, curious as to the mainsprings of, let us hope, the long since cured *maladie du siècle*, will occupy himself with the fortunes of Werther and René, Adolphe and Amiel, he will not omit to include in that strange company the amorously sentimental and sentimentally melancholic Amaury. For myself I admit I find that youth quite as entertaining as either of the more famous offspring of Goethe or Chateaubriand.

As a historian Sainte-Beuve showed remarkable aptitude, but it is as an historian of mental phases, episodes, and general events, rather than of the ebb and flow of outer weal, the conflict of kingdoms and the fortunes of internecine warfare, the rise of this house or that dynasty, the ruin of cities and the growth of States. He could have been neither a Gibbon nor a Niebuhr, neither a Guizot nor a Mommsen, not even a Macaulay or an Ampère ; but he is in the domain of historical literature what the author of "The

History of the Rise of Morals in Europe" and "The History of Rationalism" is in the sphere of ethical research, though, of course, there is a radical distinction between the method of Mr. Lecky and that of the author of "Port Royal." To the accomplishment of this immense undertaking Sainte-Beuve brought his inexhaustible patience, his almost unerring faculty of wise discrimination, his precise and scientific method of analysis and exposition, and a style which gave wings to words yoked to dry and apparently outworn subjects. Still, the work is not one that will be widely read a generation hence. Only exhaustive and definitively accurate detail could save from oblivion so lengthy a history on so remote and secondary a subject; and though in its day "Port Royal" fulfilled the need even of the student, scholars now seek their information in the less ambitious but more thorough "studies" of a score of specialists. It may safely be said, however, that no student of Pascal, or of the religious movement in the seventeenth century, will ever be able to dispense with Sainte-Beuve's masterly work.

As the literary critic, as the first who brought into the analysis and exposition of literature the methods of exact science, Sainte-Beuve must always have a high place in the literary history of the nineteenth century. Ultimately, it may be that his chief glory will lie in his having been the pioneer of a new literary art, in his having been the torch-bearer who gave light and direction to many, not heeding much whether his torch, its service done, should thereafter be seldom seen and rarely sought. His example has been of almost inestimable value, and not among his countrymen only. All of the foremost living critics of France, from the eldest and most brilliant, Henri Taine, to Paul Bourget, the late Émile Hennequin, Ernest Tissot, and Charles Morice, have learned much from him — some a life-long lesson, others guiding hints only. As for our own critics, it is, broadly speaking, scarcely to be gainsaid that with us criticism as an art has no acknowledged existence. There are brilliant exceptions who prove the rule, but they are few and their limitations are so marked as for the

most part to deserve the epithet insular.* As for the
ordinary criticism in our journals and weekly papers, the
less said about it the better for our complacency, since
little of good as against a great deal of reprobation would
have to be uttered. A change must soon come. Personally,
I doubt if it will occur till our utterly mistaken and mis-
chievous system of anonymous reviewing — whether in
magazines, weekly papers, or journals — is given up in
favour of the more just, more valuable, in every way
better habit in vogue among our neighbours. It would
be ridiculous to urge that there is no sound and honest
criticism among us; but it is hypocritical for those who
know better to pretend that unsigned critiques are as free
from jealousy, spite, and all uncharitableness, as, for the
greater part, these would be if it were not for the shield of
anonymity. It has come to this pass, that no one occupied
in the literary life ever thinks of paying attention to unsigned reviews, be they in the foremost weeklies or in the
provincial press, unless the writers be known. Praise and
blame, enthusiasm and indifference—each has to be accepted
suspiciously. The result is that literary criticism, instead
of being an interpreter and a guide, now to warn and now
to allure, is a maker of confusion, a will-o'-the-wisp of
judgment, and is no longer hearkened to or followed as of
yore. The real cure for this lamentable state of affairs is
the cultivation of the literary sentiment, of the feeling of
the sacredness of literature; and, thereafter, of scrupulous
heed, both on the part of the critics and of the cultured
public, for the exemplification of criticism *as an art*.
Mere book-noticing, of course, like the poor, we shall have
always with us: a circumstance not incompatible with the

---

* I should like to draw attention here to one of the younger and
lesser known critics who are working towards a new science of
literary criticism: I allude to Mr. John M. Robertson, whose "Essays
towards a Critical Method" (*Fisher Unwin*) is one of the few English
studies in literary criticism deserving special attention. No one can
read this book of Mr. Robertson's, or Émile Hennequin's "La Critique
Scientifique," without realising how limitedly apprehended this new
art of criticism is in England.

growth and culture of literary criticism. But possibly the best, perhaps the only feasible means to induce this fortunate result, in the first instance, would be the universal adoption of signed and responsible reviews.

In the "Notes et Rémarques" at the end of the sixteenth volume of the *Causeries du Lundi* occurs the following: "I have given no one the right to say—He belongs to us (*Il est des nôtres*)." It is this absolute independence, this many-sidedness of Sainte-Beuve, which is one of the secrets of his success. He can be an intellectual comrade of every poet, from the austere Dante to the gay Villon ; of every wit and satirist, from Rabelais to Rivarol ; of every builder up of ethical systems and every iconoclast of creeds, of the ancient Latins and Greeks as well as of the modern Germans and English ; and, moreover, at all times a comrade with an eye to the exact value of and pleasure derivable from his companion of the hour. Here, it seems to me, is his strength and his weakness. He can be *bon camarade* with every one, but he is never able to forget that he is the observer of the thoughts, speech, action, and principles of those with whom he fares. He has charming ruses for evading detection. He will laugh gaily, he will smile, he will allude to this or that scarcely pertinent matter, he will altogether diverge from his subject, he will reintroduce it casually, and possibly dismiss it lightly, and yet he will have had but one aim in view from the outset,—to analyse and estimate the writings of his author, to discover the shaping circumstances of the latter as an individual, to strip him of what is extraneous, and reveal him as he really is,—in a word, to portray him in one composite photograph, to give us a likeness of the man as well as of the author which shall be none the less true because it resolves into definite features the fleeting and indeterminate traits which we perceive now in the one now in the other. He is no believer in the doctrine of the isolation of an author from his writings ; it seems as absurd to him as it would be to assert that no notice of the prism may be taken in a study of the chemic action of light passing therethrough. But, on the other hand, the question arises if Sainte-Beuve is not apt to be misled by his own theory, having to make positive affirmations based on facts necessarily in some degree suppositions. Herein is the hidden reef of literary psychology, and even so great a critic as M. Taine is occasionally missuaded by semblances which he takes for actualities. The elder writer is content to be a careful scientific observer, and delights in artistic demonstration of his newly perceived and otherwise accumulated facts : M. Taine, M. Bourget, and the later literary analysts go further, and wish to reach down through facts to their origins, and to the primary impulsion again of the influences which moulded those origins—and, finally, by cumulative verification to transform hypothesis into demonstrable truth. But, fundamentally, both means are identical ; the basis of each is the adoption, for literary research, of the method of exact science. Sainte-Beuve hated fixed judgments ; he had none of the arrogances of his critical kindred. He neither said himself, nor cared to hear others saying, that a book was definitively good or definitively bad ; he loved the *nuances*, the delicacies and subtleties of criticism, as much as he disliked rigid formulas. Yet his studies in literary psychology, as M. Paul Bourget would call them, are not only acute but are generally profoundly conclusive : it is his suave and winsome manner that makes many think he is too complaisant to be critical, though he has himself said, that in his "Portraits" the praise is conspicuous and the criticism inobtrusive — "dans mes *Portraits*, le plus souvent la louange est extérieure, et la critique intestine." The *man* himself continually evades us, but the *critic* is always trustworthy. He has, to a phenomenal degree, the delicate *flair* which detects the remotest perfume amid a confusion of fragrances ; he knows how to isolate it, how to detach it, how to delight us with it—and then when we are just upon the verge of deeper enjoyment he proves that the scent is not so exquisite in itself after all, but owes much to the blending of the exhalations of neighbouring flowers and blossoms and herbs. While we are still wavering

between conviction and disenchantment, he explains that
it has this peculiarity or that, because of the soil whence it
derives its nurture, a thin rocky earth or loam of the valley.
Then, finally, lest we should turn aside disappointedly, he
tells us something about it which we had but half noticed,
praises fragrance and bloom again, and with a charming
smile gives us the flower to take with us, perchance to
press and put away, like sweet-lavender or wild-thyme, a
hostage against oblivion of a certain hour, a certain moment
of fresh experience.

What range for one man to cover! Let one but glance
at the contents of all these volumes : besides this novel,
these three collections of poems, here are seven volumes
of "Port Royal" (containing a multitude of vignettes
and sketches as well as carefully - drawn pictures and
portraits), fifteen volumes of the "Causeries du Lundi,"
volumes upon volumes of "Nouveaux Lundis," "Portraits
Littéraires," "Portraits des Contemporains," "Derniers
Portraits" and "Portraits des Femmes," this "Tableau
historique et critique de la Poésie Française et du Théâtre
Français au xvie Siècle," these miscellaneous essays and
studies. Then those richly suggestive "Notes," and
"Thoughts," and "Remarks" must be added, and the recent
volume edited by M. Jules Troubat, Sainte-Beuve's latest
secretary and "good friend with qualifications," and an "Introduction" here and an "Étude" there. Let us take up
M. Charles Pierrot's "Table Générale et Analytique" (forming the appendical volume to the *Causeries du Lundi*),
and glance through his painstaking analyses. Sainte-
Beuve, we find, has written no fewer than nineteen separate
studies on celebrities of the sixteenth century, among them
personages so distinct as Rabelais and Casaubon, Marie
Stuart and Montaigne ; seventy-four upon the great spirits
of the seventeenth century, including more than one careful
essay upon Pascal ; forty-three upon the men of the eighteenth
century, comprising Le Sage and Voltaire and Vauvenargues,
Rousseau and Diderot and Grimm, men of letters, men
of science, philosophers, priests, kings, and diplomatists ;

thirty, again, upon those who flourished in the reign of Louis XVI., with vivid portraits of Malesherbes and Necker, Rivarol and Beaumarchais, Condorcet and Bernardin de St. Pierre ; eleven not less thorough *études* upon the rarest spirits of the Revolution, Mirabeau and La Fayette, André Chenier, Mme. Roland ; and, at last, those brilliant essays upon the makers of our own century, from Napoleon and other generals on the one hand, and from Chateaubriand and Joubert on the other, to Gustave Flaubert, and Taine, and Théodore de Banville ; — in all, one hundred and five "portraits" of men and women of the most divers genius. To these (close upon three hundred, including the not infrequent two or even three essays upon one individual) must be added the studies upon foreign writers of ancient and modern times,—Theocritus and Firdausi, Virgil and Dante, Frederic the Great, Goethe, Gibbon, Cowper,—not to speak of a score or so of essays on various themes, from "Du Génie Critique" in the "Portraits Littéraires" (Tome i.) to "Du Roman Intime" in the "Portraits des Femmes."

It will readily be understood, therefore, that the essays which succeed these introductory words represent but a fragment of the critical work of Sainte-Beuve. The reader must be generous to the translators, moreover, for the great critic's style does not lend itself to easy reproduction. Yet, though something essential of the charm is lost, enough remains to make a translation from him well worth while ; the matter is there, though the charm of manner may escape the ablest interpreter. I cannot honestly say that in these essays Sainte-Beuve is quite as fascinating as in the original ; yet they will certainly serve to give the English reader not merely some comprehension of the intellectual range and insight of Sainte-Beuve, but some idea also of his grace of style and individual charm. They have been selected with a view to show his many-sidedness, his genuine sympathies with the most antagonistic types, his delightful method, his guiding principle.

I should like to conclude with a selection from the

several hundred detached "Pensées" of Sainte-Beuve which are often so beautiful, so clever, or so witty, which are always so suggestive ; but that is impracticable now. Those who would become more intimate with the man as well as with the writer should turn, in particular, to the two hundred and more "Notes et Pensées" in the eleventh volume of the *Causeries du Lundi,* and to the richly suggestive posthumous collection, "Les Cahiers de Sainte-Beuve." For "finis," however, I may select one, peculiarly apt to the great critic himself, as well as to the epoch. It is the cxxvii. of the "Notes et Pensées:" "Great things may be accomplished in our days, great discoveries for example, great enterprises ; but these do not give greatness to our epoch. Greatness is shown especially in its point of departure, in its flexibility, in its thought."

WILLIAM SHARP.

GOETHE AND BETTINA.[*]

1850.

IT may be remembered we have already seen Jean-
Jacques Rousseau in correspondence with one of
his admirers, whose partiality towards him ultimately
developed into a warmer sentiment. After reading
La Nouvelle Heloïse, Madame de la Tour - Franque-
ville became extremely enthusiastic, believing herself
to be a Julie d'Etange, and thereupon indited somewhat ardent love-letters to the great author, who, in
his misanthropical way, treated her far from well. It
is curious to note, in a similar case, how differently
Goethe, the great poet of Germany, behaved to one of
his admirers, who declared her love with such wild
bursts of enthusiasm. But not more in this case than
in the other must we expect to find a true, natural, and
mutual affection—the love of two beings who exchange
and mingle their most cherished feelings. The adoration in question is not real love—it is merely a kind
of worship, which requires the god and the priestess.
Only, Rousseau was an invalid—a fretful god, suffering
from hypochondria, who had fewer good than bad days ;
Goethe, on the other hand, was a superior god, calm

* *Correspondence between Goethe and Bettina.* Translated
from the German by St. Sebastien Albin.

A

and equable, in good health and benevolent—in fact,
the Olympian Jupiter, who looks on smiling.

In the spring of 1807 there lived at Frankfort a
charming young girl of nineteen years of age, though
of such small stature that she only appeared to be twelve
or thirteen. Bettina Brentano, the child of an Italian
father, who had settled and married at Frankfort, came
of a family noted for its originality, each member
having some singular or fantastic characteristic. It
was said in the town that "madness only began in the
Brentano family where it ended in other people."
Little Bettina considered this saying as a compliment.
"What others call eccentricity is quite comprehensible
to me," she would remark, "and is part of some esoteric
quality that I cannot define." She had in her much of
the devil and the imp—in fact, all that is the reverse
of the *bourgeois* and conventional mind, against which
she waged eternal war. A true Italian as regards her
highly-coloured, picturesque, and vivid imagination,
she was quite German in her dreamy enthusiasm,
which at times verged on hallucination. She would
sometimes exclaim, "There is a demon in me, opposed
to all practical reality." Poetry was her natural world.
She felt art and nature as they are only felt in Italy,
but her essentially Italian conceptions, after having
assumed all the colours of the rainbow, usually ended
in mere vagaries. In short, in spite of the rare qualities
with which little Bettina was endowed, she lacked
what might be called sound common-sense—a quality
hardly in keeping with all her other gifts. It seemed
as if Bettina's family, in leaving Italy for Germany,
had, instead of passing through France, come by the
way of Tyrol, with some band of gay Bohemians.
The faults to which I have just alluded grow sometimes graver the older one becomes, but at nineteen

they merely lend an additional charm and piquancy. It is almost necessary to apologise in speaking so freely in relation to Bettina ; for Signorina Brentano having become Frau d'Arnim, and subsequently widow of Achim d'Arnim, one of the most distinguished poets of Germany, is now living in Berlin, surrounded by some of the most remarkable men of the day. She receives a homage and consideration not merely due to the noble qualities of her mind, but to the excellency of her character. This woman, who was once such a frolic-some imp, is now known as one of the most unselfish and true-hearted of her sex.

However, it was she herself, who, in 1835, two years after Goethe's death, published the correspondence that enables us to glean an accurate knowledge of her character, allowing us—in fact, compelling us—to speak so unconstrainedly in relation to her. This book, translated into French by a woman of merit, who has concealed her identity under the *nom de plume* of *St. Sebastien Albin*, is a most curious work, enabling us to realize the difference that distinguishes the German genius from our own. The preface, as written by the authoress, is thus worded : " This book is intended for good, not bad people." This is similar to saying, " Honi soit qui mal y pense." It was quite suddenly that Bettina fell in love with the great poet Goethe, but her romantic feeling was of a purely ideal nature, for as yet she had never seen him. While musing alone one summer morn in the redolent and silent garden, Goethe's image presented itself to her mind. She only knew him through his renown and his works—in fact, through the very evil she heard spoken in relation to his cold and indifferent character. But the idea instantly captivated her imagination ; she had dis-covered an object for her worship. Goethe was then

fifty-eight years of age. In his youth he had conceived
a slight affection for Bettina's mother. For many years
he had lived at Weimar, at the small court of Charles-
Augustus, in favour, or rather intimate friendship, with
the prince. There he calmly pursued his vast studies,
for ever creating with prolific ease ; he was then at the
height of contentment, genius, and glory.

Goethe's mother lived at Frankfort. She and Bettina
became great friends, and the young girl began to love,
study, and understand the son in the person of this
remarkable mother, so worthy of him to whom she had
given birth. Goethe's aged parent—" Goethe's Lady
Counsellor," as she was called—with her noble (I was
about to say august) character, and her mind so replete
with great sayings and memorable conversations, liked
nothing better than to converse about her son. In
speaking of him *her eyes would dilate like those of a
child*, and beam with contentment. Bettina became
the old lady's favourite, and, on entering her room,
would take a stool at her feet, rush at random into
conversation, disturb the order of everything around
her, and, being certain of forgiveness, would allow
herself every freedom. The worthy Frau Goethe being
gifted with great discernment and common-sense, perceived from the very first that Bettina's love for her
son would lead to no serious consequences, and that
this flame would injure no one. She would laugh at
the child's fancy, and in so doing would profit by it.
Not a day passed without this happy mother thinking
of her son ; "and these thoughts," she would say, "are
gold to me." If not to Bettina, to whom could she
express them, before whom could she count her gold
—this treasure not intended for the ears of the profane ?
So, when the frolicsome young creature was absent,
running along the banks of the Rhine, and playing

the truant in every old tower and rock, she would be greatly missed by her dear "Lady Counsellor." The old lady would write to her in the following manner:—

"Hasten homewards. I do not feel so well this year as last. At times I long, with a certain foreboding, for your presence, and for hours together I sit thinking of Wolfgang" (Goethe's Christian name), "of the days when he was a child playing at my feet, or relating fairy tales to his little brother James. It is absolutely necessary I should have some one to whom I can converse in relation to all this, and *nobody listens to me as well as yourself.* I truly wish you were here."

On returning to the mother of the man she adored, Bettina would hold long conversations with the venerable lady about Goethe's childhood, his early promise, the circumstances attendant on his birth ; about the pear-tree his grandfather planted to celebrate its anniversary, and which afterwards flourished so well ; about the *green arm-chair* where his mother would sit, relating to him tales that made him marvel. Then they would speak about the first signs of his awakening genius. Never was the childhood of a god studied and watched in its minutest details with more pious curiosity. One day, while he was crossing the road with several other children, his mother and a friend, who were at the window, remarked that he walked with "great majesty," and afterwards told him his upright bearing distinguished him from the other boys of his age. "That is how I wish to begin," he replied ; "later on I shall distinguish myself in many different ways. And this has been realized," his mother would add, on relating the incident.

Bettina knew everything about Goethe's early life better than he did himself, and later on he had recourse to her knowledge when wishing to write his memoirs.

She was right in saying, "As to me, what is my life but a profound mirror of your own ?"

In his boyhood Goethe was considered one of the finest fellows of his age. He was fond of skating, and one fine afternoon he persuaded his mother to come and watch him sporting on the ice. Goethe's mother, liking sumptuous apparel, arrayed herself in "a pelisse, trimmed with crimson velvet, that had a long train and gold clasps," and she drove off in a carriage with friends.

"On arriving at the river Mein, we found my son energetically skating. He flew like an arrow through the throng of skaters ; his cheeks were rosy from the fresh air, and his auburn locks were denuded of their powder. On perceiving my crimson pelisse, he immediately came up to the carriage, and looked at me with a gracious smile. 'Well, what do you require ?' I said to him. 'Mother, you are not cold in the carriage, so give me your velvet mantle.' 'But you do not wish to array yourself in my cloak, do you ?' 'Yes, certainly.' There was I, taking off my warm pelisse, which he donned, and, throwing the train over his arm, he sprang on the ice like a very son of the gods. Ah, Bettina ! if you had only seen him ! Nothing could have been finer. I clapped my hands with joy. All my life I shall see him as he was then, proceeding from one archway and entering through the other, the wind the while raising the train of the pelisse, that had fallen from his arm."

And she added that Bettina's mother was on the bank, and it was her whom her son wished to please that day. Have you not perceived in this simple tale told by the mother, all the pride of a Latona : "He is a son of the gods"? These were the words of a Roman senator's wife, of a Roman empress, or Cornelia, rather than the utterance of the spouse of a Frankfort citizen !

The feeling that then inspired this mother, in regard to her son, ultimately permeated the heart of the German nation. Goethe is "the German father-land." In reading Bettina's letters, we find ourselves, like her, studying Goethe through his mother, and in so doing we discover his simple and more natural grandeur. Before the influence of court etiquette had distorted some of his better qualities, we see in him the true sincerity of his race. We wish his genius had been rather more influenced by this saying of his mother, "There is nothing grander than when the man is to be felt in the man." It is said that Goethe had but little affection for his mother, that he was indifferent towards her, not visiting her for years, though he was only a distance of about forty miles from where she lived. And on this point he has been accused of coldness and egotism. But here, I think, there has been exaggeration. Before denying any quality to Goethe it is necessary to think twice, for at first sight we imagine him to be cold, but this very coldness often conceals some underlying quality. A mother does not continue to love and revere her son when he has been guilty of a really serious wrong towards her. Goethe's mother did not see anything wrongful in her son's conduct, and it does not beseem us to be severer than she. This son loved his mother in his peculiar way, and though his conduct could not perhaps be exactly regarded as the model of filial behaviour, it cannot be said he was in any wise ungrateful. "Keep my mother's heart warm," he would say, in writing to Bettina. . . . "I should like to be able to reward you for the care you take of my mother. A chilling *draught* seemed to emanate from her surroundings. Now that I know you are near her I feel comforted —I feel warm." The idea of *a draught* makes us smile. Fontenelle could not have expressed himself better. I have sometimes thought Goethe might be defined as a *Fontenelle invested with poetry.* At the time of his mother's death, Bettina wrote to him, alluding to the cold disposition that was supposed to characterize him—a disposition inimical to all grief: " It is said you turn away from all that is sad and irreparable—do not turn away from the image of your dying mother ; remember how loving and wise she was up to the last moment, and how the *poetic element* predominated in her." By this last touch, Bettina evinced her knowledge of how to affect the great poet. Goethe responded in words replete with gratitude for the care she had shown his mother in her old age. But from that day their relationship suffered by the loss of the being who had forged the link between them. However, as I have already mentioned, Bettina was in love with Goethe. We might ask what were the signs of this feeling. It was not an ordinary affection, it was not even a passionate love, which, like that of Dido, Juliet, or Virginia, burns and consumes until the desire is satisfied. It was an ideal sentiment, better than a love purely from the imagination, and yet dissimilar to one entirely from the heart. I scarcely know how to explain the feeling, and even Bettina herself could hardly define what she felt. The fact is that, gifted with a vivid imagination, exquisite poetical feeling, and a passionate love of nature, she personified all her tastes and youthful inspirations in Goethe's image, loving him with rapture as the incarnation of all her dreams. Her love did not sadden her, but, on the contrary, rendered her happier. " I know a secret," she would say ; "the greatest happiness is when two beings are united, and the divine genius is with them."

It generally sufficed her to be thus united in spirit. Goethe, whose insight into life and human nature was as profound as his knowledge of the ideal, had from the first understood the quality of this love, and did not shun it, though at the same time he avoided too close a contact. The privilege of the gods is, as we all know, the possession of eternal youth : even at fifty-eight years of age, Goethe would not have been able to endure every day with impunity the innocent famili-arities and enticements of Bettina. But the girl lived far away. She wrote him letters, full of life, brilliant with sensibility, colouring, sound, and manifold fancies. These epistles interested him, and seemed to rejuvenate his mind. A new being, full of grace, was revealing herself to the observation of his poetical and withal scientific mind. She opened for his inspection an *un-looked - for book, full of delightful images and charming depictions.* It seemed to him as much worth his while reading this book as any other, especially as his own name was to be found on every page, encircled with a halo of glory. He called Bettina's letters " the gospel of nature." " Continue," he would say, " preaching your gospel of nature." He felt he was the *god-made man* of that evangel. She recalled to his mind (and his artistic talent needed it) the impressions and the freshness of the past, all of which he had lost in his somewhat artificial life. " All you tell me brings me back remembrances of youth—it produces the effect of events gone by that all of a sudden we distinctly remember, though for a long time we may have for-gotten them." Goethe never lavished his attention on Bettina, though he never once repulsed her. He would reply to her letters in a sufficiently encouraging way for her to continue writing. There was a strange scene the very first time Bettina met Goethe, and from the way she describes the meeting we perceive she does not write for the benefit of the cynical scoffer. Towards the end of April, in 1807, she accompanied her sister

and brother-in-law to Berlin, and they promised to
return by the way of Weimar. They were obliged to
pass through the regiments that were then occupying
the land. On this journey Bettina was arrayed in
male attire, and sat on the box of the coach in order to
see farther, while at every halting-place she assisted in
harnessing and unharnessing the horses. In the morning she would shoot off a pistol in the forests, and
clamber up the trees like a squirrel, for she was
peculiarly agile (Goethe called her the Little Mouse).
One day, when in an uncommonly frolicsome mood
she had ascended into one of the Gothic sculptures of
the Cologne Cathedral, she commenced a letter in the
following way to Goethe's mother :—

"Lady Counsellor, how alarmed you would be to see
me now, seated in a Gothic rose."

Somewhere else she says: "I prefer dancing to
walking, and I prefer flying to dancing."

Bettina arrived at Weimar after passing several
sleepless nights on the box of the coach. She immediately called on Wieland, who knew her family, and
obtained from him a letter, introducing her to Goethe.
On arriving at the house of the great poet, she waited
a few minutes before seeing him. Suddenly the door
opened, and Goethe appeared.

"He surveyed me solemnly and fixedly. I believe
I stretched out my hands towards him—I felt my
strength failing me ! Goethe folded me to his heart,
murmuring the while : '*Poor child ! have I frightened
you ?*' These were the first words he uttered, and they
entered my soul. He led me into his room, and made
me sit on the sofa before him. We were then both
speechless. He at last broke the silence. 'You will
have read in the paper,' he said, 'that a few days ago
we sustained a great loss through the death of the

Duchess Amelia' (the Dowager-Duchess of Saxe-Weimar). 'Oh!' I answered, 'I never read the papers.' 'Indeed! I imagined that everything in relation to Weimar interested you?' 'No, nothing interests me excepting yourself; moreover, I am much too impatient to read a newspaper.' 'You are a charming child.' Then came a long pause. I was still exiled on that fatal sofa, shy and trembling. You know it is impossible for me to remain sitting like a well-bred person. Alas! mother" (it was Goethe's mother to whom she was writing), "my conduct was utterly disgraceful. I at last exclaimed, 'I cannot remain on this couch!' and I arose suddenly. 'Well, do as you please,' he replied. I threw my arms round his neck, and he drew me on his knee, pressing me to his heart."

In reading this scene, we must remember it took place in Germany, not in France! She remained long enough on his shoulder to fall asleep, for she had been travelling for several nights, and was exhausted with fatigue. Only on awakening did she begin conversing a little. Goethe plucked a leaf off the vine that clustered round his window, and said, "This leaf and your cheek have the same freshness and the same bloom." My readers may be inclined to believe this scene was quite childish; but Goethe soon divulged to her his most serious and intimate thoughts. He became nearly emotional in speaking of Schiller, saying he had died two springs ago; and on Bettina interrupting him to remark she did not care for Schiller, he explained to her all the beauties of this poetical nature—so dissimilar to his own, but one of infinite grandeur—a nature he himself had the generosity of fully appreciating.

The evening of the next day Bettina saw Goethe again at Wieland's, and on her appearing to be jealous

regarding a bunch of violets he held, which she supposed had been given him by a woman, he threw her
the flowers, remarking, "Are you not content if I give
them to you?" These first scenes at Weimar were
child-like and mystic, though from the very first
marked by great intensity—it would not have been
wise to enact them every day. At their second meeting, that took place at Wartbourg, after an interval of
a few months, Bettina could hardly speak, so deep was
her emotion. Goethe placed his hand on her lips, and
said, "Speak with your eyes—I understand everything;" and when he saw that the eyes of the charming
child, *the dark, courageous child,* were full of tears, he
closed them, adding wisely, "Let us be calm—it beseems us both to be so!" But in recalling these scenes,
are you not tempted to exclaim, "What would Voltaire
have said?"

Let us abandon all French ideas in order to take a
right estimate of Goethe. Nobody has spoken more
highly of Voltaire than Goethe himself, nor has
any one understood him better as the perfect type of
French genius. Let us then endeavour, in our turn, to
render Goethe his due in taking him as the complete
type of German genius. Goethe and Cuvier are the
two greatest men of this century. Goethe's strength
lay in the breadth and universality of his mind. He
was both a naturalist and a poet, dissecting as well as
idealizing all he studied, analyzing human nature from
the scientific point of view, though not unmindful of
the poetry that is concealed in everything. There was
not a man, not a single branch of study, he did not
inquire into with the greatest curiosity and precision, anxious to discover every detail in relation
to both. In fact, he appeared to exemplify a nearly
exclusive passion for everything he studied; but

when he had found out all he wished, he would take up something new. In his splendid house, over the entrance of which was inscribed the word *Salve*, he even lavished his hospitality on strangers and foreigners, welcoming them without distinction, conversing with them in their own language, utilizing them all as subjects of analysis ; for his sole aim was to *develop his taste.* He was perfectly serene, and devoid of all bitterness or envy. When any one or anything displeased him, or seemed unworthy of a longer inspection, he would turn away and throw his glance elsewhere. He had but to choose in this vast universe ! He was not indifferent, neither was he adhesive. He was of an insistently inquiring mind, without ever being thoroughly captivated by any person or any object. His beneficence was like that of a truly Olympian god. This word does not provoke a smile on the other side of the Rhine. At the apparition of a new poet, or an original genius—a Byron, or a Manzoni—Goethe would instantly study him with keen interest, without allowing his judgment to be marred by any personal feeling —for he possessed the *love of genius.* When *The Count of Carmagnola*, by Manzoni, came to his notice, he, though knowing nothing about the author, commenced a thorough study of the work, discovering manifold intentions, manifold beauties, in the piece. One day, in his periodical essay ("On Art and Antiquity"), where he would pour out the superabundance of his thoughts, he introduced Manzoni to the notice of Europe. When he was attacked by an English review, Goethe defended him, adducing a number of reasons which certainly had never occurred to Manzoni. Then, on meeting M. Cousin, who was one of Manzoni's friends, he questioned him with an insatiable curiosity regarding the author's smallest physical and mental

peculiarities, until he could thoroughly well picture to
himself this being—this new production of nature, who
went by the name of *Manzoni*, dissecting him as he
would, in his capacity of botanist, have examined a
plant. He acted thus in relation to everything. He
was full of advice and solicitude towards Schiller. He
perceived how the young poet, so ardently enthusiastic,
was carried away by the power of his own genius.
There were great differences of opinion between them.
However, Goethe was not any the less disposed to
use his influence when Schiller wished to be named
Professor of History at Jena. Then a happy incident
bringing them together, a union took place, and Goethe
became the mentor of the genius who was still in search
of the right way.

Their correspondence, that has been since published,
shows us Goethe in the *rôle* of adviser, exercising a
healthy influence on Schiller, without any conscious
display of superiority, guiding him like a father or
brother. He called Schiller *a magnificent being.*
Goethe understood everything in the universe—everything excepting, perhaps, two things—the *Christian* and
the *hero*. As regards this, he was lacking in some
quality of the heart. He considered Leonidas and
Pascal as two *unnatural productions* of nature. Goethe
liked neither grief nor sacrifice. Seeing any one ill or
sad, he remembered how he had written *Werther*, to
rid himself of an importunate idea of suicide. "Do as
I have done," he would say; "give birth to this child
that torments you, and it will no longer injure your
entrails." His mother also knew of this remedy. She
wrote once in the following way to Bettina, who, by
reason of the suicide of a young friend, the Canoness
Gunderode, had become quite melancholy :—

"My son has said we *must exhaust by work all that*

oppresses us. When he had any sorrow he would make a poem of his grief. I have repeatedly told you to write the history of Gunderode and send it to Weimar ; my son would be pleased, and he would keep it ; moreover, it would then no longer oppress your heart."

Such was (as far as a rapid sketch can portray) the man whom Bettina loved, but in a manner that beseemed them both, that is to say, with a flame that caressed without burning. After the day of their interview, and on her return to Frankfort, Bettina wrote to him on every subject, sent him all her thoughts, at times in a tone of solemn adoration, at others in one of gaiety and fun. Her effusions are often strange, and verge on the ridiculous :—"When I am in the midst of nature, whose intimate life your mind has made me understand, I often confound your mind with this life ! I throw myself on the green sward and kiss it." She repeats, too, frequently :—"You are beautiful, you are grand and admirable, better than all I have ever known. . . . Like the sun, you vanquish the darkness of the night." At such times she addresses him as if speaking to Jehovah. But, apart from these exaggerations, she utters some thoughts of exquisite freshness and delicacy. The letter we might call " Under the linden-tree," by reason of the hollow linden which is therein described, is replete with life, the warbling of birds and the buzzing of the bees in the sunlight. When Bettina complains in this note of not being loved as she loves, she is right in exclaiming, "Am I not the bee who flies away to bring you the nectar from every flower ?" But Goethe, like Rousseau—like every poet —was only in love with the heroine of his fancy, *the ideal of his dreams.* Rousseau would not have abandoned the Julie of his creation for any Madame d'Houdetot ! Now and then there are touches of common-sense and flashes of real passion in Bettina's letters, and she complains of this inequality of exchange. "Do not sin against me," she writes to Goethe; "do not make to yourself any *graven image* to worship, while it is in your power to create a wondrous and spiritual bond between us." But this wholly metaphysical, this ethereal love—is that the true bond?

Unlike Rousseau, Goethe was withal charming to the one he kept at a distance; in a moment he would retrieve by a gracious and poetical word his apparent or real coldness. This amiable and frolicsome girl reminded him of the days when he was better, more truly happy, when he had as yet not sacrificed to the contemplation of outward things the primitive delicacy of his soul. He realized that he was indebted to her for a rejuvenescence of mind and a return to spiritual life! He often sent her back her own thoughts clothed in rhyme and in the form of a sonnet. "Good-bye, my charming child," he wrote to her. "Send me soon another letter, that I may have something to translate." She provided him with themes for poetry, and he would put them into execution. May we venture to remark, it seems to us, that though the natural blossom became in consequence an artificial flower of greater finish, it lost at the same time its tender grace and native perfume. Moreover, Goethe appeared to recognise this superiority of a rich and capricious nature, that constantly displayed itself under an ever surprising, an ever new form. "You are delightful, my young dancer; at every movement you throw us a wreath unawares!" She understood him so well, she so fully appreciated him! From Bettina's letters we can obtain not only an ideal Goethe, but a living Goethe, still grand and handsome in spite of the first touch of old age, and smiling from beneath his placid brow "with his large dark eyes, that beam with kindness when he looks at me." She felt in him the dignity *arising from the grandeur of the mind.*

"When I saw you for the first time, what appeared to me remarkable, and inspired me with both a profound respect and decided love, was the fact of your whole being expressing King David's words in relation to man — 'Every one should be king of himself.'" Goethe's dignity, that evinced itself in his talent as well as his person, harmonized with a certain elegance — not a tender or simple, but a severe and reflective grace. "My friend!" passionately exclaims Bettina in one of her letters, "I might be jealous of the Graces — they are women, and continually surround you. Where you are, is also St. Harmony." Bettina understood him in every form of his talent, in the transient and tumultuous phase of "Werther," and in the calmer and superior one that ultimately triumphed. "Superb torrent, how wildly you rushed through the regions of youth! and now, tranquil river, how peacefully you glide through the meadows!" With what disdain, not unmingled with jealousy, did she find fault with Madame de Staël, who, expecting to discover in Goethe a second "Werther," was disappointed in finding him so different!

"Madame de Staël has been twice mistaken," said Bettina; "firstly in her expectations, and secondly in her judgment."

However, this lively young girl, this restless imp, who possessed some of the ethereal spirit of Queen Mab or Titania, had also, like Wilhelm Meister's "Mignon," Italian blood in her veins. In spite of her attempts to be as German as possible, she was not altogether content with this æsthetic adoration, that did not satisfy the yearnings of nature. At times, hardly knowing what

B

she needed, she craved for more—she would have liked
to pass a whole spring with her friend. She wished
to give up her mind entirely to him, and to receive an
equal return. "Can we receive a present without
giving ourselves as a present?" she wisely remarked.
"That which is not given entirely and for ever cannot
be deemed a gift!" Goethe offered her glimpses of his
inner life, but did not give himself entirely to her.
He would write her short notes, occasionally entrusting
their composition to his secretary. Then she would be
vexed, and sulk for some time. She demanded but
little, only wishing this little to come entirely from
himself. "You have me in my letters," she said, "but
have I you in yours?" After the death of Goethe's
mother, Bettina had greater reason to complain; for
the good mother knew her son, and would explain to
the young girl how the poet's true feeling was concealed
in these few lightly written lines, that from any pen
but his would have suggested but little. "I know
Wolfgang" (Goethe) "so well," she would say; "he has
written this, his heart overflowing with emotion." But
when Bettina could no longer have recourse to this far-
seeing interpreter, she would often be doubtful, though
there was never time for real grief to creep in among
those fantastic and brilliant flashes of intellect; and
in reading Bettina's letters, we discover ourselves, like
Goethe, believing them to be but the fruits of a pleasant
illusion. "For who could reasonably believe in so
much love. It is better to accept it all as a *dream*."

If Goethe was really in love, he had often cause to be
jealous of Bettina; for she would be casually captivated
by many people and many things. I will not linger
to relate to my readers about the handsome French
hussars, and the young artists of Munich, to whom she
lectured on realistic Italian art, for Goethe's great rivals

in her youthful and enthusiastic soul were the Italian
hero Hofer, and the grand composer Beethoven. Hofer,
the hero of the insurrection of Tyrol, was Bettina's
first infidelity. In the spring of 1809, when the war
broke out everywhere afresh, and gigantic conflicts were
about to be waged, Bettina could not remain unmoved.
The sound of the bugle aroused her from her sleep.
She watched from Munich, where she was then living,
all the phases of the holy and patriotic revolt of the
Tyroleans, sacrificing themselves for the emperor who
abandoned them, and finally delivered them over to the
enemy. Her anxiety was unequalled. Instead of the
graceful fancies in which she revelled like a bee or
butterfly, Goethe was surprised at receiving letters
written in the following tone :—"Goethe, oh that I
could enter Tyrol, and arrive in time to die the death
of those heroes !" The capture and death of Hofer,
who was allowed to be shot, drew words of grief and
eloquence from her pen. Goethe's replies to these
heroic utterances were curious, to say the least.
During that period, and the days of Wagram, he was
writing his novel on *Elective Affinities,* so as to
divert his mind from the sorrows of the times.
Bettina's heart-felt cry drew from him the following
calm reflection :—"In placing your last epistle with the
others, I find it closes an interesting epoch (1807–10).
You have led me through *a delightful labyrinth* of
philosophical, historical, and musical opinions to *the
Temple of Mars,* and in everything you preserve your
healthy energy." There we perceive the moral anatomist, who appreciates and reproduces, though he does
not share the impressions of his surroundings. He
commends Bettina for her energy, but he could have
dispensed with it. From his point of view, he could
only see in all these harrowing pictures the "capricious

transformations of life," only catch in these scenes
of bloodshed a little glimpse of poetry. " You are
right," he observed, in writing to Bettina, " in saying
that the blood of the heroes shed on the soil is recalled
to life in every flower."

No—decidedly, heroism was not one of Goethe's
distinguishing qualities. Goethe has been frequently
called an Olympian god, but he was certainly not one
of Homer's Olympian deities. When such battles were
waged at Ilion, Homer's gods descended from their high
estate.

Beethoven may be considered as Bettina's second
infidelity. From the very first day she met him at
Vienna, in the May of 1810, Bettina experienced all
she had felt for Goethe—she forgot the universe. The
great composer, deaf, misanthropical, and cynical to
every one, was, from the first, confidential and full
of gracious attentions to her. He immediately went to
the piano to play and sing the most divine melodies
for her benefit. Charmed with the interest she displayed, and her frank and simple approbation, he
insisted on accompanying her home, conversing as they
walked, on several artistic subjects. " His speech was
so vehement, and he stopped so frequently, that it
required great courage to remain listening ; but all he
uttered was so impetuous and unexpected, that I completely forgot we were in the street. My people were
surprised at perceiving he was with me. After dinner
he went to the piano, of his own accord, and played for
a long time in the most marvellous way—his genius
and pride fermenting together."

It is a rare gift, and certainly a proof of genius, to
be able in such a degree to gain the confidence of men
of genius. Beethoven knew of Bettina's connection
with Goethe. He would often speak of him to her,

hoping thus to become acquainted with the great author's thoughts on art. Bettina has admirably depicted these conversations with Beethoven. She has painted in memorable words the simplicity of a genius convinced of his own strength—the grave, energetic, and passionate nature of a man who disdains his century, and has faith in the future. This Beethoven gives us the idea of a Milton. Here, it must be remembered, we are with the greatest of men, and all honour is due to Bettina for having been capable of acting the part of interpreter between Goethe and Beethoven. Goethe was touched by Beethoven's messages, and answered with feeling and compliance. They were like two kings—two *magi*, saluting one another from afar through the medium of a little frolicsome page, who was well able to deliver their messages. Even in this, Goethe preserved his character of anatomist, who seeks to discover the natural meaning of beings and things. He was enchanted at seeing such a grand *individual* as Beethoven added to his collection. "I have had much pleasure," he observed, "in contemplating this image of an original genius."

Goethe and Beethoven met two years afterwards at Toeplitz. At this meeting of two equal geniuses, similar in so many ways, and who inwardly criticised each other, Beethoven manifestly maintained the moral superiority. We have two letters from the composer to Bettina. Evidently he was touched by this young person, who was such an able listener, answering him with her fine expressive glances. After reading these letters, we are inclined to exclaim, "Why did she not love Beethoven instead of Goethe? He would have rendered her gift for gift." Beethoven was certainly as much in love with art as Goethe, and it would have always remained his principal passion. But he suffered, and his proud genius sought a melancholy seclusion. He exclaimed, with grief and sympathy, "Dear, very dear Bettina, who understands art? With whom can I converse about this grand divinity?" He could have opened his heart to her; for he added, "Dear child, for a long time we have professed the same opinion on every subject."

In 1811, Bettina married M. d'Arnim, and her relations with Goethe, though they never entirely ceased, suffered in consequence. With every exertion of the imagination, it was impossible to continue the dream as before. The connection became by degrees a remembrance — an immutable worship; and Bettina gradually buried all that which had been the incense of her youth.

I should like to have given a clearer and completer idea of a book that differs so much from our way of feeling and thinking—of a work so replete with grace, imagination, fine perception, and folly, and in which every stroke of common-sense assumes the form of a whimsical conceit.

Goethe, who happened one day to be strolling with Bettina in the park at Weimar, compared her to the Greek woman at Mantinea, who gave lessons in love to Socrates; and he added, "You do not utter one single word of sense, but your absurdities teach more than all the wisdom of the Greek woman." What could we add to such an opinion? But the day after reading this book, so as to enter fully into the truth of nature and human passion, and expel from our minds all idle fancies and imaginings, I should strongly advise the perusal of the story of Dido in the *Æneid*, a few scenes from *Romeo and Juliet*, the tale of *Francesa de Rimini* by Dante, or simply *Manon Lescaut*.

ALFRED DE MUSSET.

1857.

————

As with an army so with a nation ; it is the bounden
duty of every generation to bury their dead, and to
confer the last honours on the departed.   It were not
right that the charming poet, who has recently been
taken from our midst, should be laid under the sod
before receiving a few words of good-bye from an old
friend and witness of his first literary efforts.   Alfred
de Musset's poetry was so well known, so dear to us
from the very first ; it touched our hearts so deeply in
its freshness and delicate bloom ; he so belonged to
our generation (though with a greater touch of youth)
—a generation then essentially poetical, and devoted to
feeling and its expression !   I see him as he looked
twenty-nine years ago, at the time of his *debut* in the
world of literature, entering first into Victor Hugo's
circle, then proceeding to that of Alfred de Vigny and
the brothers Deschamps.   With what an easy grace he
made his first entrance !   What surprise and delight
he aroused in the hearts of his listeners at the recital
of his poems, *L'Andalouse, Don Paez,* and *Juana.*   It
was Spring itself, a Spring of youth and poetry, that
blossomed forth before our ravished gaze.   He was
scarcely eighteen years of age ; his brow betokened all

the pride of manhood ; the bloom was on his cheek, for
the roses of childhood still lingered there.　Full of the
pride of life, he advanced with haughty gait and head
erect, as if assured of his conquest.　Nobody at first
sight could have suggested a better idea of youthful
genius.　There seemed promise of a French Byron in
these brilliant verses of poetic fervour, the very success
of which has since made them commonplace, but which
were then so new in the poetry of France :—

"Love, plague of the world, and unutterable madness," etc.

"How lovely she is in the evening, under the beams of the
　　moon," etc.

"Oh ! decrepid old age, and heads bald and bare," etc.

"Perchance the threshold of the ancient Palace Luigi," etc.

These lines, bearing a truly Shakespearian impress ;
these wild flights of fancy, 'mid flashes of audacious
wit; these gleams of warmth and precocious passion,—
all suggested the genius of England's fiery bard.

The light and elegant verses that proceeded every
morning from his own lips, lingering soon afterwards
on those of many others, were in accordance with his
years.　But passion he divined, and wished to outstrip.
He would ask the secret of it from his friends, richer in
experience, and still suffering from some wound, as we
can see in the lines addressed to Ulric Guttinguer—

"Ulric, no eye has ever measured the abyss of the seas,"...

that end with this verse—

"I, so young, envying thy wounds and thy pain !"

When coming face to face with pleasure at some ball
or festive gathering, De Musset was not captivated by
the smiling surface ; in his inward deep reflection he

would seek the sadness and bitterness underlying it all ;
apparently abandoning himself to the joys of the
moment, he would murmur inwardly, so as to enhance
the very flavour of his enjoyment, that it was only a
fleeting second that could never be recalled. In everything he sought a stronger and more acute sensation, in
harmony with the tone of his own mind. He found
that the roses of a day failed to succeed each other with
sufficient rapidity ; he would have liked to cull them
one and all, so as to better inhale their sweetness and
more fully express their essence.

At the time of his first success there was a new
school of literature already greatly in vogue, and
developing daily. It was in its bosom that De Musset
produced his first works, and it might have seemed that
he had been nourished on the principles of this school.
He made a point of demonstrating that it was not so,
or, at least, need not have been so ; that he wrote on
the lines of no previous author ; that, even in the new
ranks, he was entirely original. Here he undoubtedly
displayed too much impatience. What had he to fear ?
The mere growth of his daring talent would in itself
have sufficed to evince his originality. But he was
not the man to await his fruit in due season.

The new school of poetry had been, up till then, of
a somewhat solemn, dreamy, sentimental, and withal
religious tone ; it prided itself on its accuracy, I may
even say strictness of form. De Musset threw over
this fastidious solemnity, exhibiting an excess of familiarity and raillery. He scorned both rhyme and rhythm ;
his poetry was in perfect *déshabillé*, and he wrote
Mardoche, followed shortly after by *Namouna.* "Oh !
the profane man, the libertine !" exclaimed the
world ; and yet, every one knew them by heart.
Dozens of verses from *Mardoche* would be taken for

recitation, though hardly any one knew the reason why, unless it were that the poem was easy, and replete with fancy, marked here and there, even in its insolence, with a grain of unexpected good sense, and that the verses were "friends to the memory." Even the most sentimental dreamers would murmur to themselves, with an air of triumph, the verse, "Happy a lover," etc. As to the Don Juan in *Namouna*, this new kind of *roué*, who appeared to be the author's favourite child— the ideal, alas! of his vice and grief—he was so fascinating, so boldly sketched; he occasioned the creation of such fine lines (two hundred of the most daring verses ever seen in French poetry), that one coincided with the poet himself in saying, "What do I say! Such as he is, the world loves him still."

In his drama, *The Cup and the Lips*, Alfred de Musset expressed admirably in his creations of Frank and Belcolore the struggle between a noble and proud heart and the genius of the senses, to which that heart has once yielded. In this piece we catch glimpses—in fact, more than glimpses—of hideous truths, of monsters dragged into the light of day from out this cavern of the heart, as Bacon calls it; but this work is invested with a glamour, an incomparable power, and even though the monster is not vanquished, we can hear the golden arrows of Apollo falling and resounding on his scales.

Alfred de Musset, similar to more than one of the characters he has depicted, said that to be an artist such as he wished, he must see and know all, and dive into the very depths of everything. A most perilous and fatal theory! And by what a powerful and expressive image he rendered this idea in his comedy, *Lorenzaccio*. Who, indeed, is this Lorenzo, whose youth has been as pure as gold, whose heart and hands were peaceful, who in the simple rising and setting of the sun seemed to see every human hope blossoming around him, who was goodness itself, and who brought his own destruction by wishing to be great ? Lorenzo is not an artist, he wishes to be a man of action, a great citizen ; he has determined upon a heroic plan ; he has decided to deliver Florence, his native town, from the vile and debauched tyrant, Alexander de Medici, his own cousin. In order to succeed in his enterprise, what does he propose undertaking? To play the part of Brutus, but of a Brutus adapted to the circumstances of the case ; and in this end, to lend himself to all the frivolities and vices dear to the tyrant whose orgies dishonour Florence. He creeps into Alexander's confidence, and becomes his accomplice and instrument, abiding his time and watching for the right moment. But, in the meanwhile, he has lived too dissipated a life ; day by day he has plunged too deeply into the mire of uncleanliness ; he has seen too much of the dregs of humanity. He awakes from his dream. Nevertheless, he perseveres, resolved to attain his object, knowing, though, that it will be all in vain. He will destroy the monster who fills the city with disgust, but he knows full well that the day she is delivered from his tyranny, Florence will take unto herself another master, and that he, Lorenzo, will only incur disgrace. Thus Lorenzo, by dint of simulating vice, and putting on evil like a borrowed garment, is at last impregnated with the evil he at first only assumes.

The tunic steeped in the blood of Nessus has penetrated his skin and bones. The dialogue between Lorenzo and Philip Strozzi—a virtuous and honourable citizen, who merely sees things in their right and honest light—is one of startling truth. Lorenzo is conscious of having seen and experienced too much, of having ventured too far into the depths of life to ever return. He realizes that he has introduced into his heart that implacable intruder ennui, which forces him without pleasure to do from habit and necessity what he at first essayed through affectation and pretence. The whole of this deplorable moral attitude is portrayed in moving words : " Poor child ! you rend my heart," says Philip ; and in answer to all the profound and contradictory revelations of the young man, he can only repeat : " All this astonishes me, and in what you relate there are things that pain, others that please me."

I am merely touching lightly on the subject. But in thus re-glancing, now that Alfred de Musset is no more, over a good number of his characters and pieces, we discover in this child of genius the antithesis of Goethe. The German writer severed himself from his most intimate productions. He cut the link between them and himself, casting his imaginary characters from him, while invading fresh fields, wherein he could capture new creations. For him poetry signified deliverance. Unlike De Musset, Goethe, from the time he wrote *Werther*—that is, from his youth upwards —to the end of his eighty years of life, was doing his best to husband his mental and physical resources. For Alfred de Musset poetry was all in all, it was himself ; it was his own youthful soul, his own flesh and blood, that he transmuted into verse. When he had thrown to others the dazzling limbs of his poetic being—limbs that at times appeared like unto those of Phaeton or a youthful god (take, for instance, the splendid invocations in *Rolla*)—he still retained his own heart, bleeding, burning, and wearied. Why was he not more patient ? Everything would have come in due course. But he hastened to anticipate and devour the seasons.

After the mimicry of passion—passion that as a child he so well divined—passion at last came of itself—real, undeniable passion. We all know how, after it had for a time enhanced the glamour of his genius, it laid waste his whole existence. An allusion to this story of passion may be permitted, considering how well it is known.

The poets of our day, the children of this generation, are not deserving of reticence on our part—considering how little reticence they have exercised themselves. Above all, in this particular episode, confessions have proceeded from two sides, and we might remark with Bossuet, were we ourselves exceptions to the rule, that there are individuals who spend their life in filling the world with the "follies of their mis-spent youth."

The world, or rather France, has in this case, it must be allowed, submitted with all good grace ; she has listened with keen interest to what appeared to her at least eloquent and sincere. Alfred de Musset was indebted to these hours of storm and anguish for the creation, in his *Immortal Nights*, of lines which have vibrated through every heart, and that will for ever stand the test of time. As long as France and French poetry exist, the flames of De Musset will live, like those of Sappho ! Let us not forget to add a *Souvenir* to these celebrated *Nights*—a *Souvenir* closely associated with these poems. The *Souvenir* describes a return to the Forest of Fontainebleau, and is of a beauty pure and touching ; and, what is rare in him, this work is imbued with infinite tenderness. In his rapid existence there was one moment of wondrous promise during the interval of his hours of intense excitement. It was at this period that De Musset's poems acquired a new subtlety of thought, a touch of irony, a mocking lightness, withal exhaling the pristine freshness which his weariness of the world had not yet destroyed. Such an elegant and essentially French treatment had not been seen since the days of Hamilton and Voltaire. This moment, though, was of short duration, for De Musset drove everything at a rapid pace ; but it was a precious moment, appearing to his friends as precursory to a greater maturity of thought. He then wrote proverbs of an exquisite delicacy, and verses always beautiful, but light, and invested with a superior ease—verses withal pregnant of wit and reflection allied to an elegant carelessness. He would burst into accents of profound melody, that recalled the harmonious sounds of other times :—

"Star of love, descend not from the skies !"

All this seemed to promise a more temperate season, and the lasting reign of a talent that was sought after in the most critical circles, as well as by the most fervent of youth. Whether it were a question of singing the first triumphs of Rachel, or the *début* of Pauline Garcia, or railing at the coarsely emphatic effusions of patriotism from the free "German Rhine," or writing a witty tale, De Musset would rise to the occasion, appropriately blending enthusiasm with satire. He verified more and more the device of the poet : "I am a light thing, flying to every subject."

He was the fashion. His books, as I have already remarked in another article, became acceptable as bridal presents, and I have noticed young husbands giving them to their wives to read from the very first month of their marriage, so as to develop in them a poetical taste. It was then, also, that men of wit and reputed discernment, the *dilettanti* that are so numerous in our

country,* presumed to say they preferred De Musset's
prose to his poetry, as if his prose were not essentially
that of a poet : only a poet could have written such fine
prose. There are people, who, if they could, would
sever a bee in two. However, De Musset gained
theatrical triumphs as well as the favour of society. It
had been discovered for some time that more than one of
the comedies composing *The Performance in an Arm-
Chair*, could, if understood and well rendered by
amateur actors and actresses, procure an hour of very
agreeable recreation. These little pieces were represented in the country-houses, where there was always
plenty of leisure time. To Madame Allan, the actress,
is due the honour of having discovered that De Musset's
stage-works were equally suitable for representation on
the public boards. It was wittily said of her, that she
brought his *Caprice* from Russia in her muff.†

The success that was gained at the Comédie-Fran-
çaise by this pretty poetical gem, proved that the
public still possessed a latent refinement in literary
taste, that merely required arousing. What, then, did
the poet wish to render him happy ? Why did he, who
was still so young, not wish to live and enjoy life ?

* An elegant writer, who passes for one of the first critics of
the day, but who has never been a good judge in relation to any
contemporary author (I mean M. Villemain, if we are compelled
to name) belonged to this particular class.

† The *Revue des Deux-Mondes* of May the 15th (page 475)
seems to contest the authenticity of this remark. But let it be
remembered that those who made it did not mean to imply that
the editor of the said *Revue*, who was for some years the able
manager of the Theatre-Français, did not think of producing
Alfred de Musset's pieces ; what was really implied was, that
Madame Allan, who had played *Le Caprice* at St. Petersburg,
played it so delightfully in Paris that every one began to appreciate De Musset's dainty composition.

Why did he not return the smiles that greeted his presence ? Why did his genius, now influenced by a greater calm, not reawaken the old inspiration, which would have been purified by his later finer shades of taste ?

De Musset was essentially a poet ; he wished to feel. He belonged to a generation whose password, whose first vow, inscribed in the depths of the heart, was " Poetry, poetry itself, poetry before anything." " During my youth," remarked one of the poets of this period, " I desired and worshipped nothing beyond passion," that is to say, the living part of poetry.*

De Musset disdained adopting what is called wisdom, but which seemed to him merely the gradual decay of life. It was impossible for him to transform himself. Having attained and gone beyond the summit of the mountain, it seemed to him that he had come to the end of every desire ; life had become a burden to him. He was not one of those to whom the pleasure of

* Somebody well known to me—an intimate friend of De Musset, and who shared with him in this life of imagination and unbridled desire—has even dared to inscribe a thought, which I have stolen, unknown to him—a thought that describes fully, indeed more than fully, the kind of irregularity and vehemence of passion so dear to the generation called the children of the century :—"At times I picture to myself an ideal Elysium, where every one will join his favourite group, and find again those whom he resembles. My group—as I have already stated elsewhere—my secret group is that of the incontinent, of those who are sad, like Abbadona, mysterious and dreamy even in the very bosom of pleasure, and for ever pale and wan in their voluptuous tenderness. De Musset, on the contrary, has had for his ideal, ever since his earliest days, the delights of nocturnal revels ; his group is that of the Duchess of Berry (daughter of the Regent), and of little Aristion of the Anthology, who danced so well, and who could drink the contents of three goblets, one after the other, her brow decked with wreaths."

criticism could supply the place of artistic production ; of those who can find interest in literary work, and who are capable of studying arduously, in order to avoid passions that are still in search of prey, without having any really serious object. He could but hate life from the moment (using his own language) that it was no longer sacred youth. He considered life not worth living unless mingled with a slight delirium.

His verses are steeped in these sentiments. He must often have experienced a feeling of anguish and defeat in reflecting on the existence of a superior truth, of a severer poetical beauty, of which he formed a perfect conception, but that he had no longer the power of attaining.

On a certain occasion, one of De Musset's most devoted friends, and whose recent death must have been a grievous omen to him—Alfred Tattet, whom I happened to encounter on the Boulevards—showed me a scrap of paper, containing some pencilled lines, that he had found that very morning on the table at De Musset's bedside. The poet was at that time staying with him in his country-house, in the Valley of Montmorency.†

---

* To live and enjoy meant one and the same to him. " Joy ! joy ! and death after !" that was his device. During De Musset's second youth, when happening to mention that he was reading *Werther* and *La Nouvelle Héloïse*, and devouring all the sublime vagaries of which he had so often made fun, he added : " I shall perchance venture too far in that sense, as in the other. But what matter ? I shall still march onward." In fact, hurry on until extinction. What a frightful moral and physical hygiene !

† My memory is very clear on this point. M. Edmund Texier believes that they were written in another country-house of M. Tattet, at La Madeleine, near Fontainebleau ; but it was really at Bury, in the Valley of Montmorency, that they were written.

Here are the verses stolen from him by his friend, and since published, but they only possess their full meaning when one knows they were written during a night of utter exhaustion and bitter regret :—

> " I have lost my strength and life,
> My friends and my joyous mood ;
> I have even lost the pride
> That made me trust my genius.
>
> When I discovered truth,
> Methought she was a friend ;
> When I understood and felt her,
> She had already wearied me.
>
> And yet she is immortal ;
> And those who have lived without her
> Have ignored everything.
>
> God speaks, and I must answer.
> The only thing that remains to me
> Is sometimes to have wept."

Let us remember his first songs of the Page or Amorous Knight—

> " To the hunt, the happy hunt ! "

—a matutinal sound of the horn,—and in placing it at the side of his final sorrowing lines, we seem to perceive the whole of De Musset's poetical career illustrated in the two poems representing glory and pardon. In the beginning, what a glorious train of light ! Then, what gloom, what shadow ! The poet who has been but the startling type of many unknown souls of his day,—he who has but expressed their attempts, their failures, their grandeur, their miseries,—his name, I say, will never die. Let us, in particular, engrave this name on our hearts. He has bequeathed to us the task of getting old,—to us, who

could exclaim the other day, in all truth, on returning from his funeral : "For many years our youth
has been dead, but we have only just buried it
with him !"   Let us admire, continue to love and to
honour in its best and most beautiful expression, the
profound and light spirit that he has breathed forth in
his poems ; but withal it behoves us not to forget the
infirmity inherent in our being, and never to boast of
the gifts that human nature has received.

LETTERS OF
LORD CHESTERFIELD TO HIS SON.

1850.

In every age there have been treatises written with a view to forming the Honourable Man, the Well-bred Man, the Courtier, and the Accomplished Gentleman. When reading, in a following age, these diverse works on politeness and the conduct of life, we immediately detect portions of them that are as equally out of date as the fashions of our grandfathers ; the pattern has evidently changed. If by chance the book has been written by a man of sense, who has known and understood mankind, we cannot fail to profit by the study of the models given to preceding generations. The letters Lord Chesterfield wrote to his son represented a perfect school of manners and knowledge of the world. They are particularly interesting from the fact that in writing them he never thought of suggesting a model of behaviour, but only of privately forming an excellent pupil. They are confidential letters, that were suddenly brought to light, betraying all the secrets and ingenuity of an anxious parent. If, in reading them to-day, we are struck by the importance given to mere details and different little points in dress, we are not any the less impressed by the lasting portions of the book—those parts that are in keeping with the thought and observation of all times. This solid portion of the work is more considerable than we should believe when only glancing at it casually. In striving to educate his son as a polite member of society, Lord Chesterfield pursued a different course to Cicero ; for, instead of composing a treatise on " The Duties," he wrote letters which, by reason of their combination of good judgment and lightness of touch, —of a certain frivolous tone intermingled with a more serious grace— might take the mean between *The Memoirs of the Chevalier de Grammont* and *Telemachus.*

Before expatiating on the subject, we must first know something about Lord Chesterfield, one of the most brilliant wits of his day, and one whose name has been closely associated with France. Philip Dormer Stanhope, Earl of Chesterfield, was born in London on the 22nd of September 1694, the same year as Voltaire. He was the descendant of an illustrious race He was fully conscious of its worth, and he desired to uphold the honour of his name. However, he could not refrain from ridiculing the pride of birth, and, in order to resist the glamour of pedigree, he hung among the portraits of his ancestors, two faces of an old man and woman ; under one was the inscription, "*Adam* de Stanhope," under the other, "*Eve* de Stanhope." Thus, though sustaining the honour of his birth, he repudiated all the chimeras of lineage. Chesterfield's father did not undertake his education ; he was consigned to the care of his grandmother, Lady Halifax. From an early age he wished to excel in all directions ; and this feeling of ambition, that he endeavoured, in after years, to awaken in the heart of his son, is, in evil as well as good, the principle of every great achievement. Having no one in his

early youth to advise and direct him, he more than
once made a wrong choice in selecting the object of his
emulation, and conceived a false idea of honour. He
confesses having indulged, at a period of inexperience,
in drink and other excesses. He had no natural inclination to habits of intemperance, but assumed them in
deference to his desire to be considered a man of pleasure.
His practice in relation to gambling was governed by
the same wish to distinguish himself. In the first
instance he gambled with a sense of indifference, but
later on he could not live without it, and in consequence compromised his fortune for a long time.
"Take warning by my conduct," said he to his son;
"choose your own pleasures, and do not let others
choose them for you."

This desire to excel and gain distinction was
frequently put to good account; his early studies were
excellent. He was sent to Cambridge, and learnt all
that was taught there; he pursued the study of civil
law and philosophy; he followed the mathematical
lectures given by the blind scholar Saunderson. He
read Greek fluently, and wrote in French long accounts
of his progress to his old tutor, a refugee clergyman,
called Jouneau. Lord Chesterfield had in his childhood learnt our language from a Normandy lady's-maid.
The last time Chesterfield visited Paris, in 1741, M.
de Fontenelle told him his accent was similar to that
of Normandy, and asked whether his first lessons in
French had been given him by any one from those parts.

After passing two years at Cambridge University, he
travelled over the Continent, according to the custom
of the young noblemen of his country. He visited
Holland, Italy, and France. From Paris he wrote to
this same M. Jouneau on the 7th December 1714:—

"I shall not tell you what I think of the French,

because I am being often taken for a Frenchman, and more than one of them has paid me the highest possible compliment, by saying, '*Monsieur, you are quite one of ourselves.*' I shall only tell you that I am impudent ; that I talk a great deal very loudly, and with an air of authority ; that I sing ; that I dance in my walk ; and, finally, that I spend immense sums in powder, feathers, white gloves, etc."

Here we see him in his mocking, satirical, and somewhat insolent humour, making his points for the first time at our expense ; later on he will render full justice to our good qualities.

In the Letters to his son he has given a description of himself as he locked the first day of his *entrée* into good society, when still covered with the rust of university life. He was shy, awkward, and silent, and could only summon sufficient courage to remark to a beautiful lady near him, "Madam, do you not think it extremely warm to-day ?" But Lord Chesterfield wrote thus to his son, so as not to discourage him, and to show him to what an extent a young man can alter to his advantage. He gives himself as an example, in order to embolden his son and gain his confidence. I should not think of considering this anecdote as absolute truth. If Chesterfield was for a time awkward in society, the period must have been of short duration.

Queen Anne had just died ; Chesterfield hailed with delight the accession of the House of Hanover, of which he became one of the avowed champions. At the opening of his public career he secured a seat in the House of Commons, and began his political life under favourable auspices. However, a circumstance, trivial to all appearances, kept him, it is said, in check, and somewhat paralyzed his eloquence. A member of the House, who was gifted with no special talent save that

of mimicry, imitated to perfection the speakers to whom
he responded. Chesterfield feared ridicule (it was one
of his weaknesses), and on certain occasions he preserved
a greater silence than he wished, for fear of incurring
the mockery of his colleague. At the death of his
father he inherited the earldom, and entered the House
of Lords, where he found more scope for the display of
his graceful tact and polished eloquence. Nevertheless,
he evidently appreciated the floor of the House of
Commons more than that of the House of Lords, as an
arena wherein was exhibited greater political aptitude,
and greater debating power. "It is surprising," he
remarked afterwards, in relation to Pitt, at the time
that great orator consented to enter the Upper House
under the title of Lord Chatham,—"it is surprising
that a man in the plenitude of his power, at the very
moment when his ambition has obtained the most
complete triumph, should leave the House which procured him that power, and which alone could ensure
its maintenance, to retire into that Hospital for
Incurables, the House of Lords."

It is not for me to criticise the Earl's political career.
Nevertheless, if I may risk a general assertion, let me
mention that his ambition was never entirely satisfied,
and that the brilliancy of his public life concealed many
shattered plans and broken hopes. Twice, in the two
decisive moments of his political career, he failed.
When young, and in the first flush of ambition, he
staked everything in the cause of the presumptive heir
of the throne, who became later George II. He was
one of those who, on the accession of this prince, anticipated his favour and a share of power. But this clever
man had not pursued the right course to catch the rays
of the rising sun. For a long time he had paid court
to the prince's mistress, believing she was destined to

great power, while he had neglected the legitimate wife, the future queen, who alone possessed real influence. Queen Caroline never forgave him. This was the first blow to his political fortune. He was then thirty-three years old, and full of ambitious hopes. He had been too impatient, and pursued a wrong direction. Robert Walpole, to all appearances much less keen and dexterous, had employed better measures, and had calculated more wisely.

Thrown into the Opposition party, more especially since 1732 — when he was compelled to resign his functions at Court—Chesterfield worked for six·years with might and main, diligent in the destruction of Walpole's ministry. Walpole, however, did not fall until 1742. But the Earl failed to immediately gain a footing in the new Government. It was more with an honorary than a real title, that two years afterwards, in 1744, he entered office, first as Ambassador at the Hague and Viceroy of Ireland, then as Secretary of State and member of the Cabinet (1746–48).

In short, Lord Chesterfield, though always an important politician in his country, either as one of the leaders of the Opposition, or as an able diplomatist, was never an influential minister of State.

In politics he certainly possessed the intuition and foresight that belong to a great breadth of mind, but these qualities were more pronounced than the patience, perseverance, and practical every-day firmness so necessary to politicians in power. In truth, we can say of him, as it is said of La Rochefoucauld, that politics made an accomplished moralist of the incomplete man of action.

In 1744, at the age of only fifty years, his political aspirations seemed partly to have exhausted themselves ; his health obliged him to seek seclusion. We now know the object of his secret ideal and his real ambition. He had had, in 1733, before his marriage, a natural son by a French lady, a certain Madame du Bouchet, whom he had met in Holland. He fostered a deep affection for this child. It was in all sincerity that he wrote to him : "From the very first day of your life the dearest object of mine has been to make you as perfect as the weakness of human nature will allow." All his wishes and affection were centred in his son, and, either as Viceroy of Ireland or Secretary of State in London, he would always find time to write him lengthy detailed letters, to direct him in every action of his life, to perfect him in serious accomplishments as well as in good-breeding.

Lord Chesterfield, whose writings we are so fond of reading, was a man of mind and experience, and, as a result of his eventful career, we are initiated in all the secret springs of political and public life. From his youth upwards he was a friend of Pope and Bolingbroke ; he introduced Voltaire's and Montesquieu's works into England, and he corresponded with Fontenelle and Madame de Tencin. He was made a member of the Academy of Inscriptions. He united in him the wit of the two nations, and in more than one clever essay, but more particularly in the Letters to his son, shows himself to be an agreeable and consummate moralist—in fact, one of the masters of the science of life. He is the Rochefoucauld of England.

Montesquieu, after the publication of his *Esprit des Lois*, wrote to the Abbé Guasco, who was then in England :—"Tell Lord Chesterfield that nothing flatters me so much as his approbation, but that, as he is reading me for the third time, he will be better able to tell me what there is to correct and rectify in my book ; nothing could instruct me better than his observations

and his criticisms." It is Lord Chesterfield, who, conversing on one occasion with Montesquieu in respect to
the readiness of the French nation for revolutions, and
their dislike to slow reform, gave utterance to the
saying which fully describes its history : "You French
know how to make barricades, but you never raise
barriers." Lord Chesterfield had a deep admiration
for Voltaire ; he remarked in regard to *The Century
of Louis XIV.:* "Lord Bolingbroke had taught me
how to read history, Voltaire teaches me how it should
be written." Nevertheless, with that practical common-
sense that rarely forsakes clever men on the other side
of the Channel, he disapproved of Voltaire's indiscre-
tion. When already aged and in seclusion, Chesterfield
wrote thus to a French lady of his acquaintance :—

"Your good authors are my principal resource :
Voltaire especially charms me, with the exception of
his impiety, with which he cannot help seasoning all
that he writes, and which he would do better carefully
to suppress, for one ought not to disturb established
order. Let every one think as he will, or rather as he
can, but let him not communicate his ideas if they are
of a nature to trouble the peace of society."

In this letter, indited in 1768, he merely repeated
what he had said twenty-five years previously, in
writing to Crébillon's son, who was a singular corre-
spondent, and still more singular confidant, as regards
morality. Both their letters had relation to Voltaire,
the first having relation to his tragedy *Mahomet,* and
the daring passages this work contained.

"What I do not pardon him for, and that which is
not deserving of pardon in him," wrote Chesterfield,
"is his desire to propagate a doctrine as pernicious to
domestic society as contrary to the common religion of
all countries. I strongly doubt whether it is permissible

for a man to write against the worship and belief of
his country, even if he be fully persuaded of its error,
on account of the trouble and disorder it might cause ;
but I am sure that it is in no wise allowable to attack
the foundations of true morality, and to break necessary
bonds which are already too weak to keep men in the
path of duty."

In these reflections, Chesterfield was not mistaken
in his opinion of Voltaire's great inconsistency.   In
short, his inconsistency was as follows : Voltaire, who
looked upon men as fools or children, and who could
hardly ridicule them sufficiently, placed nevertheless
in their hands loaded fire-arms, without considering
what use they might make of these weapons.

Lord Chesterfield himself, I must admit, has been
accused by the Puritans of his country of having been
guilty of a breach of morality in the Letters to his son.
The severe Johnson—who, moreover, was not impartial
in his criticism of Chesterfield, believing he had cause
to complain of the Earl's conduct as regarded himself
—remarked at the time the Letters were published,
that "they taught the morals of a courtesan and the
manners of a dancing-master."

Such an assertion is simply an injustice ; and if
Chesterfield, in this particular case, dwells so fully on
grace of manner, and places so much value on all that
contributes to render a young man agreeable, it is
because he has already attended to the more solid part
of his son's education.   Moreover, his pupil was not
lacking in qualities of honour, but in those that help
to render a man affable and gracious.   Though many of
the ideas in Chesterfield's epistles may appear strange,
expressed by a father to his son, all these letters are,
nevertheless, animated by a spirit of true tenderness
and wisdom.   Had Horace been blessed with a son, I

verily believe he would have spoken to him in a somewhat similar tone.

The Letters begin with the rudiments of education
and instruction. Chesterfield teaches his son the first
elements of history and mythology in French. I am
far from regretting the publication of these first letters ;
they contain excellent advice. Young Stanhope was
scarcely eight years old when his father compiled a
little method of rhetoric, within the child's capacity,
and endeavoured to teach him elegant language and
distinction in his mode of expression. He exhorts him
above all to pay *attention* to all he undertakes, and gives
this word its full value. It is *attention* alone, says he,
that grafts objects in our memory : " There is no surer
mark of a mean and meagre intellect in the world than
inattention. All that is worth the trouble of doing at
all deserves to be well done, and nothing can be well
done without attention." He frequently repeats this
maxim, and applies it to different subjects, in proportion as his pupil becomes older and better able to
understand the term in its full meaning. No matter
whether it is question of work or pleasure, he wishes
everything to be well and thoroughly done in its proper
time. " When you read Horace, pay attention to the
accuracy of his thoughts, to the elegance of his diction,
and to the beauty of his poetry, and do not think of
the *De Homini et Cive* of Puffendorf ; and when you
read Puffendorf, do not think of Madame de St.
Germain ; nor of Puffendorf, when you speak to
Madame de St. Germain." But this free and strong
power of directing one's thoughts by an effort of the
will, is peculiar only to great or singularly good
minds.

M. Royer-Collard used to remark : " What was
most wanting in these days was *respect* in the moral

order, and *attention* in the intellectual order." Lord
Chesterfield would, though in a less serious manner,
have been capable of giving utterance to the same idea.
He had soon felt what was lacking in this child, whose
spiritual growth had become the object of his life.

" On sounding your character to its very depths,"
he said to him, "I have not, thank God, discovered
any vice of heart or weakness of head so far ; but I
have discovered idleness, inattention, and indifference,
defects which are only pardonable in the aged, who, in
the decline of life, when health and spirits give way,
have a sort of right to that kind of tranquillity.   But
a young man ought to be ambitious to shine and
excel."

It is precisely this sacred fire which makes the
Achilles, the Alexanders, and the Cæsars—"To be the
first in all one undertakes."   But nature had neglected
to implant, in the honest but essentially mediocre soul
of Chesterfield's son, this maxim of great hearts and all
illustrious men.   " You appear to lack," said his father,
"that *vivida vis animi,* which excites the majority of
young men to please, to strive, and to outdo others.'
" When I was your age," he says again, " I should have
been ashamed for another to know his lesson better, or
to have been before me in a game, and I should have
had no rest till I had regained the advantage."   This
little course of education by letter offers a ceaseless
dramatic interest ; in reading these epistles we follow
the efforts of a delicate, distinguished, and energetic
nature, such as Lord Chesterfield's, battling with an
honest but indolent one, struggling against an inert
temperament, and wishing to create, at any sacrifice,
an accomplished, agreeable, and original masterpiece ;
though, after all his striving, he merely produces a
fairly good imitation.

What sustains, in fact what touches the reader in this struggle in which so much skill is expended, and the same advice continually repeated, is the true fatherly affection that animates and seems to inspire this refined and excellent master. He is patient as well as incisive, full of wonderful resource and dexterity, and indefatigable in sowing in this barren soil the seeds of elegance and grace. Not that this son, the object of so much culture and zeal, was in any way unworthy of his father. It was said that nobody could be clumsier and more awkward than he, and Johnson is supposed to have made a remark of the same nature. These are, however, gross exaggerations. It appears, according to more impartial evidence, that Mr. Stanhope, though far from attaining a high standard of elegance, had in reality the tone of a well-bred, polite, and discreet man. But do not my readers feel that it was precisely these qualities which made matters so hopeless? It would have perhaps been better to have totally failed, and only to have succeeded in creating an original character in an inverse sense, instead or wasting care and money in the production of an ordinary, insignificant man of the world.

Chesterfield must have been grievously disappointed, and those who are not fathers themselves might smile pitifully at his fruitless efforts.

From the very first, Chesterfield considered France as the most suitable country in which his son could gain polished manners and a certain gentleness that cannot be acquired in later years. We glean from certain private letters, written to a lady in Paris, called, I believe, Madame de Monconseil, that Chesterfield intended sending his son there from his childhood.

"I have a boy," he wrote to this friend, "who is now thirteen years old : I freely confess to you that he

is not legitimate ; but his mother was well born, and
was kinder to me than I deserved. As to the boy,
perhaps it is partiality, but I think him amiable : he
has a pretty face ; he has much sprightliness, and I
think intelligence, for his age. He speaks French
perfectly ; he knows a good deal of Latin and Greek,
and he has ancient and modern history at his fingers'
ends. He is at school at present, but as they never
dream here of forming the manners of young people,
and they are almost all foolish, awkward, and un-
polished—in short, such as you see them when they
come to Paris at the age of twenty or twenty-one, I do
not wish my boy to remain here to acquire such bad
habits ; for this reason, when he is fourteen, I think of
sending him to Paris. As I love the child dearly, and
have set myself to make something good of him, as I
believe he has the stuff in him, my idea is to unite in
him what has never been found in one person before—
I mean the best qualities of the two nations."

He then enters into the details of his plans, and the
means he intends taking : an English tutor in the
morning, a French teacher in the afternoon, and, above
all, the help of refined society. The war that broke
out between France and England obliged the father to
postpone this plan of Parisian education, and it was
not until 1751, at the age of nineteen, that the young
man visited Paris. He had already travelled through
Switzerland, Germany, and Italy.

This most solicitous father had arranged everything
in a manner conducive to his son's success and welcome reception in Paris. The young man resided at
the Academy with M. de la Guérinière. In the
morning he attended to his studies, and the rest of the
day he devoted to society. "Pleasure is now the last
branch of your education," writes this indulgent father ;

"it will soften and polish your manners, it will incite you to seek and finally to acquire *graces.*" On this point the parent is unsparing in his remarks. He incessantly repeats his admonitions touching elegance of manner, for without the *graces* every effort is fruitless. "If they are not natural to you, cultivate them," he exclaims. He seemed to forget that, to be able to cultivate them, one must already possess them.

Three ladies, friends of his father, were particularly requested to watch over him and counsel him at the commencement. These so-called governesses were Madame de Monconseil, Lady Hervey, and Madame du Bocage. Chesterfield considered them only essential during the first period of his son's sojourn in Paris; he wished the young man to act afterwards independently, and choose for himself some charming and more familiar guide. In regard to the delicate question of women, Chesterfield breaks the ice as follows:—"I shall not talk to you on this subject like a theologian, or a moralist, or a father," he says; "I set aside any age, and only take yours into consideration. I wish to speak to you as one man of pleasure would to another, if he has taste and spirit." He inspires him with that good taste by which he can indulge in his pleasures, with a due regard to a refined association in respect to the gentler sex, while he will be led to avoid those relationships which tend to demoralize. His principle was that "an honourable arrangement is befitting a gallant man." His morality in this respect was contained in this verse of Voltaire: "There is never any evil in good company." Such passages as these induced the grave Johnson, in a sense of modesty, to turn his head away; we, in our modesty, only smile.

The serious and the light are at every moment aptly blended in these Letters. Marcel, the dancing-master,

D

is frequently recommended ; Montesquieu, the same. The Abbé de Guasco, a parasite of Montesquieu, is also referred to as a useful person for giving introductions here and there.

"Between you and me," writes Chesterfield, "he has more knowledge than genius ; but *a clever man knows how to make use of everything*, and every man is good for something. As to the Président of Montesquieu, he is in all respects a precious acquaintance ; '*He has genius, with the most extensive reading in the world. Drink of this fountain as much as possible.*'"

Among the authors whom Chesterfield commends at this period to his son's notice, are La Rochefoucauld and La Bruyère :—

"If you read some of La Rochefoucauld's maxims in the morning, consider them, examine them well, and compare them with the originals you meet in the evening. Read La Bruyère in the morning, and see in the evening if his portraits are correct."

But these excellent guides have not any other utility save that of a chart. Without personal observation and experience they would be useless, and would even lead one into as many mistakes as would a map if one wished to gain a complete knowledge of towns and provinces. Better to read one man than ten books. Here are some remarks worthy of these masters of morality :—

"The most essential of all knowledge, I mean the knowledge of the world, is never acquired without great attention, and I know a great many aged persons who, after having had an extensive acquaintance, are still mere children in the knowledge of the world."

"Human nature is the same all over the world ; but 'ts operations are so varied by education and custom, that we ought to see it in all its aspects to get an intimate knowledge of it."

"Almost all men are born with every passion to some extent, but there is hardly a man who has not a dominant passion to which the others are subordinate. Discover this governing passion in every individual ; search into the recesses of his heart, and observe the different effects of the same passion in different people. And when you have found the master passion of a man, remember never to trust to him where that passion is concerned."

"If you wish particularly to gain the good graces and affection of certain people, men or women, try to discover their most striking merit, if they have one, and their dominant weakness, for every one has his own, then do justice to the one, and *a little more than justice to the other.*"

"Women, in general, have only one object, which is their beauty, upon which subject hardly any flattery can be too gross to please them."

"The flattery which is most pleasing to really beautiful or decidedly ugly women, is that which is addressed to the intellect."

If at times he seems to despise women, he makes amends elsewhere for his apparent scorn. Whatever he may think, he does not permit his son to revile the fair sex :—

"You appear to think that from the day of *Eve* to the present time they have done much harm : as regards *that lady*, I agree with you ; but from her time history teaches you that men have done more harm in the world than women ; and, to speak truly, I would warn you not to trust either sex more than is absolutely necessary. But what I particularly advise you is this : never to attack whole bodies, whatever they may be."

"Individuals occasionally forgive, but bodies and societies never do."

In all directions Chesterfield recommends circumspection and a certain impartial discretion, even in relation to the rogues and fools with which the world abounds. "After their friendship there is nothing more dangerous than to have them for enemies." His is not the morality of Cato nor of Zeno, but that of Alcibiades, Aristippus, and Atticus.

Referring to religion, in answer to some rather decided opinions of his son, he says :—

"The reason of every man is, and ought to be, his guide ; and I should have as much right to expect every man to be of my height and temperament, as to wish that he should reason precisely as I do."

In everything he advocates what is good and just, but does not advise one to be an indiscriminate champion. Even in literature, he says, we should tolerate the weaknesses of others. How different is this wisdom to our severe practice of criticism !

He does not, however, counsel untruth ; he is strict on this point. His precept is this : not to express all one thinks, but never to tell a lie.

We see that Chesterfield can treat subjects seriously as well as pleasantly. He remarks continually that the mind should be firm as well as pliant, and that one's real decision of character should be concealed by a gentleness of manner. The Earl appreciated the awakening earnestness of France in the eighteenth century, and perceived her latent redoubtable fecundity of ideas. According to him, Duclos was right in observing, in his *Reflections*, that "a germ of reason was beginning to develop itself in France." "What I can confidently predict," adds Chesterfield, "is that before the end of this century the trades of king and priest will have lost half their power." Already, in 1750, he clearly foresaw our Revolution.

From the very first he fortified his son against the idea that the French are purely frivolous :—

"The cold inhabitants of the north look upon the French as a frivolous people, who sing and whistle and dance perpetually ; this is very far from being the truth, though the army of *fops* seem to justify it. But these *fops*, ripened by age and experience, often turn into very able men."

His ideal was to unite in oneself the respective merits of the two nations ; but, even if the English were possessed of this combination, he seems to award the preference to France :—

"I have said many times, and I really think, that a Frenchman who joins to a good foundation of virtue, learning, and good sense, the manners and politeness of his country, has attained the perfection of human nature."

Chesterfield himself united to a certain degree the good qualities of the two nations, with an additional feature eminently characteristic of his race. He had imagination even in his humour. Hamilton possesses this distinctive quality, and applies it to his French wit. The great philosopher Bacon is nearly a poet in his style. We can hardly say this of Chesterfield, and yet he evinces more imagination in his wit than we ever meet with in Saint-Evremond or in any of our subtle moralists. In this respect he resembles his friend Montesquieu. If, in the Letters to his son, we are able, without undue severity, to point out certain passages of a slightly corrupt morality, we can, by way of compensation, find some serious and most excellent ones ; those, for instance, in which he mentions Cardinal de Retz, Mazarin, Bolingbroke, Marlborough, and many others.   It is a book abounding in felicitous thought and happy observations.

Chesterfield desired to educate his son for the diplomatic service.   At first he found some difficulty in carrying out his plans, from the fact of the illegitimacy of his child.   In order to still captious objections, he secured for him a seat in Parliament ; it was the surest means of vanquishing the scruples of the court. During his maiden speech, Mr. Stanhope hesitated for a moment, and was obliged to refer to his notes.   He would not attempt to address the House a second time. He succeeded better in diplomacy in one of those minor positions where solid worth suffices.   He filled the office of envoy-extraordinary at the court of Dresden. But his health, which had always been feeble, prematurely gave way, and his father, to his unutterable grief, lost him at the age of thirty-six (1766).

By reason of his numerous infirmities, the Earl lived at this period in complete seclusion, his most painful ailment being that of total deafness.   Montesquieu had formerly remarked to the Earl, when finding that his sight failed him : "I know how to be blind." Chesterfield could not say he knew how to be deaf.   In consequence of this infirmity, he wrote oftener to his friends generally, and particularly to those in France. "The exchange of letters," he remarked, "is the conversation of deaf people, and the only link which connects them with society."   He found his last solace in his charming country-house at Blackheath, to which he had given the French name of "Babiole." He occupied himself with gardening, and the cultivation of melons and pine-apples.   It pleased him to vegetate "in company with them."

"I have vegetated here all this year," he wrote to a French friend (September 1753), "without pleasures and without troubles : my age and deafness prevented the first ; my philosophy, or rather my temperament (for one often confounds them), guaranteed me against the last. I always get as much as I can of the quiet pleasures of gardening, walking, and reading, and in the meantime *I await death without desiring or fearing it.*"

He avoided undertaking any lengthy literary work, feeling too weak for such an effort ; but from time to time he sent agreeable articles to a periodical publication, *The World.*

These articles are in keeping with his reputation for refinement and good-breeding ; but nothing can equal the quality of the work which he himself did not consider a literary production—letters he expected no one to read, and which are to-day the finest legacy of his authorship.

He lingered through a somewhat premature old age. He frequently made witty remarks in relation to this sad subject. Speaking of himself and one of his friends, Lord Tyrawley, who was equally old and infirm, he remarked : " Tyrawley and I," he said, " have been dead two years, but we do not wish it to be known."

Voltaire, in spite of his assumption of a moribund condition, was far better preserved than his contemporary, Lord Chesterfield.   The French philosopher wrote to the Earl the following letter, signed " The old Invalid of Ferney : "—

" May you enjoy an honoured and happy old age, after having passed through all the vicissitudes of life ! May you enjoy the pleasures of mind, and preserve your health of body. Of the five senses that have fallen to our share, you have only one which is enfeebled, and Lord Huntingdon assures me you have an excellent digestion, which is well worth a pair of ears.

It may perhaps be for me to decide whether it is the saddest to be deaf, blind, or the victim of a bad digestion. I can judge of these three conditions, having thoroughly examined the matter, but for a long time I have not, dared express a decided opinion on trifles ; with how much more reason should I therefore hesitate in expressing myself on such an important subject. I am content in believing that if you have the sunlight in the beautiful house you have built, you will secure a few tolerably happy moments; this is all one can hope for at our age. Cicero wrote a beautiful treatise on old age, but he did not prove by the facts of his life the truth of his work ; his latter years were extremely unhappy. You have lived longer and more happily than he. You have had to do with neither Dictators nor Triumvirs. Your lot has been one of the most desirable in this great lottery in which the good numbers are so rare,—a lottery in which the greatest of prizes—perennial happiness—has never been gained by a single human being. Your philosophy has never been ruffled by chimeras such as have sometimes perplexed fairly good brains. You have never in any way been a charlatan, nor the dupe of charlatans, and this I consider as a very uncommon quality, a quality contributing to the glimpse of happiness we are allowed to enjoy in this short life."

Lord Chesterfield died on the 24th of March 1773. In mentioning his charming course of worldly education, we have not deemed it inopportune, even in a democracy, to take a few lessons in the conduct of life and good-breeding, and to accept them from a man whose name is so intimately associated with that of Montesquieu and Voltaire, who, more than any of the countrymen of his day, has shown a singular predilection for our nation ; who has appreciated, perhaps more than

we deserve, our amiable qualities ; who has understood
our serious qualities ; and of whom we might say, with
a full sense of sympathetic admiration, that his mind
would have been French, had it not exhibited, in its
humour and flights of fancy, that indescribable quality
of the imagination which bears essentially the impress
of his race.

DE BALZAC.

1850.

A REAL study relating to the life and works of the
celebrated novelist who has but recently been taken
from our midst, and whose sudden death has caused
universal sorrow, would form a work of considerable
dimension ; but the moment for this has not yet come.
It is not beseeming to make moral inquests of this kind
on those who have only recently passed away—above
all, when the departed one was replete with strength,
promise, and fertility. All that is due to the memory
of a renowned contemporary at the moment that death
has claimed him as his own, is to point out, in a few
emphatic words, his merits, his ability, and the delicate
yet potent charms by which he has influenced his
century. I will endeavour to do so in relation to
Balzac, putting aside all personal feeling,* merely making use of the rights reserved to unbiassed criticism.
Balzac was a portrayer of the manners of our century,
and was keener in his penetration and more original

----

* Look in the *Revue parisienne*, of August 25, 1840, for
M. de Balzac's article in relation to myself. If I have forgotten
it, I do not for one moment fear that other people remember it.
Such judgments as his only condemn in the future those who
have expressed such opinions.

than any other author of that *genre.* Early in life he appropriated the nineteenth century as his special subject. He threw himself ardently into the study of these times, and never once abandoned the theme. Society, like a woman, requires a special painter to delineate it in accordance with its own taste. He was the painter of society, and was unique in its portrayal. He invented a new method of painting this age of ambition and frivolity,—an age which prides itself on its unprecedented characteristics,—thereby gaining its highest applause. He was born before the fall of the Empire ; so, during his childhood, he knew the imperial epoch, and contemplated it with that clearness and fine penetration peculiar to children—that instinctive knowledge that afterwards ripens into keen judgment, but of which the fresh lucidity remains for ever unequalled. Some one belonging to the same age as himself has said : " As a child I felt things so keenly, that my sensations could only be likened to having a knife every moment piercing my heart." Balzac, in this characteristic, was of similar temperament. His childish impressions, resulting later in analysis and portrayal, are characterized by a singular depth of feeling, and it is precisely these impressions that lend such life and delicacy to his ideas. He had already attained manhood at the time of the Restoration, and saw it in its entirety from the most advantageous point of view—that is, as an artistic observer in the crowd, poor and struggling with the hungering envy of genius and human nature, with all that longing which gives a foretaste of debarred luxuries. He was beginning to gain his reputation at the time when the new Government was proclaimed in July 1830. He saw the administration of that Government from above as well as below, and his opinion was perfectly unbiassed. He has

delightfully portrayed the characteristics of that period
in the presentment of his middle-class types. Balzac
lived through the three epochs (all utterly unlike each
other) that form the half of this century, and his works
are in measure the reflection of that period. Who, for
instance, has drawn a better picture of the old beaux
and beauties of the Empire? Who, above all, has
given us a more delightful sketch of the duchesses
and countesses at the end of the Restoration—these
women of thirty, waiting with vague expectation to
be depicted in literature? Who has more accurately
described the unctuous *bourgeoisie,* triumphant under
the dynasty of July, the already extinct class of
the *Birotteaux* and *Crevels?* Balzac had an immense
field before him. He determined soon in life to
delve into its very depths. He surveyed it entirely,
leaving no stone unturned, yet he found his ground
too narrow in proportion to his capacity for literary
ardour. Though it was his apposite and delicate
observation in relation to the higher orders which
gained him the hearts of the aristocratic society,
an entrance into which he had always aspired, he
was not content with merely observing, but often
created new characters.

*The Woman of Thirty, The Deserted Woman, The
Female Grenadier,* were the first productions that
conquered the attention of his readers. The idea
on which *The Woman of Thirty* was based, was not
entirely original. Since the existence of civilised
society, the woman of that age has held an important
place. During the eighteenth century—a century
which had leisure to give a touch of refinement to
all its ideas—a court ball was given on the Shrove
Tuesday of 1763, called the "Mothers' Ball." The
young girls formed the audience, and no woman

under thirty was permitted to dance. The young girls sang a song :—

> *Il est plus d'un mois pour les fleurs,*
> *Et toutes les roses sont sœurs.*

Here, again, is the prettiest verse of this song :—

> *Belles qui formez des projets,*
> *Trente ans est pour vous le bel age ;*
> *Vous n'en avez pas moins d'attraits ;*
> *Vous en connaissez mieux l'usage ;*
> *C'est le vrai moment d'être heureux ;*
> *On plaît autant, on aime mieux.*
> *Enfants de quinze ans,*
> *Laissez danser vos mamans !*

We perceive the eighteenth century taking up the idea for one evening. But our century has seriously grasped the subject, and the theory regarding the woman of thirty, with all her advantages, superiority, and matured perfections, has only arisen in our day. Balzac is the originator of this theory—a theory one of the truest of all in his system of psychological studies. This little book was the beginning of his success. Through his having guessed so well at first, women henceforth believed in him implicitly.

Balzac was certainly successful in France, but his European renown was greater, his talent less contested by other nations. The particulars we could give on this subject would appear fabulous. Balzac described the manners of his day, and his very success on this point may in itself be considered as one of the most curious illustrations of the spirit of that period. More than two centuries ago, in 1624, Honoré d'Urfé,—the author of the famous novel *L'Astrée*, — then living at Piedmont, received a serious letter from twenty-nine princes or princesses and great lords or ladies of

Germany. The writers informed him they had adopted the names of the heroes and heroines in *L'Astrée*, and had formed a clique called the "Academy of True Lovers." They urgently requested a sequel to the book. That which occurred to D'Urfé was repeated in the case of Balzac. For a time, society in Venice conceived the idea of taking the names of his principal characters, and playing their respective parts in real life. During an entire season the town abounded with Radignacs, Duchesses of Langeais, and Duchesses of Manfrigneuse, more than one actor or actress being, for a fact, bent upon adhering faithfully to his or her part. The author, in his initiation of these reciprocal influences, strikes the keynote of human nature, exaggerating to a certain degree its peculiar tendencies. Society is flattered, and puts into practice what the author had merely imagined. Thus, that which at first appeared an exaggeration, becomes at last incontestable truth. Not only in Venice, but in Hungary, Poland, and Russia, Balzac's works were considered law. The slightly fantastic portions of his novels, that incurred a somewhat severe criticism in his own country, disappeared at this distance—in fact, added one more attraction to his writings. For instance, his descriptions of rich and fantastic furniture, amassed according to the freaks of his imagination, became a reality. These highly coloured pictures, that were to us as mere dreams of an artistic millionaire, were accurately copied by other nations, and it became the fashion to furnish one's house *à la Balzac*. How could the author remain insensible to these echoes of fame—heralds of future glory!

Believing in these echoes, and inspired by a lofty sense of ambition, his strong and fertile imagination was stimulated to draw upon all its resources, and to give forth productions of every kind. Balzac had the physique of an athlete, and all the fire of an artistic nature in love with glory. The vast work he had planned necessitated the use of these mental and physical forces. Only in these days are to be found such organizations, nearly herculean in their physical strength, producing in rich abundance for twenty years.

In reading Racine, Voltaire, and Montesquieu, we do not for one moment think of questioning whether they were physically strong or not. Buffon was an athlete, but his style does not indicate his physical strength. The classic writers of those days only wrote with their brains—with the essentially intellectual part of their being. But in these times it is otherwise. By reason of the immense labour that society forces a writer to perform in a short space of time, by reason of the necessity for an author to be rapid as well as emphatic, he has not leisure to be platonic. The entire physical organization of the author is brought into action, and betrays itself in his works. He does not merely write with his head, but with his blood and his muscles. In analyzing the qualities of a writer, his physique should be taken into consideration. Balzac prided himself on being a physiologist, and he certainly may be considered as such, though his science of life was less accurate than he himself believed. His physical nature and that of others play a conspicuous part in his works, and are the more evident in his moral descriptions. I do not wish in any way to detract from his merit, his peculiarities being characteristic of the picturesque literature of these days.

One day, Monsieur Villemain, who was very young at the time, was reading to Sièyes his *Eulogy on Montaigne*—that charmingly fresh *éloge*, the first he had ever written. Coming to the passage where he says, "But in reading Rousseau, I should be fearful of dwelling too long on those guilty weaknesses that we should always keep out of sight,"—Sièyes interrupted him, remarking, "But no—we should allow them to be near us, so as to study them at a closer proximity." Here we see the physiologist above all in search of truth, opposed to the literary scholar, who requires good taste in preference to all else. Shall I venture to admit I am like Sièyes? This is also admitting that I resemble Balzac. But on two points I differ from him. I admire that particular *efflorescence* in the delicate portions of his writing (I can find no other term), by which he imparts to everything an appearance of life, but I cannot accept, under the pretext of physiology, the abuse of this particular method. I cannot admire his enervated and luxurious mode of writing—that deliciously corrupt style, imbued with a nearly Oriental voluptuousness, and at times more supple than the frame of an ancient mime. Does not Petronius, in the midst of describing different scenes, regret the decline of the *oratio pudica*—that chaste style which does not abandon itself to every movement? On another point Balzac is faulty as a physiologist and an anatomist—he had more recourse to his imagination than to scientific facts. Skilful in his moral dissections, he has certainly discovered new channels, though many are of his own creation. At a certain point in his analyses the real *plexus* ends where the imaginary *plexus* begins, he himself not being able to distinguish the one from the other. Like himself, the majority of his readers have confounded them, especially his women readers. Balzac had an avowed weakness for the precepts of Swedenborg, Van-Helmont, Saint-Germain, and Cagliostro, and of others similar to them—in fact, the author was subject to illusions. Balzac professed to be scientific, but in reality he possessed a kind of physiological *intuition*. In speaking of this, Chasles remarks with great penetration : "It has been continually repeated that Balzac was a keen observer and analyst. He was better or worse than that, namely, a seer." He generally failed in all he had not comprehended at first sight, no amount of after thought being able to supply this deficiency of conception. How many things he was able to comprehend at a single glance ! Conversing with you, apparently absorbed in his work, he would, in view of his own advantage, question you and listen to your response ; though, even when he had not apparently listened, and had been seemingly pre-occupied, he would retire, having imbibed all the knowledge he had wished to acquire, and would after-wards astonish you in describing all that he had silently gained. As I have already stated, he was from youth upwards immersed in his work. He was wont to confound with the world of reality that little world which he partly depicted from exoteric observation, and partly created in the recesses of his own brain. He held converse with his own creations ; he mentioned them frequently as intimate acquaintances. He had created them in such verisimilitude, that, having once brought them into being, they remained for ever with him.

Balzac's real power requires defining ; it was that of a copious nature, full of ideas, of types and of inventions, ever creating, never wearied. It was that power he possessed, and not the other, which is doubtless the truer power—a power by virtue of which a writer system, atizes his work, he meanwhile remaining superior to his creations. It may be justly said that Balzac was under the sway of his own work, and that his talent often rushed away with him, like the steeds of a four-horsed chariot. I do not wish that every author should be precisely similar to Goethe, with his marble brow, far above "the ardent cloud ;" nor do I concur with Balzac, who has more than once in his writings expressed the opinion that an author should dive head-foremost into his work, "like Curtius into the gulf." Such phases of talent evince much fire and passion, but frequently lack solid worth.

In order to illustrate Balzac's true literary theory, we need only quote his own words ; for instance, if I take *Les Parents Pauvres,* his last and most powerful novel, published in this very journal,[*] I discover the author's favourite ideas and *secrets* (if he ever fostered any) in his description of the Polish artist, Wenceslas Steinbock. According to what he writes : "A great *artiste* is in these days a prince without a title ; he has glory and riches before him ; but this glory cannot be acquired either in playing or dreaming ; it is the reward of obstinate labour and ardent concentration of purpose. You have ideas in your brain ? Well, what of that ! And so have I ideas. . . . What is the use of having anything in your soul, if you do not put it to account ?" That is what Balzac thought, and he never spared himself hard work in the execution of an idea. "To conceive," said he, "is to enjoy—it is like *smoking magic cigarettes ;* but unless you put into execution that which you have conceived, your conceptions evaporate into mere dreams." "Constant work," he says again, "is the law of art, like that of life—for art is idealized creation." Moreover, the *artiste, par excellence*—the poet—does not wait for orders or commands ; he produces to-day, to-morrow,

---

[*] *Les Parents Pauvres* appeared, first of all, as a serial in the *Constitutionnel.*

always ; hence his habit of labour, hence the perpetual knowledge of the difficulties he must undergo in order to retain his *intimate relationship* with the Muse and her creative powers. Canova lived in his studio, and Voltaire in his study. Homer and Phidias must have done likewise." I have expressly quoted this passage, because, notwithstanding the praise he bestows on the quality of industry,—an eulogium that does honour to himself,—we still perceive the influence of the modern spirit, the singular disregard with which Balzac forfeited the very beauty that he professed to pursue. Neither Homer nor Phidias lived thus in *intimate relationship* with the Muse ; they always knew and received her in her chaste austerity. According to De Bonald, "The Beautiful is always austere." These words are like immoveable and sacred columns, that I only wish to point out in the distance in order that our admiration for a man of genius, and the regretful homage we are extending to his memory, may not induce us to overstep the confines of artistic taste.

Balzac speaks again of those *artistes* who meet with "an overwhelming success, in itself sufficient to crush those whose shoulders are not strong enough to bear it—a circumstance that often occurs." Indeed, there remains a greater test for the writer than the battle he has to fight sooner or later—that is, the day following the victory. He must be endowed with real strength to be able to bear all the glory, to be neither terrified nor discouraged, so as not to sink under the blow, like Léopold Robert. Balzac has proved that he possessed this peculiar strength. He would often converse pleasantly on the subject of glory. "I am well acquainted with glory," he would say. "I was once travelling with some friends in Russia. As night was

drawing near, we went to a castle to ask for shelter.
On our arrival, the hostess and her ladies hastened to
welcome us, one of the latter running immediately to
fetch some refreshments. In the meanwhile, the
conversation became animated. When the lady returned, bearing them, she heard these words : 'Well,
M. de Balzac, you think, then, that'— She made a
movement of joyous surprise, and let the tray fall,
everything being broken to pieces. Is not that glory ?"
Thus expatiating, he would make his listeners smile,
smiling himself the while, though he none the less
enjoyed the feeling of glory. It sustained him in his
work. The most intellectual of his followers, Charles
de Bernard, who has since died, did not possess this
incentive. In his epicurism, Bernard doubted everything, and his remarkable works bear the stamp of his
peculiar cynicism. Through Balzac's very fervour, his
writing gained in warmth and animation, an exquisite
delicacy underlying his enthusiasm. The whole of
Europe was to him like a park, where he had only to
stroll to meet with friends, admirers, and sumptuous
hospitality. The little half-withered flower he would
show you, he had plucked the other morning, on his
return from the Villa Diodati ; the picture he would
describe to you he had seen yesterday in the palace of
a Roman prince. To him it appeared but a step from
one capital to another, from a villa in Rome, or from the
Isola-Bella, to a castle in Poland or Bohemia. With a
touch of his magic wand he had access to every spot !
The *Isola-Bella* (The Beautiful Island) was not merely
a dream to him. That which had seemed to him for
years to be only a poetical illusion, was at last bestowed
upon him by one of those devoted women whom he
had idealized.

All the artists of the day were his friends, and he

has conferred on them a place of honour in his writings. He was passionately fond of works of art, of painting, sculpture, and antique furniture. When he found leisure (and he frequently discovered means of obtaining it, giving up his days to whatever pleased his fancy, and his nights to work), he loved to hunt up the "fine bits," as he called them. He had ferreted all the bric-à-brac shops in Europe, and would converse for the hour about them. Therefore, the wonderful and dazzling descriptions of china and furniture that we find in his books, are life-like in their colouring—those descriptions that from another pen would have appeared like the mere imaginings of an artistic brain. His descriptions are too lengthy, but the light and shade which envelop them are generally true to art. The reader feels affected, even when the result is not equal to the trouble the author appears to have taken. Through his gift of colour he charmed all painters ; they recognised in him a *confrère*, who had mistaken his vocation and gone astray in the paths of literature. He did not appreciate the art of criticism ; he had made his way in the world in spite of censure, and his genius was not one that could be either guided or moderated. He writes in relation to a sculptor, who had become idle from mere discouragement : "Having again become an artist *in partibus*, he met with much success in society ; he was consulted by a number of amateurs, and became a critic, like all the weak men, whose *debut* promises more than they are able to perform." This last trait may be true in relation to a sculptor or painter, who, instead of working seriously, passes his time in discussion and argument, but this idea of Balzac's, that is continually being utilized by a whole school of young writers, is both an error and an injustice. But, as it is difficult to define power and impotence, let us pass on to something else.

Had Balzac been able to tolerate a sincere and intelligent Aristarchus, such a guide would have been of infinite use to him, considering how his luxuriant nature, which lavished itself without restraint, required control.

There are three points to be observed in the writing of a novel—the characters, the action, the style. Balzac excelled in the portrayal of his characters ; he imbues them with life, he stamps them with indelibility. Though they may be sometimes over-coloured, and at other times just the reverse, they nevertheless always possess some intrinsic worth. Through him we make refined, charming, and jovial acquaintances, and sometimes others that are far from agreeable ; but in either case we are certain not to forget one or the other. Not content in merely well depicting his characters, he gives them singular and appropriate names, through which they are grafted for ever on our memory. He attached the greatest importance to the baptism of his *dramatis personæ.* According to Sterne, he attributed a certain occult power to names in deference to either ironical or descriptive nomenclature. The *Marneffes*, the *Bixious*, the *Birotteaux*, the *Crevels*, are thus named by him, in virtue of some confused anomatopeia, by which the man and his name resemble each other. After the characters comes the action. On this point Balzac is faulty ; his action often flags, digresses, and becomes exaggerated. As to his style, it is delicate, subtle, fluent, and essentially picturesque. I have often wondered what effect a book of Balzac's would produce on a mind nourished hitherto on ordinary French prose, in its simple frugality—a class of mind that no longer exists—a mind formed by the reading of Nicole and Bourdaloue, whose homely and serious style "goes a long way," according to La Bruyère.

This last-mentioned author has also said : "For all thought there is but a single expression, and that is the good one." In his writing, Balzac appears to ignore this wise maxim of La Bruyère. He makes use of a series of vivid and capricious expressions, that are withal indefinite—one might almost call them *attempted expressions.* His publishers knew it well. In the printing of his books he would continually alter and revise each proof. Metaphorically speaking, the mould itself was perpetually bubbling, thereby preventing the concretion of the metal ! Could not the most sympathetic criticism—for instance, that of his friend and associate, Louis Lambert—have guided him into the path of sober ideas, not with a view of staying the torrent of his genius, but rather to temper his mind with a few axioms that I believe to be essential in all art and in all literature ?

"Clearness is the varnish of the masters." — *Vauvenargues.*

"A work of art should only express that which elevates the soul and pleases it in a noble manner. The feeling of the artist should not overstep those limits— it is wrong to venture beyond."—*Bettina to Goethe's mother.*

"Common sense and genius are of the same lineage, wit being only collateral."—*Bonald.*

I wish that he who so greatly admired Napoleon, and whom his great example dazzled, as he has dazzled so many others,—I wish he had abandoned for ever his senseless and puerile comparisons, and, if he found it absolutely necessary to look for his ideal of power in military life, he had put to himself the following question—a question worthy of a good place in French rhetoric : " Who is the grander of the two, an Eastern conqueror leading on numberless hordes, or Turenne defending the Rhine at the head of thirty thousand men ? " But a man's nature cannot be altered by force, and as death has closed the career of this great man, let us, in all gratitude, accept the bounteous inheritance of the talent that is no more. The author of *Eugénie Grandet* is immortal. The father (I was about to say lover) of *Madame de Vieuménil* and *Madame de Beauséant* will always retain his place on the most secret and safe-guarded shelf of the boudoir. Those in search of gaiety, mirth, and satirical humour, should not forget the illustrious *Gaudissarts*, the excellent *Birotteaux*, and all their race. There is, in fact, pabulum for every mind.

Were I not limited to the confines of this article, I should like to discuss Balzac's last work, the which, in my opinion, is one of the most remarkable of the day, though not the most flattering to modern society. *Les Parents Pauvres* (The Poor Relations) shows us his vigorous genius in its maturity, giving itself full scope. Human degradation has never before been so completely exposed to view. The first part of this novel (*La Cousine Bette*) abounds in characters that are life-like, in conjunction with certain exaggerations that the author appears incapable of avoiding. To begin with, Bette, who gives her name to the book, is one of these over-coloured types. This poor creature, whom we perceive first of all as a simple peasant of the Vosges, rough, badly clothed, and rather envious, though really neither bad nor designing, hardly seems the same person who is suddenly transformed into a woman of the world, nearly beautiful in appearance, and infernal in her perverseness—a real Iago or female Richard the Third ! Such things do not occur in real life—this creature belongs to the race of the *Ferragus* and the *Treize.* Our corrupt and vicious society does not allow of such revengeful hatred and cruelty. Certainly our sins are not small, but, on the other hand, our crimes are not so great. Other characters in the book are profoundly true, and above all, that of the Baron Hulot, with his mad love of women, which gradually brings him to utter ruin and disgrace ; and Crevel, excellent in every way, in his manner, deportment, and jokes—in fact, the very incarnation of *bourgeois* vice, in all its vulgar pomposity. In this work we have no longer to do with human whims and folly. Vice is the main-spring ; it is social depravity which forms the principal matter of the book. The author revels in this illustration of sin, and at times his *verve* leads us to suppose he is making sport of vice. There are a few pathetic scenes, but the unhealthy ones predominate. The story is full to overflowing with the sap of impurity ; those infamous *Marneffes* seem to infect the whole book. This remarkable novel, when well read and digested, would lead to reflections, not merely in relation to Balzac, but in relation to all of us writers—children, partly mysterious or openly avowed, of a sensual literature. Some (true sons of René) have hidden or rather veiled their sensuality under the form of mysticism, while others have publicly revealed theirs.

Though Balzac was an ardent admirer of Walter Scott, of whom Lamartine poetically exclaimed,—

"The noble sentiments arising from the pages,
Like so many perfumes from the odorous sands,"—

he failed to take to heart the example of the Northern Magician. He failed to inhale his universal charm of purity and health—those salubrious breezes which penetrate even through the conflict of human passion.

After reading *Les Parents Pauvres*, one feels inclined to plunge into the perusal of some healthy book, to throw oneself into Milton's "pellucid streams." Were this a less incomplete work, and I at liberty to give full scope to my thoughts, I might draw a lengthy comparison between Balzac's talent and that of his most celebrated contemporaries—Madame Sand, Eugène Sue, and Alexandre Dumas. With an equally low opinion of human nature, Mérimée might be taken as a contrast to Balzac, as regards his style and general treatment of a subject. He is a man of taste and accurate judgment, who, even when exaggerating an idea, evinces a certain discretion and reticence in its treatment, and was as keenly sensitive of ridicule as Balzac was deficient in that particular susceptibility. Much as we admire Mérimée's vigorous manner, we cannot refrain from regretting the entire absence in him of that enthusiasm which Balzac possessed in excess. George Sand, needless to say, is a grander and surer writer than Balzac; she never experiments in her mode of expression. She is a great painter of nature, and especially of landscapes. As a novelist, she is good in the original conception of her characters, but they rapidly drift towards a certain ideal of the Rousseau school — an ideal that becomes nearly systematic. Her *dramatis personæ* do not live throughout the book; at a certain moment they become merely lay figures. She never traduces nor embellishes human nature; she endeavours to idealize it, but in so doing, distends her characters out of all reasonable proportion. She attacks society in the abstract, but at the same tim emphasizes the merits of the individual.

In a word, the masterful power she exhibits in her descriptions is not to be found in the creation of her characters. As to her style, it is of the first quality. Eugène Sue is perhaps equal to Balzac in invention and fertility of imagination. He constructs grand plots; his characters are life-like, and deeply impress the reader; while he is strong in dramatic construction. His details, however, are sometimes weak. They are numerous and varied, but are not characterized by that originality and delicacy of touch we perceive in Balzac. Sue endows some of his characters with a certain humour, though he occasionally degenerates into affected eccentricity. Both writers spurn pure and healthy subjects, being prone to dissect that which is corrupt and artificial. Sue is incapable of writing so abundantly and subtlely as Balzac on subjects that deal with sin. In fact, Sue was mistaken in not entirely following the instincts of his own nature, instead of consulting the modern system exemplified in his last novels—a transgression of which Balzac was never guilty. Balzac was at least faithful to his own instincts and favourite inspirations. As to Dumas, everybody knows his prodigious fervour, his easy *entrain*, his happy construction, his witty and flowing dialogue. Unlike Balzac, he covers immense canvases without ever tiring his brush or his readers. Of the three last-mentioned writers, Balzac may be considered the most analytic. The revolution of February was a blow to him. The entire structure of the refined civilisation, such as he had always longed for, appeared to be on the eve of giving way. For a moment he fancied he would lose his ideal Europe and his ideal France. He was, however, equal to the occasion, and meditated describing the new society, now presented to him under its fourth form. I might give the sketch of his last planned work, which he discussed with such enthusiasm. But wherefore speak of a mere dream? He is dead of heart disease, a death frequent among the men of these days, who exhaust their vitality by overwork. Frédéric Soulié, whom it would be unjust to forget in grouping together the principal stars of modern literature, died three years ago of the same disease. Perhaps over the grave of one of the most versatile of these writers, it is opportune to repeat that this literature has formed its school and had its day. We may think to-day that its strongest sap is exhausted. But let it make a truce, let it rest for a time, affording the opportunity to society of reposing after its excesses, so that society may present new and calmer pictures· of itself to painters of a healthier inspiration. Within these last years a strong competition arose between the most powerful representatives of this active, absorbing, and inflammatory literature. The mode of publishing in magazines, that obliged the writer to startle his reader in every new chapter and arouse his curiosity, led to great exaggerations in the colouring and effects of the novel, a strain that could not be sustained much longer. In admiring the intrinsic merit of these men, whose talents were not stimulated by influences conducive to a higher development, let us hope, in view of the welfare of our future society, for the possession of pictures none the less vast, but more peaceful and comforting; let us hope, too, for a calmer life for those who depict them—a life with an inspiration equally as fine as in the past, but milder, healthier, more natural and serene.

THE MEMOIRS OF SAINT-SIMON.

1851.

No literature is richer in memoirs than the French literature. The first memoirs we ever possessed, in our language, were those of Villehardouin, written at the end of the twelfth century. Our prose already then evinced those simple, clear, and natural qualities which it will undoubtedly always retain, with an added tone of epic grandeur it has not for ever preserved. Villehardouin's work remains as the first monument on the horizon. Afterwards comes a succession of capital historical pictures, drawn by witnesses and contemporaries, Froissart, Commynes, and many others following. By a series of unbroken memorable accounts, we thus arrive at the periods of Louis XIII. and Louis XIV., periods abounding in these peculiar kind of testimonies. The Memoirs of Cardinal de Retz appeared to have attained the height of perfection as regards interest, movement, moral analysis, and vivid colouring. It seemed as if nothing could ever surpass them. But then those of Saint - Simon appeared, invested with such qualities of breadth, logic, expression, and colour, that they may be considered as the most valuable collection of memoirs in existence. In bringing them to a close, the author had the right of judging them as follows :—" I believe I might say that, up till now, no memoirs have ever contained more varied, more detailed, and more thoroughly tested information ; nor have there ever existed any that form a more instructive or curious collection."

These long Memoirs, that were not completely published until 1829–30, had for a long time been known and discussed by historians and men of an inquiring mind. Duclos and Marmontel continually made use of them for their histories of the Regency. In her letters to Horace Walpole, Madame du Deffand made frequent mention of Saint - Simon's Memoirs. The Duke of Choiseul had lent her, by way of a great favour, the manuscript deposited at the Foreign Office. She frequently speaks of this work, and her impressions of the book appear to vary in the course of reading. At first she finds the Memoirs simply amusing, " although the style is *abominable*," she says, " and the portraits *badly done*,"—that is to say, roughly painted, and in peculiar colours. But soon the feeling of truth gets the better of her : she is overwhelmed ; she regrets that Walpole is not with her to enjoy this incomparable book. " You would have infinite pleasure," she writes, " *unutterable* pleasure ; he would take you out of yourself." This is how the Memoirs affect all those who read them with continuity ; they take you out of yourself, and carry you back, whether you will or not, into the midst of the living scenes they describe. The existence of these Memoirs was a horror to the people who knew that in this book they and theirs were unmercifully treated and branded with letters of fire. Voltaire, who had depicted the century of Louis XIV. in a complimentary manner, with so much ability and charm, and who was warned of the contradictions which Saint-Simon's authority might one day raise up against him, conceived the idea of refuting in part these Memoirs. During his last visit to Paris, he was planning this refutation. It seems to me that, as regards the century of Louis XIV., Voltaire was more patriotic than veracious. Speaking of certain documents of and despatches from Charmillart in his possession, and which afforded him information dishonourable to the ministry of 1701 to 1709, Voltaire wrote to Marshal Noailles (1752):—"I have been sufficiently prudent not to make use of them, being more anxious to consider the glory and good of my nation than to utter unpleasant truths." This point of view differs greatly from that of Saint-Simon, of whom it has been justly said that he was "as inquisitive as Froissart, as penetrating as La Bruyère, and as vehement as Alceste."

Saint-Simon was born in January 1675. His father, already old, had been a favourite of Louis XIII., and owed to this prince the possession of his fortune. Brought up by a refined and virtuous mother, young Saint-Simon exhibited at an early age an innate taste for reading, and a particular liking for history. In studying the historical memoirs that existed from the time of Francis I., he conceived in his early youth the idea of noting with his pen all he saw, that it might be published after his death. He was determined to keep his secret purpose *to himself*, and to preserve his manuscript under lock and key to the end of his days. This was an exceptional display of prudence in one so young—a prudence which signalized his fitness for the work he had undertaken. At nineteen years of age, when in the army, he began his Memoirs, in July 1694. From that time he was sedulous in his observation, and ever diligent in putting on paper all the information he gained. When afterwards, in seclusion, he gave the finishing touches to his Memoirs, he consequently worked on the original notes he had daily inscribed. It cannot therefore be alleged by those who desire to depreciate the authenticity of the Memoirs, that he compiled them long after the events, merely from remembrances, which, being distant, would have been necessarily blurred.

Saint-Simon's public and political life was simple, and would hardly be worth mentioning were it not for the fact of his having been an observer and a historian. He entered the army at an early age, retiring after a few campaigns, by reason of an injustice which had been done him. Married to the daughter of the Marshal de Lorge, he frequented the best circles, leading at the same time an extremely virtuous life. On every occasion he displayed a great eagerness to uphold the rights of the aristocracy, and in their vindication became entangled in several contests and lawsuits. His propensities, even in those days, made him incur ridicule, and gave him a reputation for eccentricity. In spite of his virtue, Saint-Simon was on terms of great intimacy with the future Regent, the Duke of Orleans. When this prince was pursued by infamous accusations, he stood to the front on his behalf, a circumstance which afforded him the opportunity of exercising a real and active influence in the first measures adopted by the Regency. It may be remarked, in the first steps he then took, he, for the first and only time in his life, associated himself with matters of a political character. He worked with might and main for the restoration of the power of the nobility, which, to him, more particularly comprised the dukes and the peers. In deference to this object, he endeavoured to diminish the powers of the law and the rights of the Parliament, while labouring to tear the usurped rank from Louis XIV.'s bastards, who had been made legitimate, and whom he looked upon with the greatest abhorrence. Ultimately he held temporarily an honorary embassy in Spain ; immediately after, he retired from public life, dying in 1755, at the ripe age of eighty years.

Touching one of these quarrels of etiquette and prerogative raised by Saint-Simon, Louis XIV. could not refrain from observing : " It was a strange thing that since Monsieur de Saint - Simon had left the service, he only thought of studying rank and bringing actions against every one." Saint - Simon was undoubtedly possessed of the mania of differentiating rank. Above all, he was passionately fond of observing and dissecting character ; he was a great physiognomist, added to which he could penetrate the mysteries of any intrigue. He noted his knowledge and various impressions in a vivid, ardent, and fanciful style, up to that time unequalled by any other author in power of expression. Chateaubriand remarked that " Saint-Simon wrote *à la Diable* for immortality." Saint-Simon acted as the spy of his century, but Louis XIV. was unconscious of his real function. What a formidable spy he was, prowling on every side with a hungry curiosity. " I examined every one *with my eyes and ears*," he continually avows. The secret he is seeking, and which he finally tears from the very bowels of the earth, is exposed to our view in a language full of animation, and nearly furious in its ardour. His language palpitates with joy and anger, and we often imagine that Molière would have indulged in a like manner of expression had he taken history as his subject.

It is said that Saint-Simon was never able to perform a useful part in the management of State affairs. I am

F

inclined to believe this statement ; for he is too
incisive in his observation, too rebellious in his moral
impressions, and his genius is too impetuous, to allow
of his commanding political method and tact. A man
with his peculiar qualities is only fitted to notice, to
discover, and to criticise what others do.   It was,
however, reserved to him to write all he knew, and
have it published for the benefit of posterity.

Monsieur de Noailles, a writer and *confrère* whom I
greatly honour by reason of his serious mind and
elevated character, proclaimed himself as an adversary
of Saint-Simon.   De Noailles, in his *History of Madame
de Maintenon* (vol. i. p. 285), has made accusations
against him I cannot endorse, considering the extremely
sweeping character of his imputations.   The historian
might in measure be excused, considering the fact that
it was natural he should indulge in a spirit of retaliation,
having regard to the spiteful and injurious manner
with which Saint-Simon spoke of his ancestor, Marshal
de Noailles, in relation to Madame de Maintenon.
These are family quarrels that we cannot enter into.
If, however, the historian professes to have expressed
an impartial and historical opinion, worthy of his
judgment, may I be allowed to suggest that he has
not rendered to Saint-Simon the justice this great
observer and writer deserves in so many ways, particularly as regards his *sincerity*, his *uprightness*, and
his *love of truth*, all of which are made manifest in
defiance of his errors and his hatred.   He never fails
to exhibit a certain *honest, manly courage*, even in his
excesses.

In history there are two ways of considering events
and people.   One is to estimate them as they appear
on the surface, in their specious and proper arrangement, in their more or less grave and noble behaviour.

This is an easy view, when it is the question of an age such as that of Louis XIV.—an age over which there presided so much decorum. It is from this point of view that Voltaire himself, M. de Bausset, Fénelon, and the historian Bossuet, and many others, have written respecting this illustrious reign. The great moralist La Rochefoucauld has defined the *gravity* of certain individuals as "a mystery of the body invented to conceal the defects of the mind." Indeed, most people who possess this apparent solemnity have every reason for dreading a familiar contact; they are in fear of being *sounded*, so to speak, in their weak points. It is thus with certain periods. Towards its decline the reign of Louis XIV. was in great need of this special gravity and ceremony, in order to protect itself from over-penetrating minds. These minds, after choosing the characters they are about to portray, do not hesitate to sound them to their very depths and piti-lessly unmask them. It is the moralist and painter of human nature, rather than the so-called historian, who possesses the art of disrobing people and exhibiting them in their true light. Though differing in their form of expression, Molière, Cervantes, Shakespeare, and Tacitus, all possessed this insight into human nature. Saint-Simon was a moralist as well as a historian, and it is this admixture of the qualities of both which constituted his originality.

In his Memoirs, Saint-Simon begins by asking himself with a grave sincerity whether it is allowable to write and to read history, more especially the history of his day. In order to understand his peculiar scruples, we must remember he was pious and devotional—often seeking retreat at the monastery of the Trappists, in the intervals between his quarrels and his slanders. He knew full well how utterly inconsistent with

charity weie the views he took of human nature.   " Is
not an innocent ignorance," he would ask himself,
" preferable to a knowledge so alien to charity ? "   But
he responds boldly to his own question, and in realizing
that the Holy Ghost Himself had condescended to
inspire the first writers of history, he persuaded himself, with much ingenuity, that the Holy Ghost would
approve of what he was undertaking, and that it was
permitted to him as a writer not to remain in a ·blinded
and duped condition in the presence of wicked and
intriguing people.   He thus explained his mission :
" The wicked, who have already so many advantages
over the good, would have a yet greater triumph if
the good were not able to discern and consequently
to avoid the wicked. . . . Charity, which imposes so
many laws, could not, however, impose the law of not
seeing men and things as they really are."   He therefore pursues his particular vocation, believing that,
in so doing, he is not guilty of any great sin.   In
his Introduction he gives a full definition of history,
according to his conception, and concludes with a moral
obvious to any truly religious person ; he remarks that,
if the multitude of individuals who are the actors in
history, " had been able to perceive in the future the
result of their efforts, of their vigilance, and of their
intrigues, nearly all of them would have stopped short
at the beginning of their career.   They would have
forsaken their opinions and most cherished pretensions,"
and realized that here below all is emptiness and
vanity.

Did Saint-Simon, in his furious animosity against
those he pursued, fulfil all he promised to himself?
Was he able to withstand passions that were irreconcilable with the austere principle of charity as defined
by him ?   Did he write with a sense of true justice ?

No—certainly not. Nevertheless, on finishing his Introduction, one should immediately read the four or five pages which terminate his last volume under the title of Conclusion. In these pages he boldly justifies himself, while at the same time he evinces a sincere repentance for any injustice he may have committed. He sacrificed everything to truth, and exclaims : " It is this very love of Truth that has been so injurious to my good fortune. I have often felt it was so, but I have preferred truth to everything, and could never stoop to deception ; I may say, I have even cherished truth against my own interests." However, in spite of his holding his head so high on the subject of truth, he admits that he has not been entirely impartial ; his strong feelings overbalance his judgment. " We are delighted," he says, " with straightforward and true people ; we are annoyed with the knaves with which the Court is infested ; we are even more disgusted with those who have done us some injury." " Stoicism is a beautiful and noble chimera. It were useless priding myself on being impartial." Praise and censure proceed from his heart according as Saint-Simon is affected. In short, his only aim in what he writes is to put truth even before feeling, save here and there, where his own nature is at fault ; he wishes *the very essence* of his Memoirs to testify the sincerity and truth of the book in its entirety. In this we perceive Saint-Simon's integrity of purpose, and, save the restrictions we have just made in relation to the historian's invincible antipathies, all his writings are consistent with the spirit of an honest man. What, in fact, does he say in speaking of his father whom he has just lost ? After describing him in an elevated tone, tinctured by a true filial affection, he does not hesitate to exhibit his parent at a certain period of his life as offering his services to Louis XIII.,

with a view to convey a somewhat dishonourable
message to Mademoiselle d'Hauteville—an offer which
was repudiated by the king, and for which the monarch
called him to order. Apart from this, the portrait of
his father is one of extreme grandeur. He, however,
over-colours the picture in representing his sire with all
the qualities of some grand feudal lord ; he exaggerates
in saying the blood of Charlemagne runs in his father's
veins. But we admire this very illusion, for the sake of
the dignified filial affection it displays. The pages
where he describes this aged man, faithful to the very
last to the memory of Louis XIII., exhale a real eloquence of heart, and testify to a nobility of race. He
pictures his venerable father attending regularly every
year at St. Denis, on 14th May, the annual funeral
service of the deceased monarch ; he depicts his father's
indignation at finding himself at last alone at the tomb
of the departed ruler. Saint-Simon, the son of this
favourite of Louis XIII., had a grand idea of the nobility
—an idea in accordance with our primitive independ-
ence. Strange as it may appear, after Richelieu, and
under Louis XIV., Saint-Simon would have liked the
nobility to be invested with legislative power in the
State, such as that order possessed in the time of Clovis
and Pepin.

Saint-Simon's first descriptions relate to his campaigns. He begins with the siege of Namur (1692).
His first pictures are full of life and freshness ; he then
portrays the monastery of Marlaigne, near Namur, with
its adjoining hermitages, and the beautiful scenery, in
a style far more graphic than we are accustomed to find
in the reign of Louis XIV.

The historian cannot refrain from discussing everything that is presented to his gaze, and from presenting
all he contemplates. His Captain Maupertuis and his

friend Coesquen are sketched in a few felicitous touches, and in the person of the former he already begins to criticise and demolish the importance of those he describes. Indeed, nearly all these great people, when scrutinized more closely (I am even speaking as regards the peerage), seem most inferior beings. Saint-Simon's curiosity is not thoroughly aroused until just before the marriage of his friend, the Duke of Chartres, the future Regent, with one of the bastard daughters of Louis XIV. "For several days I had noticed something (touching this marriage), and as I imagined there would be some interesting scenes, my curiosity rendered me extremely vigilant." Saint-Simon drafts with a master-stroke the various scenes that took place at the time of this marriage. He shows us Louis XIV., in his inexorable majesty, over-awing his whole family; he describes the weakness of the young prince, who, in spite of his first resolution, finally agrees to everything; he gives us a presentment of his mother, the haughty German woman, who finds she is obliged to consent to the alliance, striding rapidly up and down the gallery of Versailles, and "gesticulating with all the fury of Ceres after the rape of her daughter Proserpine;" he does not forget either to mention the vigorous box on the ears she inflicts on her son before the whole court, at the moment when he comes to kiss her hand. In these descriptions we see the painter in the full swing of his genius. The Princes of Lorraine, used as infamous tools towards persuading the Duke of Chartres to acquiesce in this marriage, are qualified in merciless terms. Saint-Simon does not belong to those discreet writers of the French school, those slaves of the court, who, before expressing an opinion, ascertain whether it be universally held. He has the frankness of the primitive Gaul—in fact, of the ancient Franks. Somebody has said of the historian, that when he writes

badly and uses forced expressions, he uses the language
of one of the early Barbarians. No ; Saint-Simon, even
then, is no other in reality than the last comer among
the conquerors. In every page of his book there is
scene after scene, and the characters seem to breathe
before your very eyes. The Duke du Maine marries.
Monsieur de Montchevreuil, who had been the Duke's
tutor, remains with him as gentleman of the chambers.
" Montchevreuil," says the author, " was an extremely
worthy and unpretentious, but very dull man ; his wife,
who was a Boucher-D'Orsay, was a big, thin, sallow-
looking creature, who had a *silly laugh*, and showed
much of her large, ugly teeth ; she was pious beyond
measure, and comported herself with great correctness.
She only required the traditional wand to become a
perfect fairy. In spite of her utter lack of mind, she
had so captivated Madame de Maintenon, that," etc.
The Memoirs are all written in this style. The
dramatis personæ seem literally to converse with us.
One person, as in the world of reality, follows upon
another, and we have enough to do to make our way
through this great crowd of individuals. We have
hardly time to breathe in the presence of this ceaseless
comedy. Saint-Simon excels in detail as well as in
the general grouping of his characters.

His history might be likened to a fresco of Rubens,
which has been boldly painted without any regard to
previous careful drawing, and in which the faces stand
out all the more vividly by reason of these dashing
strokes of the brush. His work is similar to a great
historical fair held in the gallery of Versailles. The
painter revels in his depictions, evincing, however, a
lack of artistic power in the management of his outlines. He is himself the first to acknowledge this
defect : "I was never an *academical* subject," he re-

marks ; " I have never been able to shake off the habit
of writing rapidly." If he had revised his work he
would have spoilt and crippled it ; he was right in
letting it remain as it was, vast and full of movement,
and somewhat extravagant in many ways.

There is much to select from in a painting of such
dimensions. I shall make choice of two vast scenes,
and point out a few of Saint-Simon's great qualities.
One of the scenes is the picture he gives us of the
Court at the time of the death of Monseigneur, son of
Louis XIV. The second is that which signalizes, in a
measure, the happiest day of the historian's life. It is
that of the Council which consummates the degradation of the Duke of Maine and the legal destruction of
the legitimated bastards.

In both these scenes Saint-Simon does not merely
play the part of an inquisitive man ; he has personal
interest in both. But in the first of these his individual
feeling keeps itself within bounds. He retains before
all else the capacity of painter and moralist, and does
not display, as in the second scene, his vices and his
excesses—I may even say, the ferocity of his vindictive
nature.

It is in the month of April of the year 1711. The
royal family has not yet lost any of its members,
when suddenly it is reported that the son of Louis
XIV., Monseigneur, a stout man of about fifty years of
age, who in the order of nature appeared destined
very shortly to occupy the throne, has fallen dangerously
ill at Meudon. At this news, all the ambitions, fears,
and hopes of the courtiers are aroused. Saint-Simon is
truthful, and here he proves by his admissions, that if
needful he can cherish truth, though he does so against
his own interests. He was on bad terms with Monseigneur and with his followers ; therefore the sudden

news of the prince's dangerous condition was most
agreeable to the historian.   This he confesses without
hypocrisy : " I passed the day," he says, " in inward
conflict, my Christian feelings struggling against those
of the man and the courtier."   But, in spite of all his
efforts, his nature gets the better of him, and he abandons
himself to hopes of a smiling future.   Saint-Simon was
on very good terms with the little Court of the Duke of
Burgundy, who, on his father's—the Monseigneur's—
death, would be on the eve of ascending the throne.   While
Monseigneur was dying at Meudon, " the Court at Versailles," remarked   Saint-Simon, "presented   quite a
different scene.   The Duke and Duchess of Burgundy
were openly holding Court there, and this Court *resembled the first dawn of day."*   During five days every
one is in suspense—a suspense that Saint-Simon fully
describes.   At last, Monseigneur, who appeared to be
recovering, has a relapse, and dies.   As soon as the
Court hears he is dying, the courtiers flock towards the
Duchess of Burgundy, to worship the rising sun.   At
this point Saint-Simon draws a picture which surpasses
all that can be imagined as regards sagacity and genius
in the portrayal of human nature.   At the very first
rumour of Monseigneur's relapse and approaching death,
Saint-Simon hastens to the Duchess of Burgundy, and
finds all Versailles assembled there,—the ladies in
undress, the doors open, and everything in confusion.
He seizes with eagerness the most splendid opportunity
he has ever found, of reading at first sight the faces of
these actors : " This spectacle," he says, " absorbed all
the attention I could muster in the midst of the
different feelings that assailed my soul."   In contemplating each countenance, he exercises his faculty of
moral dissection.   He initiates his work by observing
the two sons of the dying man, then scrutinizes their

wives, and, by degrees, each who is interested in the great event.

"*All those present,*" he exclaims, with a joy he can hardly suppress, "*expressed by their faces what they felt; it was only necessary to have eyes, without any knowledge of the Court, to distinguish the interests depicted on the different countenances, or the vacuity of those who were uninterested; these individuals were perfectly calm, while the others were affected with sorrow, or trying to preserve a decent gravity to hide their relief and their joy.*"

In saying that it suffices *to have eyes* in order to decipher the diverse interests written on the human countenance, Saint-Simon seems to imagine everybody is gifted with the same penetration as himself. He appears to ignore the fact that penetration so prominently developed is a gift, which happily has not fallen to the lot of many of us. If every one could so easily read the hearts of others, and see through their hidden motives, all friendship, good understanding, and social intercourse would for the most part perish. Such a gift is not easy to manage with discretion ; it is difficult to refrain from its abuse. Solomon has said in his Proverbs, "As in water face answereth to face, so the heart of man to man." But it is difficult to follow the mandates of wisdom, when one can fathom so well the souls of other men. It is hard, even if one does not prostitute this power from interested motives, to refrain from frequently hating and despising others, and from showing one's antipathies and feelings. The fault, and in part the glory, of Saint-Simon as a writer consisted in the indulgence of his fiery and flaming passions, incited by his gift of second sight.

He finds, then, great pleasure in contemplating this crowd assembled at Versailles, and again confesses his own feelings in relation to the decease of Monseigneur.

As only the news of his relapse and not his death had already spread, Saint-Simon was not perfectly reassured. "I feared, in spite of myself," he remarked, "that the invalid might possibly recover, and I was extremely ashamed of this fear." Every man has had moments in his life when his own thoughts have made him blush. Saint-Simon knows it well, and proves it in relation to himself. Having made his own confession, he unhesitatingly enters upon a sort of universal dissection of souls. We might liken him in the midst of this bewildered crowd to a wolf in the sheepfold.

At a certain hour of the night, when positive news of Monseigneur's death has arrived, Saint-Simon shows us, in this great gallery at Versailles, a vast scene, the apparent confusion of which conceals a sort of arrangement of the various figures.

At the end of the gallery, in an open salon, sit the two princes, sons of the deceased, the Duke of Burgundy and the Duke of Berry, each with his princess at his side. They are seated on a sofa near an open window, with their backs towards the gallery. "Every one is in confusion, and those ladies in most familiar intercourse with the Court are sitting at the feet of their friends." "The grouping is *mirrored;* you see the picture."

Then follows the description of the apartments in the gallery. At the other side in the *first* rooms—that is to say, in those the farthest from the drawing-room of the princes—stand the valets, who cannot withhold their *groans* in their despair at losing so vulgar a master—a master "so exactly made for them." Among these disconsolate valets there are others who are more circumspect, and who have been ordered by their masters to watch this moving scene,—the valets, these Figaros of the period, hastening to hear the news, "and who demonstrated by their mien *what shops they swept.*"

Then after the valets came the courtiers *of every description.* "The majority—that is to say, the fools—*drew sighs from their heels,* and, with eyes wild and tearless, praised Monseigneur, but always uttered the same praise, that of goodness." After the fools we have those who are keener; there are even some sincerely grieved and shocked. Again, there are the politic—thoughtful, and reflecting by themselves over the consequences of such an event; and others who assume great gravity and formality in order to conceal their lack of grief. They are fearful of betraying themselves by too free a manner.

"*But in the expression of their eyes they afford compensation for the lack of external agitation. In spite of their efforts, they can be distinguished from the rest of the courtiers; they shift their position, as if uncomfortably seated or standing in an uneasy position; they appear to avoid each other's glances; a certain indefinable freedom, a certain sparkle, seems to pervade their whole person, in spite of their attempts at assuming a rigid demeanour.*"

After having exhausted with a subtle curiosity, and described with a surpassing eloquence, the various attitudes of those assembled at Versailles, Saint-Simon returns to his two princes and princesses in the large salon. There he studies their countenances, which he delineates in the finest and most precise shades. We might liken him to a Hippocrates at the bedside of a dying man, studying every symptom, every twitching of the face, and delivering his opinion of the disease with all the authority of a master. But in this case Hippocrates cannot keep cool; he gives vent to the sense of joy and feeling of satisfied curiosity; he exclaims in the midst of this multitude of objects,—

" *It is one of the greatest delights at Court to those who know how to enjoy such a pleasure, to look around and fathom the hearts of those about us. On such an occasion as this, the first disturbance caused by the surprise to the observed facilitates our inspection; we are astonished to find lacking in some of the individuals qualities for which we gave them credit, and in which they are deficient, probably for want of heart or mind; then, again, we discover in others more than we expected; all these discoveries form a keen enjoyment.*"

Two or three comical incidents, such as the circumstance in relation to the arm of the *fat, sleeping porter*, which he suddenly stretches out near the sofa, and the apparition of Madame in full court dress, weeping and howling as loud as she can with grief, without knowing why, are intermingled with the scenes of mourning, so as to add a touch of brightness ; for Saint-Simon never forgets to be true to nature. At last, towards the end of this night, every one goes to bed, exhausted with emotion, and those who are the saddest sleep the best ; but the historian, still intoxicated with the pleasures of moral dissection, does not sleep long. He arises at seven in the morning. "But I must admit," he remarks, " that such a wakefulness as this is sweet, and such an awakening delicious."

The second scene that I recommend to those who wish to revel in the picturesque genius and inexhaustible passion of Saint-Simon, is the one describing the Council of the Regency, in which the Duke of Maine was disgraced (August 26th, 1718). Again the writer cannot sleep for joy during the few nights preceding this grand day, which shall relieve his smothered anger and avenge him of so many insults. We must remember that in this second scene, so replete with dramatic interest, he is the counsellor and instigator. He has wound up the machine ; he delights in watching it gradually work, and strike the eyes of those who do not expect the blow, and he revels in their consternation. In this description he is less disinterested than in the scene relating to Monseigneur's death ; he shows too visibly the gratification of his vindictive cruelty. The poor Duke of Maine and all his adherents are scourged with the lash of his venom. When once Saint-Simon falls furiously upon any individual, he does not release his hold ; he tramples his victim under foot. One should read the page in which Saint-Simon describes the moment when, in the Council of the Regency, the Duke of Orleans declares his resolution of giving back to the bastards of Louis XIV. the simple rank of peers. All the machinations devised against these fallen favourites are revealed. A gloom passes over the faces of the lookers-on—of the Villars, the Tallards, the D'Estrées, and other members of the Council. The varying shades of sadness are graphically rendered. Saint-Simon, who pretends to have no knowledge of the secret, and who restrains his exultation within decent bounds, gives us a marvellous picture of the nearly sensual intoxication of his joy.

" *Thus constrained,*" he remarks, " *I attentively studied the faces of those around me; immoveable as if nailed to my seat, I was full of the keenest joy, and of the most delightful restlessness. I revelled immoderately in the enjoyment persistently longed for and at last realized; the very captivity of my transports enforced me to a state of anguish, but this anguish filled me with a sense of voluptuousness which I never felt before or since this memorable day. How inferior are the pleasures of the senses to those of the mind, and how true it is that our ultimate satisfaction is proportioned to the troubles we have undergone.*"

We already perceive in this presentment that the author has not sufficient control over his feelings, and we should notice this defect the more were I to give further quotations which exhibit the development of this scheme of action. He is for ever experiencing different emotions, and is never wearied of giving them expression. In order to fully represent his feelings, he unconsciously pushes language to its last limits. In his hands it is like a steed who has run his race, and is exhausted by the effort, his rider the while remaining full of energy, and requiring the quadruped to perform what he can no longer accomplish ; in fact, language fails to convey to the fullest, Saint-Simon's super-abundance of joy and passion.

Let us examine the remarkable jubilation we have just witnessed, and let us boldly say : Such was the man who utters no lie, who dissimulates not, who makes himself no better than he really is, and who betrays with his own pen himself as well as others. With passions so ardent and so persistent as those he confesses, he must undoubtedly have often been mistaken, have frequently exaggerated, and imagined what did not exist. Though he was unjust and rash in more than one detailed statement, I do not think there is much extrava-gance in his history when taken in its entirety. He had the greatest abhorrence of servility and baseness, and he had a horror of the slavery of man, arising in a too mean devotion to his own· narrow interests. He deplored the ruin of the State caused by unbridled selfishness ; in short, he hated what then constituted the deeply-rooted corruption of Courts—a corruption which has not ceased to be the greatest evil amongst the communities of men. Imagine for a moment a Saint-Simon no longer at Versailles, but in one of the great modern assemblies, and ask yourself what he would see there.

Therefore, without pretending to warrant the truth

of the historian's opinion of such and such a person, and taking into full consideration his sagacious and nearly animal instinct,— an instinct which rarely deceived him,—we can hardly say that in the main he has either calumniated his century or mankind. If he has slandered it, he has done so in a manner worthy of Alceste, and with that degree of anger which is the stimulant of potent souls and the sap which gives colour to genius.

For all that, Saint-Simon was in the composition of his *ensemble* not quite a superior writer. Though possessing great qualities of mind and singular gifts, he was unable to control and group the mass. He also failed to give to his opinions that proportion and harmony the possession of which banishes all appearance of vanity or prejudice. He was, so to speak, the victim of his own instincts.

If the length of this essay were not limited to a certain number of pages, I might mention a hundred curious and amusing things relating to Saint-Simon ; my readers would smile at his opinion of Voltaire, and of everything in relation to law and literature ; they would smile, too, at his aristocratic propensities. I happen to know several rather amusing verses, in which he is called "The Greffier of the Peers," "Little Huzard of the Regent of France," and some other more or less witty lines in relation to him. But when we have but a short space for the treatment of a subject, we can only dwell on its serious part. Saint-Simon wished impossibilities for the nobility of his day—this nobility already so greatly in subjection. Like Boulainvilliers, he wished to reinvest it with its power, splendour, and independence, and endow it with a legitimate share of legislative and sovereign authority. He forgot that the nobility, never of any great importance in France, and at that time devoid of real basis, was no longer more than a Court nobility ; he little guessed that, in less than twenty-five years after his death, the most chivalrous supporters of the Aristocracy would be the first to change their idol, and become adherents of the Revolutions. He was indignant at the sight of these servile courtiers—this race of the Villeroys, the Dangeaux, and the D'Antins. He failed to foresee in the near future the other extreme, which would have equally grieved him ; he had no perception that noblemen would become leaders in a democratic move-ment—the Mirabeaux, the Fayettes, the Lameths, and his very own descendant figuring as the most eccentric of democrats. Nevertheless, though Saint-Simon appeared too late to be able to render to the French nobility its political and patrician influence (as our national con-dition was no longer conducive to such a change), he has, at least, given in his own person to the aristocracy, the greatest and most vigorous writer it has ever possessed. This member of the nobility, who was once ridiculed, now ranks between Molière and Bossuet as one of the most glorious v 'ters of France.*

* Since this I have written a longer account of Saint-Simon on the same lines, to be used as an introduction to the correct edition of the *Memoirs,* published by Chéruel (Hachette Library).

CAMILLE DESMOULINS.*

1850.

AFTER discoursing on the language of the age of Louis
XIV., as represented in its flower and elegance by the
most charming pupil of Madame de Maintenon, and
after having discussed the literary style of the eighteenth
century in its fulness and vigour, with Jean-Jacques
Rousseau as its most brilliant exponent, I have decided
on writing on the subject of the manner of literary
expression appertaining to the period of the Revolution,
and associating with these comments reflections upon
Camille Desmoulins, who may be looked upon as
the most talented writer in that department to which
he devoted his efforts. In the above, we have three
periods all opposed to each other. By comparing
them, our thoughts dwell long on what consists in
perfection, progress, and corruption, evolved during
these times.

One of my honoured fellow-critics has out-
stripped me in the *Journal des Débats*† in speaking

* *Biography of Camille Desmoulins.* By M. Edward
Fleury.

† Article by M. Cuvillier Fleury, commenced in the *Journal
des Débats* of the 3rd November, and completed in the numbers
of the 24th November and 1st December.

of Camille Desmoulins, but he has not said his last word on this subject. I regret having to express here my ideas before being able to profit by all of his. Moreover, my views are restricted, and, without actually avoiding the political side of the question, I shall confine myself as much as possible to all that concerns taste and language.

Camille, in his last work, entitled *The Old Cordelier*, was bold enough during the time of the Revolution to utter the words of peace, in spite of the fact that up to that date he had been himself an anarchist. In this utterance he aroused the furious anger of the tyrants, and a bloody sacrifice ensued, the result being his consecration in history as martyr of humanity. We always think of him in this supreme attitude. Nevertheless, if we wish to study him in the capacity of a man and writer, and not to bow down to him as to an idol, it is necessary to examine him at the beginning of his career, and in his successive actions and writings. During his imprisonment, Desmoulins wrote thus to his wife : " My justification lies complete in my *eight* republican volumes. It is an easy pillow on which my conscience slumbers while I await the decision of the Court of Justice and posterity." Poor Camille had strange illusions in reference to the revolutionary tribunals, and even as regards posterity. The *Study* which Monsieur Fleury has just published, and the numerous extracts this writer has taken from Camille Desmoulins' papers and pamphlets, from 1789 to 1793, hardly conduce to gain him honour and greatness in the eyes of posterity—I mean, in the eyes of sensible people, under every administration, and in all times. I wished to see the text with my own eyes, so have lying before me on my writing-table the eight volumes of the *Revolutions of France and Brabant*, a journal published by Camille from December 1789 to the end of the year 1791. These volumes, on which he declared he could rest and fall asleep with so much confidence, make, I must admit, an extremely bad pillow. I have also the greater portion of his pamphlets and smaller compositions. After glancing over them, my impression remains the same as when I had finished reading M. Fleury's extract, and is, in fact, if anything, worse.

I cannot, however, be oblivious of Camille Desmoulins' last written utterance. Strange to say, he finished well after beginning badly. Those in prison in December 1793, and in January 1794, often spoke, after their deliverance, of the wonderful impression they received when reading the first numbers of *The Old Cordelier.* Six months before Thermidor, this pamphlet appeared like the first sunbeam struggling through the prison-bars. The man who procured for his persecuted though innocent fellow-men such a gleam of hope, and who ultimately paid for this noble deed with his head, deserves to have much forgiven him. But let us immediately add, he stood in great need of forgiveness.

Camille Desmoulins was born in 1760, at Guise, in Picardy. His father was lieutenant-general in the bailiwick of this town. Camille was sent to Louis-le-Grand College, where he was a companion of Robespierre. One of Camille's relatives obtained him a scholarship, to which he did honour. His literary and classical studies appear to have been both excellent and varied, and his knowledge of antiquity as great as could be found in those days in a well-informed pupil of the university. His revolutionary style is interlarded with quotations from Tacitus and Cicero, and other Latin authors. He adapts these quotations to existing circumstances, with a touch of gaiety and parody. This is one of his peculiarities. It seems strange that a writer who professed before all else to address the people, should have thus written Latin at random, and constantly have indulged in allusions only to be understood by those who had gone through a course of sound learning.

In one of the first numbers of his journal (*The Revolutions of France and Brabant*), he felt compelled to justify himself on this point :—

"*My dear reader, I beg of you to pardon me for making use of quotations. I am not oblivious to the fact of its being considered pedantic in the eyes of many people; but I have a weakness for the Greeks and the Romans. It seems to me that nothing elucidates the ideas of an author so well as comparisons and illustrations. These additional touches in my Journal are like so many wood-cuts with which I embellish my periodical paper. As to the sentences I quote from ancient writers, convinced of the great sense contained in the following maxim of the Community of Bunglers, 'Nihil sub sole novum' ('Nothing new under the sun')—plagiarism on plagiarism,—I thought it as well to be the echo of Homer, Cicero, and Plutarch, as to be that of the clubs and coffee-houses, which resorts I greatly esteem.*"

Indeed, he had a great liking for coffee-houses, and he curiously blends the style and tone of these places with his quotations from Tacitus and other ancient authors. Speaking, in one of his first writings, of the Café Procope, near the district of the Cordeliers, he says, in allusion to the witty men who frequented it in the eighteenth century : "Nobody can enter there without experiencing the religious feeling by reason of which Pindar's house was preserved from the flames. It is true we have no longer the pleasure of hearing there Piron, Voltaire, etc." Piron and Pindar! This association of the names of two such different men is essentially characteristic of Camille Desmoulins. He enters a coffee-house with a religious feeling, and he would willingly make fun of the gospel.

Desmoulins became a member of the Bar. Being briefless, he was consequently free in 1789, and ready to play the part of an agitator, a pamphleteer, and journalist. From the very first he took up these occupations with such ardour and energy, that they appeared to have been always his true vocation. He began by writing odes and poems; he has been accused of composing verses in honour of Brienne and Lamoignon. Here, however, are some lines of a lay he admits having written, and in which he celebrates Necker at the time of the opening of the States-General. This verse is written in a tone equally solemn as *The Ode to Namur* and the poems of Jean-Baptiste Rousseau :—

" *What do I hear? What shouts of joy resound on every side? Whence comes this sudden ectasy of the children and the aged men? Necker descends the mountain; reason alone accompanies him; in him the people hope still. Holy laws, laws for ever lasting! In his hands he holds the two tables! He is about to overthrow the golden calf.*"

The "mountain" Necker descended was supposed to represent Mount Sinai, and was not as yet the famous mountain where we shall soon perceive Desmoulins. Sunday, the 12th of July 1789, two days before the capture of the Bastille, it was Desmoulins who mounted a table in the Palais-Royal, and announced to the Parisians the dismissal of Necker. Then followed that well-known scene, in which he drew his sword, showed his pistols, and *hoisted* a cockade as a sign of hope and freedom. He was not, however, a born orator; his personal appearance was far from agreeable, and he was hesitating in his speech ; he was only an orator on that particular day. But he soon became and remained a long time one of the brightest, maddest, and most skilful writers of the democratic and anarchical party. He was the first instigator of the Revolution ; he continued to be its promoter, pressing forward the chariot down the rapid slope, until the day when he suddenly resolved to turn round and order *the wheel to be locked.* His orders were not heeded, and he was dashed to pieces beneath the chariot which he had originally impelled.

The first two pamphlets that appeared before his journal are *Free France* and *The Speech of the Lantern to the Parisians.* *Free France* is a purely republican and democratic pamphlet. When we have taken into consideration the agitation of those times, and the excitement which seemed to turn every head, we do not even then feel in a proper frame of mind for reading Camille Desmoulins' first pamphlet ; we do not as yet feel as if we had *attained its level* (style of the times), for many portions of this pamphlet are not only foolish but atrocious. For instance, in speaking of the defeat of the enemies of the public welfare, he says :—

"*They are compelled to crave pardon on their knees. Maury has been kicked out by his landlord; D'Esprémenil has been even hooted by his lackeys ; the Keeper of the Great Seal has been disgraced in the midst of the populace; the Archbishop of Paris has been stoned; a Condi, a Conti, a D'Artois have been publicly consigned to the infernal gods. Patriotism spreads daily with the rapidity of a great fire. Young men are fired with enthusiasm; the aged men for the first time fail to regret the days gone by ; they blush for them.*"

This final stroke is worthy of a writer, but the rest is only worthy of a revolutionary instigator. Again, what are we to say of the following, addressed to those who were not content with the pure zeal of a disinterested patriotism, but who needed a more *powerful motive of action* ?—" *Never will richer prey have been offered to the vanquishers. Forty thousand palaces, hotels, castles,—two-fifths of the property of France for distribution, —will be the prize of valour. Those who pretend to be our conquerors will be conquered in their turn. The nation will be purged, and the foreigners, the bad citizens, all those who give precedence to their own interest before the public good, will be exterminated.*"

It is true that immediately afterwards Camille adds : " But let us turn from these horrors." Nevertheless, he thinks so little of this last exhortation, that in one part of his pamphlet he lingers with satisfaction over the summary execution of the unfortunate Launay, Flesselles, Foulon, and Berthier. " What a lesson for their equals," he exclaims, " in the fact of the Surveyor of Paris meeting the head of his father-in-law at the end of a broomstick, and, an hour afterwards, his own head, or rather the shreds of his head, at the end of a spear ! "

I will leave out further odious particulars. Do not for one moment believe, my readers, that the description of these blood-curdling details is in any way repulsive to him, nor that the feeling of humanity which is aroused in him too late, evinces here the least sign of existence. He makes a point of adding :—" But the horror of their crime surpasses the horror of their punishment." In another passage he praises the hasty lawful proceedings taken by the " Savetier de Messine," that man " eaten up with the zeal of public welfare," who himself made a point of executing in the evening, with the help of an air-gun, the guilty creatures whom he and his workmen had privately condemned during the day.   Can we have the courage, in such a pamphlet, to notice the presence of a certain fiery talent, of something peculiarly adapted to win over unreflecting men ?

The second pamphlet, *The Discourse of the Lantern to the Parisians,* in which Camille justifies himself for having taken the nickname of "Attorney-General of the Lantern," is a production of the same delirious order.   We might justly ask what is Camille's lantern. Whether it is the simple lantern of Sosius or Diogenes, of which he himself speaks at the end of his *Claim in favour of the Marquis of Saint-Huruge* (1789) : "As for me, gentlemen, nothing can prevent my following you with my lantern to lighten your footsteps.   When so many men are striving to pass motions in the National Assembly, Diogenes will not alone remain idle ; he will roll his tub into the town of Corinth." Or is it not rather a question of the other terrible lantern, with its broken glass, and from behind which one threatens to seize all the passers who are displeasing. Undoubtedly, it is of this lantern that Desmoulins speaks ; it is this lantern which he holds and playfully dances before the eyes of his adversaries ; it is with this lantern that he toys in the manner of a "spoilt child," as Robespierre said, and—as we should say—in the manner of an insolent, careless, and cruel urchin, whose knowledge of good and evil comes to him later on by fits and starts, and who ultimately perishes by what he has wantonly sported with.   In reading the nonsense, the invective, and the buffoonish bravado of this public insulter, who ultimately becomes humane, and finally a victim, we feel inclined to continually exclaim : "Nescia mens hominum fati sortisque futuræ" ("Oh, how ignorant is man of his own destiny, and of the fate that awaits him to-morrow !")

In speaking in *The Lantern* the day following the night of the 4th of August, after bestowing much praise on the Assembly and the Parisians, he says :—

"It is time I add just complaints to these eulogiums. How many rascals have just escaped me ! Not that I like too expeditious a justice ; you know that I showed signs of displeasure at the time of Foulon's and Berthier's execution ; twice I broke the fatal tape. I was strongly convinced of the treason and misdeeds of these two scoundrels, but the carpenter was too precipitate in the matter. I should have liked an interrogatory."

You perceive the tone, the sportiveness, and the fitness of this gaiety. Cruel and merciless child, when will you attain manhood ? when will you have the ordinary feeling of humanity ?

This pamphlet, so execrable in its spirit and *tendency*, certainly contains some exceedingly witty portions, and real *verve*. Monsieur de Lally, in the middle of the night of the 4th of August, when privileges were being conferred on every side, was found in the act of exclaiming, with an impulse of loyal sentimentality : "Long live the King ! long live Louis XVI., restorer of French Liberty ! "

"*It was then two hours after midnight, and good Louis XVI., doubtless in the arms of Morpheus, scarcely expected this proclamation, nor to receive on rising a medal. Neither did he imagine he would have to sing with all the Court a troublesome* Te Deum *for all the good he had just been doing. Monsieur de Lally, nothing is beautiful except the true !* "

Monsieur Target having begun a speech to the king with the following words, "Sire, we bring to *the feet of your Majesty*," was interrupted by cries of "Down with the feet ! " This same Target had demanded a demurrer for the abolition of the fisheries right, and he received an address of thanks from the "eels of Melun." Thereupon Camille exclaims : "Frenchmen, you are still the same bright, amiable, and satirical people. You air your grievances in the shape of vaudevilles, and in the provinces you give your vote to the tune of 'Marlborough.'" In his celebration of the night of the 4th of August, Camille introduces a kind of hymn, in which he commences by parodying those of the Church, and ends by alluding to the nocturnal revels of Venus :—

"Haec nox est. . . . Frenchmen, it is to-night, not on the Holy Sabbath, we have escaped from the miserable bondage of Egypt. This night has exterminated the wild boars, the rabbits, and all the game which devoured our crops. This night has abolished the tithes and the perquisites. This night has abolished the tributes and dispensations. . . . The pope will no longer levy a tax on the innocent caresses of two cousins. The lustful uncle" . . .

But here it becomes too loose in tone. He continues this peculiar style throughout two pages :—

" Oh ! disastrous night, disastrous for the High Court of Justice, the registrars, the attorneys, the secretaries, under-secretaries, for the solicitous beauties, the porters, valets, the lawyers, the creatures of the King, and for all birds of prey ! Night disastrous for the Leeches of the State, the Financiers, the Courtiers, the Cardinals, for the Archbishops, the Abbots, the Canons, the Abbesses, the Priors, and the Under-priors ! But oh ! night most delightful, o vere beata nox ! for thousands of young Nuns, Bernardines, Benedictines, Visitandines, for they will be visited." . . . .

Here we see Camille beginning to reveal his saturnalian tastes, his dream of a republic flowing with milk and honey—this republic which he nearly inaugurated the 12th of July in the Palais-Royal, and by which his imagination was for ever affected. He desired Paris to resemble Athens, and the free-thinkers of the *Port-au-Blé* to be as polite as the female grass-vendors of Piræus ; he wished to suppress the police, and to let the news-vendors hawk the papers in the middle of the streets. Entire freedom of action, or at least speech, was Camille's eternal and only receipt for universal happiness. Even in the *Vieux Cordelier*, after he had evinced a sort of repentance, he says : "I shall die with the opinion that to render the Republic of France happy and flourishing, a little ink and one guillotine would have sufficed." Apparently he alludes to the guillotine of Louis XVI.

Camille, the future writer of the *Vieux Cordelier*, is perfect in his pamphlet of *The Lantern* as regards drollery and natural talent. He strides over every period, and couples names in a most astonishing manner ; for instance, that of Louis XVI. he links with the great emperor Theodosius ; that of Monsieur Bailly, with the famous Theban, Epaminondas. He is full of mad daring, facetious and irreverent fancies, and unbridled boldness, blended here and there with flashes of wit. He is carried away by the flow of his own verbosity, and strings his words together into a sort of Litany. This journalist was imbued with some of the spirit of a Figaro and a Villon. He is the *Clerc de la Basoche* perched on the table of a coffee-house, and raised to the important position of a political agitator. Have you ever seen those impudent urchins, striding boldly along in front of a regimental band, and who mimic the fifer and the drummer, and especially the man with the big drum ? Camille Desmoulins is the sham *fifer* of the Revolution, who makes merry till the day when he learns, to his own cost, that we cannot play with impunity with the tiger. I am told

Monsieur Michelet called him "a blackguard of genius.'
I think, after reading his *Discourse of the Lantern*, and
his *Revolutions of France and of Brabant*, it is quite
enough to call him a blackguard of *verve* and talent.

It would be only too easy to prove all this by giving
samples from his writings. I am boasting, though, when
I say too easy, for it would be difficult, and oftener
impossible, to quote from Desmoulins, by reason of the
coarseness and cynicism of his passages, even of those
pregnant of a certain degree of wit. I will not deny
that under his defiant and undisciplined imagination
he conceals a feeling of patriotic inspiration and a
sincere love of liberty and modern equality. Perhaps
in the storming of the old administration and in the
complete overthrow of the feudal Bastille, it was
necessary to have these foolhardy fifers, these lost
children, marching in advance of the pioneers of the
regiment; but in reading Camille in these days, there
seems in every page an utter lack of common sense;
it is only in the amusing passages that we can find
any trace of reasoning. We discover the indications
of a frenzied mind rather than those of a fervent heart.
It seems as if the writer had in his brain a burning
coal incessantly turning, and leaving him no rest.

Mirabeau, with his superior penetration, saw from
the very first the advantage he could reap by the
services of this zealous youth, and the necessity of not
making an enemy of him; he took him to Versailles,
employed him as secretary for a fortnight, then watched
over him at a distance, and so impressed the young
man with the idea of his patron's genius, that later,
when completely emancipated and at the height of
his rebellion, Camille still respected the great tribune,
though he often poisoned his admiration with some
inevitable insult. "You know principles better than

I," said Mirabeau one day, in flattering him, "but I know men better." *

Danton, like Mirabeau, influenced Camille, and kept him in his power till the very last. In fact, the young man was only an impetuous writer in the service of a stronger brain.

In the Confederation of the sixteenth century there were burlesque, buffoonish, and satirical preachers—the democratic journalists of those days—avowed champions of the "Seize," who advocated anarchy and rebellion in the market-places and in the district of Saint-Eustache. During the Revolution, Camille Desmoulins played the part of these preachers; he resembles them in his jokes, and is analogous to them in sprinkling his discourse with Latin quotations, which he adapts to the occasion, and converts into burlesque.

The Revolutions of France and of Brabant (1789–91) are nothing but a long and continual insult to the public powers that the first Constitution endeavoured to establish or rather preserve, after regenerating them. This work is nothing but a defamation, often of the most slanderous description, of all the most prominent men of the day, and whom Camille now and then praised only to vilify all the more afterwards. The degree of licence and invective in which the writer of this journal indulges, surpasses all imaginable bounds. The paper was published every

* We read as follows in the sixth secret note of Mirabeau to the Court, dated the 1st July 1790:—" As Desmoulins appears to belong to the secret Council of the *Jacobins*, and as this man *is to be easily won over by money*, it will be possible to find out more about the Confederation " (vol. ii. p. 68, of the *Correspondence between the Count Mirabeau and the Count de La Marck*, 1851). We cannot contest such a testimony as this. Mirabeau knew Desmoulins thoroughly.

Saturday, with an engraving which generally represented a caricature. The author, in accordance with
the title of "*Revolutions of Brabant*," alludes to the
revolutionary feeling which was commencing to make
itself manifest in the provinces of Belgium. He dwells
on all that is most likely to arouse the curiosity of the
French. " Every publication," he remarks in his prospectus, " from the book in folio to the pamphlet ; all
the play-houses from Charles the Ninth's Theatre to the
Punch-and-Judy show ; every corporation, from the
Parliament to the Fraternities ; every citizen, from the
President of the National Assembly, who represents the
legislative power, to Monsieur Sanson, *representative of
the executive power*,—all these, I say, will be submitted
to our weekly review." Sanson was the executioner.
Camille's jokes always contain some *allusion to the
guillotine ;* he never ceases being the cruel, cunning
ape, amusing himself with pointing out in the distance
the edge of the sanguinary blade. The beginning of
the prospectus promises many things, and the writer
keeps his pledges fairly well. If we were merely to
consider this journal as a testimony of a distant past,
we could point out many striking portraits and many
amusing caricatures. Every time that the author feels
that his *verve* is on the wane, he revives it by pulling
to pieces the Abbé Maury or Mirabeau—Tonneau. He
is amusing as regards certain people, but in relation to
the majority of men I can find no apter expression than
by saying he is both odious and infamous. Other men
raised the actual scaffold for the execution of Bailly,
but nobody beforehand worked with a greater zeal
towards its erection, and no one was more successful in
preparing the implements of torture. Camille is the
true type of the generation who, on entering life, have
no respect for any individual or anything that has

preceded them. He said in his *Free France:* "Death extinguishes instantly." "It is for us who exist, who are now in possession of this Land, to make the laws in our turn." In other words, as the people are never in full possession of this Land, and never masters of an open field, it is necessary to drive out those who hesitate to abandon their rights and *position,* and who attempt to prevent the aggrandizement of the pro- letariat. Camille devotes himself to what he deems the necessary mission of driving out, and by means of his journal devotes himself incessantly to his cynical operations ; he cries down all the virtue, enlighten- ment, and moderation existing in the Constituent Assembly, and destroys this Assembly day by day, by attacking its influential members and depreciating all its works.

We cannot excuse him on the grounds of ignorance or thoughtlessness. He knows full well what he is doing ; he has the genius of a true journalist ; he justly estimates the power of the implement he wields, which in time, he says, nothing can resist. He inflames men's opinions and men's passions in the way they best like, and he boasts of being always six or even eighteen months in advance of others in the advocacy of the public cause. He has the instinctive knowledge of attack : in a glance he guesses his adversaries' weak points, and all means appear to him legitimate for the destruction of the enemy.

On the occasion of the issue of the so-called *Marc d'Argent* decree, which imposed certain monetary con- ditions in regard to eligibility for government office, Camille declares that this decree makes France an *aristocratic government,* "and that the institution of this decree is the greatest victory the *bad citizens* have ever gained in the Assembly. In order to conceive the

H

absurdity of this decree, it is sufficient," he adds, "to say Jean-Jacques Rousseau, Corneille, and Mably would not have been eligible." According to his hateful habit of disrespect as regards the creeds of others, he abuses the clergy who have voted for the measure. After loading them with insulting epithets, he says : " Do you not see that your own God would not have been eligible ?" He continues to bring in the name of Jesus in his invective. Then, after positively declaring his theory, which was subversive to all constitutional power, he adds : "Every one is aware of my profound respect for the holy decrees of the National Assembly ; I am only speaking so freely of this decree because I do not regard it as such." Among the edicts issued by the Assembly, Camille chooses those that serve his purpose, and considers the others as being of no account, on the pretext that they have been voted by a majority formed by the members of the clergy and nobility—members more numerous in the Assembly than they should have been. He goes on to ask what would have happened if, on leaving the Assembly, the members who had voted for the decree had been assailed by the people, shouting :—" You have just cut us off from society because you were the strongest in the Chamber ; we, in our turn, cut you off from the number of the living because we are the strongest in the street ; you have killed us civilly, we kill you physically." It is true that Camille adds, "if the people had picked up stones, he would have opposed himself with might and main against their act of stoning." It would be then indeed time for him to interfere. Just as Camille makes a distinction between *decree* and *decree,* so he distinguishes insurrection from stoning. It would be difficult to differentiate the meaning of the two words.

The writer who professes this theory, immoral both

from a social and human point of view, is the same who, in his first number, gives us Cicero's treatise on "The Duties" as *the masterpiece of common sense.* Here is one more inconsistency.

A few passages of a somewhat elevated tone, a few pages (*vide* Number 4) such as would have been written by Milton in the capacity of a pamphleteer, are not sufficient to induce us to shut our eyes to all his hateful theories, or to the insults with which Camille pursues the men who are in fact the most worthy of being honoured ; nor can we be oblivious to his detestable views, even when we read the termination of a letter addressed to his father (*vide* Number 7). At that time he accepted the *rôle* of public *accuser* and *informer*—a *rôle* that he afterwards cursed in the very depths of his heart. In a controversy with La Harpe, he does not hesitate to say :—

"*I am endeavouring to reinstate this word inculpation. . . . Under existing circumstances, we find it is necessary this word should be honoured, and we will not allow M. de La Harpe in his capacity of academician to abuse his authority as a lexicographer, and banish a word because it happens to displease Monsieur Panckoucke.*"

These pitiable words should be placed in front of the third number of *The Old Cordelier*, which fully atones for them.

André Chénier had published, in August 1790, *Advice to the French as regards their Real Enemies.* In this work he strove, with the moderation and firmness that characterize his noble pen, to draw the boundary line between true patriotism and the false enthusiasm which leads to destruction. He said : "The National Assembly has committed faults, because it is composed of men ; . . . but this Assembly is the last anchor which sustains us and prevents our destruction." He rebuked in energetic and scorching words—but without naming any one in particular—those false friends of the lower orders, those men who, through ostentation and violent demonstrations, gained the confidence of the people in order to incite them to rebellion ; he upbraided "the men to whom every law is burdensome, every restraint insupportable, and all government odious ; men for whom honesty means the most trying of all yokes. They hate the old administration, not because it was bad, but from the very fact of its being an administration." Camille did not fail to recognise his own portrait in what Chénier wrote. When attacking in his Number 41 the members of the *Society of 1789*, who separated themselves from the Club of the *Jacobins*, Desmoulins spoke of their manifesto as the work " of some unknown André Chénier," but not he of the "Charles IX. Theatre." Among André Chénier's letters we find the following in relation to Camille :—

"*My friends have made me read Number* 41 *of the* Revolutions of France and Brabant. *I had already seen a few extracts from this journal—extracts in which absurdities, often most atrocious, appeared to me to be sometimes blended with fairly amusing fancies. Yet I have been still more diverted in reading this Number* 41, *in which the author profusely scatters his honourable insults on the whole* Society of '89, *and on me in particular. He quotes from my work all the severe names I have given to the marplots, the calumniators, the corrupters, and enemies of the people, and he imagines these names are intended for him. He says: 'See how we are treated. See what is said of us.' In thus betraying the simplicity of his conscience, he seems to me more amusing than in anything I have ever seen emanating from his pen. If you yourselves have read this Number* 41, *I am sure that, like me, you have smiled at the thought of a man recognising his own portrait in a book where no names are mentioned, and in which he finds general mention of a number of authors who, by reason of their writings, by reason of a long succession of deeds fully proved, are treated as seditious agitators, hungry marplots, and bloodthirsty men. I am sure you must have smiled to find him openly declare that he fully understood that all these insults were intended for him. I must admit I was astonished at such stupidity on the part of a man who is not supposed to be entirely devoid of brains. I consulted my friends, and asked them whether they thought I was obliged to retaliate, and make him blush for his folly and extraordinary injustice; whether I ought to destroy—as far as it lay in my power—the venom which overflows in his last work. They unanimously observed that when an author distorts the meaning of what he quotes, and accuses you of intentions never manifest, it beseems a man of honour to remain silent, because it is beneath his dignity to take up his pen against a writer to whom one can only reply by giving him the lie; to wish to make such a man blush is simply a rash enterprise, and beyond all human power. It is useless to endeavour to discredit his discourse, because he is too well known to be dangerous ; even among his so-called partisans he is merely looked upon as a buffoon, who at times can be diverting enough; his friends despise him, and their contempt is even greater than that of his enemies, for his friends know him better. I yielded to these various reasons, fully appreciating their force and truth.”*

This cutting retaliation of Chénier, this condemnation from the pen of an honourable man, is worth appending to the eight volumes of the *Revolutions of France and Brabant* as the ignoble brand significant of their character. The fact that both Camille Desmoulins and André Chénier were finally victims of the

Revolution, is not in itself a sufficient reason to confound the one with the other. Let us give each his due ; let us avoid lowering in the public opinion the man who in times of violence, cowardice, and frenzy, belonged to the small‧ number of men who never swerved from their rule of duty.

The Republic, which had long been predicted by Camille, at last made its appearance. The day following the 10th of August, he and Danton were raised, or "*hoisted*," as he says, to the post of general secretary in the Ministry of Justice. They quitted this post together, and took up a corresponding position in the Convention. As a pamphleteer he continues his *rôle* of instigator. In his *Brissot Unmasked*, and more especially in his *History of the Brissotins*, he brings charges against the whole *Gironde;* he makes a point of showing that the men he insultingly calls *Brissotins*, are conspirators, royalists, and instruments of intrigue and venality. He remarks agreeably of Brissot : " I am vexed with myself for having failed to realize sooner that Brissot was the partition wall between Orleans and La Fayette,—a wall like that between Pyramus and Thisbe,—and through the crevices of which the two factions have unintermittently communicated with each other." It was with similar dainty touches, scarcely suitable even for a theatrical paper, that the senseless Camille gradually helped to deprave the public opinion and secure victims for the guillotine. He pointed out with supreme arrogance all the factions that were then at war with each other, until the day when the last vanquished were crushed at the feet of his friends and his kindred.

"*Danton, Robespierre, and Lindet—these deputies of every department, these mountaineers of the Convention, this rock of the Republic—have at last triumphed,*

while the other men have been all vanquished in their
turn; Maury the Royalist by Mounier-les-deux-Chambres;
Mounier-les-deux Chambres by Mirabeau-le-Veto-Absolu;
Mirabeau-le-Veto - Absolu by Barnave - le-Veto-Suspensif;
Barnave-le-Veto-Suspensif by Brissot, who wished for no
other veto but his own and that of his friends."

Camille believed himself to be one of the most solid
portions of this unbreakable rock, which apparently
exclaimed to the waves, "You shall come no farther!"

The execution of the *Girondins*, in October '93, was
a great blow to him. It is said he nearly fainted on
hearing the sentence of their death, and exclaimed,
"It is I who have killed them!" At last the feeling
of humanity triumphed, and, finding his new opinions
coincided with his party interests, he took up his
journalistic pen again, with a view to publishing (in
December '93) the first numbers of *The Old Cordelier.*

In reading this pamphlet, we require much deep
reflection to discover in it a regression to common sense
and ideas of moderation and justice. At first one
would imagine it were written under the direct inspiration of Robespierre, considering the abundant praise
that is bestowed on this wicked and ambitious man, and
considering the emphatic way in which Desmoulins
extols his "sublime eloquence." In order that his new-
found moderation should be well received, Camille feels
more than ever the necessity of disguising it under
the red cap of liberty. He is not even ashamed of
calling Marat *"divine."* Two years previously he was
less polite to this demoniac. On one occasion, when at
variance with him, Camille wrote thus : "*In spite of
the insults, Marat, that you have thrown at me for the
last six months, I declare that as long as I see you acting
extravagantly on your revolutionary principles, I shall
persist in praising you, because I think we should defend*

our liberty, like the town of St. Malo, not only with men, but with dogs." *

Marat is apparently treated with greater consideration in *The Old Cordelier ;* but we can understand that this consideration is merely due to politic reasons. In the beginning of that work we see the man has gone so far astray, that, in order to return to the right path, he finds it absolutely necessary to again go through all the mud and mire of the past. Neither can he avoid revisiting the old scenes of bloodshed ; not only does he commend Marat and Billaud-Varennes, but several times he extols the guillotine of the 21st January, and exclaims, in the tone of a hero : " I was a revolutionist long before any of you ; indeed, I was more—I was a *brigand,* and I glory in it."

The national delirium and disorder must have indeed been great in those days for such words as these to have been considered reasonable and indicative of a return to a milder form of thought. Everything is relative in this world, and Camille, the anarchist of yesterday in his struggle with the wretched Hébert, is the embodiment of the civilisation—in fact, the embodiment of the social genius of his day. He is similar to Apollo fighting against the serpent Python. Desmoulins must have had much courage to remark, in the second number of his paper, that Marat had reached the apex of *patriotism,* and that beyond this point love of country could go no further ; everything beyond Marat being naught else but frenzy and exaggeration - -" deserts, savages, glaciers, and volcanoes." He perceived, though late, that the revolution must have a limit.

The third number of *The • Old Cordelier* more fully expresses Camille's ideas. Under the pretext of trans-

* *Revolutions of France and Brabant,* Number 76.

lating Tacitus, he draws a picture of the "suspects" of the Republic, enumerating them as did the Latin historian those who were suspected during the tyranny of the Roman emperors. Beneath the cloak of raillery he becomes seriously eloquent, and decidedly courageous. In the fourth number he grows more explicit : " I think quite differently from those who say that the ' Terror ' should be considered as the order of the day. On the contrary, I believe that our freedom would be consolidated and Europe vanquished if you had a *Committee of Clemency.*" The word is uttered ; he may endeavour afterwards to enfeeble its meaning. The cry of suffering hearts has responded to his words, but the rage of the tyrants is not to be abated.

To Camille is due the honour of being the first to exclaim to the group of oppressors and Terrorists on the day of his separating himself from them : " No— Liberty is not a nymph of the opera, nor a red cap, nor a dirty shirt, nor rags. Liberty is happiness and reason. . . . Do you wish me to recognise her, to fall at her feet, and shed my blood for her ? Open the prison-doors to the two hundred thousand citizens whom you please to call ' suspects.' " Such utterances as these, marked by the eloquence of a Tacitus, atone for much, especially when expressed aloud and alone in the midst of the stupid, insensible crowd.

The following numbers of his journal are neither characterized by good taste nor sustained force. Even had he possessed these qualities, he would still have felt compelled to reproduce all the more in words the picture of his riotous surroundings, more especially as he was endeavouring for the first time to withdraw from taking an active part in the doings of his fellows. With the exception of a few eloquent and witty passages, his *Old Cordelier* is similar in spirit to his preceding works ; he is incoherent, indecent, and continually coupling together the most conflicting images and names ; for instance, he mentions Moses in the same breath as *Ronsin,* and calls the Saviour a *Sansculotte;* while he expresses indignation at the masquerade of the apostate Bishop Gobel ; in short, he makes use in that work of all the slang of the day. His style is slipshod, devoid of dignity, and lacking in self-respect and respect for others—qualities peculiar to every healthy soul.

As I have already said, Camille evinces in one part of *The Old Cordelier* a touch of real eloquence ; it is in Number 5, when he speaks of selling his life, and appears ready to sacrifice it in the cause of humanity and justice ; it is when, on addressing his colleagues of the Convention, he exclaims :—" *Oh, my fellow-workers, I will say to you what Brutus said to Cicero, We have too great a fear of death, exile, and poverty.*—' *Nimium timemus mortem et exilium et paupertatem.*' *Is this life worth living at the expense of honour ? All of us have reached the summit of the mountain of life. Nothing remains to us but to descend it through a hundred vicissitudes, that even the most obscure man cannot avoid. This descent will not offer to our gaze any unknown landscapes. Any joys we may yet discover in this descent were offered to King Solomon in a manner a thousand times more delightful than we can ever expect them to fall to our lot. Yet in the midst of his seven hundred wives he spurned all this furniture of happiness, exclaiming, ' Wherefore I praised the dead which are already dead more than the living which are yet alive. Yea, better is he than both they, which hath not been, who hath not seen the evil work that is done under the sun.*' "

But even here we see that Camille cannot sustain his elevated style. The idea of Solomon with his *furniture of happiness* spoils the whole effect of his speech. Even in the midst of his emotion, he cannot refrain from exhibiting the wildly comical side of his imagination. Camille is always the same. To the very last he associates, as we have already seen, the names of Pindarus and Piron, that of Corneille and Mathieu ; he links together the name of the Palais-Royal—God forgive me !—and that of the gospel. I might quote the next page in this Number 5 of *The Old Cordelier*, as it is perhaps more irreproachable in its eloquence. He commences with these words : " Let us occupy our-selves, my colleagues, not in defending our life, like so many invalids." This page is perhaps the only really beautiful one in the work—a work which, appear-ing as it did during one of the most disastrous crises of a great nation, assuredly deserves to remain as a token of generous repentance. But this work will never be ranked among the writings that do honour to the human mind.

A place of honour is only reserved for healthy works ; for those devoid of these strange amalgamations which represent unworthiness of thought and language ; for those works in which patriotism and the feelings of humanity exclude any kind of reference to blood-thirsty men, and in which there figure no inappropriate pleasantries. Again I say, a place of honour is only reserved for those works that do not offend any one's conscience or literary taste by the grotesque juxta-position, for instance, of *Loustalot* and *Marat*, between Tacitus and Machiavelli on the one hand, and Thrasy-bulus and Brutus on the other hand.

What a longing we feel after reading these pages, encrusted with mire and blood—pages which are the living image of the disorder in the souls and morals of those times,—what a need we experience of taking up some wise book, where common sense predominates, and in which the good language is but the reflection of a delicate and honest soul, reared in habits of honour and virtue. We exclaim, "Oh, for the style of honest men—of men who have revered everything worthy of respect ; whose innate feelings have ever been governed by the principles of good taste ! Oh, for the polished, pure, and moderate writers ! Oh, for Nicole's *Essays ;* for Daguesseau writing the Life of his father ! Oh, Vauvernargues ! oh, Pellison ! "

I have but one more word to say in relation to Camille Desmoulins. He died on the scaffold the 5th of April 1794. A week afterwards his young wife was sacrificed in the same way. Camille, who had fallen in love with this young Lucille, had married her on the 29th of December 1790. From among the *sixty* people, deputies and journalists, who signed his marriage contract, there remained on December 1793 (at the time he began *The Old Cordelier*) but "two friends," Danton and Robespierre. All the others had by this time emigrated, or were imprisoned or executed. He had *five* witnesses at his marriage—Pétion, Brissot, Sillery, Mercier, and the ever dear Robespierre. These five witnesses dined with the young bride and bridegroom on their wedding-day. We know what ultimately became of the five men. All of them excepting Mercier—who only escaped death by imprisonment—perished by a violent death, in consequence of the deed of the other guest, the dear Monsieur Robespierre. The hyena had entered the sheepfold, and out of the inveterate instinct of his cruel nature, had strangled all he found.

DIDEROT.*

1851.

———

THE latest studies in relation to Diderot are all alike in their tendency. They accord him his proper rank in literature without exemplifying any undue disapproval, anger, or enthusiasm. The marked qualities of his genius, his character, and his rich intellectual nature, are justly estimated in these criticisms, while his extravagances are reproved and explained. In some measure this explanation lessens the gravity of his faults. M. Génin has shown us that certain passages of Diderot expressing a positive atheism must have been written by his impetuous editor, Neigeon, who took the liberty of inserting his own comments in his master's manuscript. In philosophically discussing Diderot's anti-religious doctrines, Bersot endeavours to prove that this philosopher was nearer a certain lofty conception of the Deity than he himself believed. Indeed, it often appears that he lacks but one ray of light with which to enlighten all his thoughts. We might say of Diderot what he himself remarked regarding a pastoral view at Vernet, when twilight had darkened the landscape : " *Let us wait till to-morrow, when the sun will have risen.*"

* *Study on Diderot*, by M. Bersot, 1851.   *Works selected from Diderot*, with a notice by M. Génin, 1847.

Yet in spite of all we may say, we can never prove that Diderot was an unconscious believer, nor even a *deist*, according to the true acceptation of the word. Moreover, a discussion on this particular point would be too delicate and intricate for me to approach. But I shall have much pleasure in expressing my opinions on Diderot from a literary and moral point of view.

Diderot was born at Langres in 1713. Like Rollin's parent, his father was a cutler. From his early childhood he possessed to a high degree the quality of family affection—a quality he had inherited from his people, for he came of a simple and worthy race. He was the eldest child of the family ; he had a sister of an extremely original character, an excellent-hearted girl, who would not marry, because she wished to remain at home to attend to the needs of her father. She was "lively, bright, active, and determined, easily offended, slow in recovering her good-humour, and heedless of the present and the future ; she would not allow herself to be imposed upon by anything or any one ; she was free in her actions, and freer still in her speech—in fact, a sort of *female Diogenes.*" In this description we can see in what way Diderot resembled his sister, and where he differed from her. She was the branch which remained in its wild and uncultured state ; he was the bough that was grafted, cultivated, and full of blossom. He had a brother to whom he bore no likeness in any way ; this brother, possessed of a peculiar temperament, was extremely sensitive and reserved, and rather odd in mind and character. He was canon of the cathedral at Langres, and was considered one of the most pious men of the diocese. Proceeding from this strong middle-class stock, but gifted by nature with the addition of broad capacities, Diderot was first of all the black-sheep of the family ; afterwards he became its

glory. He began his studies with the Jesuits of his
native town, who would have liked to make him one of
their own ; then his father sent him to the College
d'Harcourt in Paris. On leaving school, he continued
living in Paris (1733-43). His life there was a hap-
hazardous one ; he tried any number of professions
without actually deciding on one in particular ; he
accepted any work he could find, and continued to study
and eagerly devour every kind of literature. He gave
mathematical lessons, which he prepared on the road
as he sauntered along. In the summer-time he would
stroll through the Luxembourg Gardens "in a grey
fustian coat with torn cuffs, and black woollen stockings
darned at the back with white thread ;" then, with
that wild and ardent look which characterized him in
those days, he would enter the shop of Mdlle. Balbuti,
the pretty librarian of the *Quai des Augustins*—she
afterwards became Madame Greuze, — he would say,
" Mademoiselle, I require the *Tales* by La Fontaine, if
you please, or Petronius . . ." and so on. Here he
demonstrates a defective side of his character—a side
we shall too often have reason to discuss. In short,
before his marriage—a love-match he made at the age
of thirty—Diderot continued leading a too hap-hazard
existence. His genius—for one could not give another
name to such a breadth and power of diverse faculties
—was so well able to conform itself to his peculiar
mode of life, that we cannot believe he was fitted for
any other kind of existence. We are inclined to think
that in thus adapting his genius to a variety of employments he followed his real vocation. His great work—
his, so to speak, individual work—was *The Encyclopedia*.
The librarians who had conceived the first idea of this
literary enterprise, instantly discovered, on interviewing
him, that they had found the man they required. They

there and then decided on carrying out their vast project. Diderot embraced the idea with so much zeal, and presented the scheme in so brilliant a light, that he succeeded in gaining the approval of the pious Chancellor Daguesseau, who consented to confer his patronage on the enterprise. Daguesseau was its first patron. During more than twenty-five years (1748–72) Diderot was firstly, with the assistance of D'Alembert, and afterwards alone, the prop, the pillar, and Atlas of this great enterprise. At times he seemed to bend under the burden, yet for ever he retained his smiling serenity. He was entrusted with the task of writing the *History of Philosophy*, which, it is true, he failed to discuss in an entirely original manner. He also wrote the *Description of the Mechanical Arts*, in which he perhaps evinced a greater originality. Three to four thousand copper-plates were designed under his supervision. However, the labour and responsibility evolved by the entire direction of this vast enterprise never succeeded in completely absorbing Diderot's attention, nor in blunting the vivacity of his humour.

Towards the close of his life, he heaved a sigh of regret on looking back at the past, and exclaimed, "In truth, I know a great number of things, but nearly every other man knows his particular trade much better than I mine. This superficial acquaintance with every branch of study is the consequence of my insatiable curiosity and my want of money. My poverty has always prevented my giving myself up to any special section of human knowledge. All my life I have been compelled to take up employments for which I was unfitted, and abandon those for which I had a natural inclination." I rather fancy he was mistaken in speaking thus, and that this variety of occupations was really in accordance with his own tastes. He has remarked that, in the province of Langres, the changes of the atmosphere are such that, in the course of twenty-four hours, the weather is successively hot, cold, and stormy, and he adds that it is but natural this change-ability in the climate should influence the tempera-ments of those who are subject to it. " From his earliest childhood a *Langrois* is accustomed to turn with every wind. The head of an inhabitant of Langres can be only compared to a weathercock ; but, in spite of the vol-atility of their desires, emotions, and ideas, the *Langrois* are slow of speech. As for myself, *I have the character-istics of my country*, and it is only through living in the capital, and through a constant attention of mind, that I have been able in some measure to correct my faults. I am constant in my tastes." I will allow he was con-stant in his tastes, but he was certainly extremely variable in his impressions. He admits this in looking at his own portrait, painted by Michel Vanloo—a portrait in which he could scarcely recognise himself. " My children, I must inform you this is not myself. In one day I wore a hundred different expressions of face, according to how I was affected. I was calm, sad, dreamy, tender, violent, passionate, and enthusiastic, but I was never such as you see me there." He adds—for it is necessary we should see him well from the very first :—" I had a large forehead, very sparkling eyes, somewhat coarse features, and quite the head of an ancient orator ; I had a look of good-nature which nearly approached an expression of stupidity—a stupidity which verged on the clownishness of olden times."

Let us therefore picture to ourselves Diderot as he really was, according to the unanimous testimony of all his contemporaries, and not as his artist friends, Michel Vanloo and Greuze, have painted him. The latter painter

I

made him resemble Marmontel, if we are to judge from the engraving taken from his picture of Diderot. " His large, open, and softly moulded forehead, bore," we are told by Meister, " the impress of a vast, luminous, and fertile mind." He adds that Lavater recognised in his physiognomy the indications of a timid, unenterprising character. Indeed, we have reason to believe that in spite of his daring mind, his spring of action was some-what weak. By the means of a little skill, one could do what one liked with him. With all his sudden and rapid eagerness, he lacked self-confidence. " His profile," again remarks this same Meister, " was characterized by a sublime and manly beauty ; the outline of his upper eyelid was delicately curved ; his eyes habitually expressed great sensitiveness and softness, but when he grew excited they blazed with fire. His mouth suggested an interesting mixture of subtlety, affability, and good-nature." That is a picture of the man who was not really himself until he became animated—a circumstance which often occurred. Then his head would assume an appearance " of nobleness, energy, and dignity." All Diderot's contemporaries declare that those who have only known him through his writings have not known him at all.* He, who was so affable and frank towards every one, shunned, however, fashionable society. He was never able to accustom himself to the salons of Madame Geoffrin, Madame du Deffand, Madame

* President de Brosses, in his letters from Paris, written in 1754, describes his meeting with Diderot, to whom he was intro-duced by Buffon : " I wished to become acquainted with this furiously metaphysical head." After he has seen him, he adds : " He is an extremely nice, amiable fellow ; he is a great philo-sopher and arguer, but rambles greatly in his talk. Yesterday, when he was in my room from nine to one o'clock, he digressed at least twenty-five times from the main subject of his discourse. Oh ! Buffon is much clearer than all those kind of people."

Necker, nor to those of any other fine ladies. He would sometimes frequent them, but left them as soon as possible. Madame d'Epinay, with the help of Grimm, succeeded, after much trouble, in inducing him to visit her ; she deserved being successful, considering her lively appreciation of the great author. " Four lines from the pen of this man," she remarked, " make me ponder more, and interest me more, than a complete work by any of our so-called *beaux-esprits.*" The Empress of Russia, the great Catherine, succeeded also, by dint of the superiority of her mind and the graciousness of her manner, to tame the philosopher. As we know, he visited her at Saint-Petersburg, and it is not sure whether he did not sometimes treat her as a friend in their long conversations. " Proceed," she would say, when she saw him by chance hesitating before giving utterance to some freedom of speech ; " *between men* all is allowable." During the farewell evening he spent with her, he commenced *weeping bitterly;* and on her addressing to him a few kind and friendly words, she nearly followed his example. One had to get accustomed to his natural outbursts. If he had not given way to them, he would have appeared somewhat constrained. He was only perfectly at his ease with his intimate friends. In their society he gave full play to his rich, powerful, imaginative, and ardent nature, fascinating all those who listened to him. It was impossible to know him without liking him.

It has been said of the Abbé Morellet, who was a strict observer of method and correctness, that even when he walked, "he drew his shoulders forward, so as to be nearer himself." This posture was quite the reverse of that assumed by Diderot. We picture him open-chested, with his head forward, and his arms stretched out, always ready, if you pleased him ever so little, to embrace you at first sight. His attitude was but the reflection of his mind.

If the *Encyclopedia* was in Diderot's time considered his principal social work, his principal glory in the eyes of the men of to-day consists in his having been the first to create the emotional and eloquent style of criticism. It is through this that he has become immortal, through this that he will be for ever dear to us journalists of every sort and condition. Let us bow down to him as our father, and as the founder of this style of criticism.

Before Diderot's time, the French style of criticism had been, firstly, as offered by Bayle, of a precise, inquiring, and subtle tone. Fénelon represented criticism as an elegant and delicate art, while Rollin exhibited its most useful and honest side. From a due sense of decency, I refrain from mentioning the names of Fréron and Des Fontaines. But nowhere yet had criticism acquired anything like vividness, fertility, and penetration; it had not yet found its soul. Diderot was the first to find it. Naturally inclined to look over defects, and to admire good qualities, "I am more affected," he remarked, "by the charms of virtue than the deformity of vice ; I quietly turn away from the wicked and *fly forward to meet the good.* If there happens to be a beautiful spot in a book, a character, a picture, or a statue, it is there that I let my eyes rest ; I can only see this beautiful spot, I can only remember it, while the rest I nearly forget. What do I become when everything is beautiful ! " This inclination to welcome everything with enthusiasm — this sort of universal admiration—undoubtedly had its danger. It is said of him that he was singularly happy "in never having encountered a wicked man nor a bad book." For even if the book were bad, he would unconsciously impute to the author some of his own ideas. Like the alchemist, he found gold in the melting-pot, from the fact he had placed it there himself. However, it is to him that all honour is due for having introduced among us the fertile criticism of *beauties*, which he substituted for that of *defects*. Chateaubriand himself, in that portion of the *Genius of Christianity* in which he eloquently discourses on literary criticism, only follows the path opened by Diderot.

The Abbé Arnaud said to Diderot : " You possess the reverse of dramatic talent ; the dramatist must transform himself into all characters ; you, on the contrary, transform them into yourself." Though Diderot was in no wise a dramatic poet, though he was not equal to this style of sovereign creation and impersonal transformation, he possessed, on the other hand, to a high degree, that faculty of *semi*-metamorphosis which is the highest triumph of criticism, and which consists in the critic putting himself in the place of the author, and taking the latter's point of view of the subject—in short, it consists in reading every work *according to the spirit that has indited it.* He excelled in adopting voluntarily, for a time, the mind of others. The spirit of other men would inspire him to a greater degree than they themselves had been inspired. Thus absorbed in the writings of others, his heart as well as his brain would become kindled with enthusiasm. He was the great modern journalist of his day ; he was the Homer of his *genre*, always intelligent, warm, expansive, and eloquent. He was continually wrapped up in others, and even if he were buried in the depths of his own ideas, he would be always ready to welcome those of other men. His mind was eminently hospitable, and disposed to befriend every one and everything. Indeed, he would give to all those he criticised, be they

authors, speakers, or artists, a feast instead of a
lesson.

He shows the same beneficence in his admirable
Salons de Peinture. One day, Grimm, who was sending to several sovereigns of the North letters containing news of literature and the fine arts, requested
Diderot to write him an account of the *Salon* of 1761.
Up to that time Diderot had discoursed on varied
questions, but had not yet made any particular study
of the *beaux-arts.* So as to satisfy the wish of his
friend, he bethought himself, for the first time, of
examining what he had till then merely glanced at,
without any deep reflection. The result of his observation and reflection was the creation of this work, containing some marvellous *causeries*—a work which has
really created in France the criticism of the fine arts.

I know the objection usually raised against these
fine discourses on art, and which is more particularly
provoked by Diderot's *Salons.* The objection is
that they are, so to speak, *at the side* of the subject ;
that they treat the subject from the literary and
dramatic point of view — the point of view most
acceptable to the French. Madame Necker wrote thus
to Diderot : " I continue to be infinitely amused by
the perusal of your *Salons. I only care for painting in
the form of poetry,* and it is thus that you have been
able to translate all the works, even those of the most
ordinary description, of our modern painters." Here
is an eulogium which, according to a few people of
taste, is the highest criticism. " In fact," say the
latter, " the peculiarity of the French is to judge
everything, even form and colour, with their mind.
As there is no language that can express the fine shades
of form, and the variety of effects of colour, we are
reduced, for the want of being able to express what we

feel, to describing other sensations, which can be
understood by every one." Diderot incurs this reproach more than any other critic. He merely takes
the pictures he sees as a pretext or motive for those he
creates in his own imagination. Nearly every one of
his articles is divided into two sections ; in the first he
describes the picture placed before him ; in the second
he suggests his own. However, when such writers are,
like him, imbued with their subject, and impregnated
with vivid artistic feeling, they are useful as well as
interesting. They lead you on, they fix your attention,
and while you are following them and listening to
them, your latent sense of form and colour is aroused
and quickened. From some mysterious cause that
words cannot define, you become in your turn a good
judge and connoisseur. From the very first we notice
how the *literary* instinct of Diderot predominates in
his criticism of the pictures. A painter has represented
the reception of *Telemachus* by *Calypso*. The young
hero is represented relating his adventures seated at
table, and Calypso is offering him a peach. Diderot
considers the presentation a *stupidity*, and that Telemachus exhibits much more ability than either the
nymph or his painter, for the traveller continues to
relate his adventures without accepting the fruit. But
the critic remarks, if this peach were well offered, if
the light fell on it in a certain way, if the expression
of the nymph corresponded with the general effect, if,
in short, the painting were from the brush of a Titian
or a Véronèse, this peach might have been a masterpiece, in spite of the *stupidity* suggested to our mind
by the offering. In a picture our ears have no function
to perform ; we are all eyes. The account of the
adventures of Telemachus we cannot hear, consequently
the fact of the offer of the peach interrupting the

story of the speaker can be only a secondary consideration.

In a great number of cases, though, Diderot gives
utterance to these just and striking remarks more as a
painter than a critic. For instance, in addressing M.
Vien, who has painted a Psyche, advancing with a
lamp in her hand to take the sleeping Cupid unawares,
he says :—

" *Oh! what a lack of mind there is among our painters;
what a small knowledge they possess of nature. Psyche's
head should bend towards Cupid, while the rest of her
body should be leaning backwards, in the position one
assumes when approaching a place one fears to enter, and
whence one is ready to fly, with one foot resting on the
ground, the other but lightly touching it. Should Psyche
let the light from her lamp fall on the eyes of Cupid?
Ought she not rather to hold it away, and interpose her
hand so as to dim the brightness? This would, moreover,
be the means of giving light and shade to the picture in an
extremely striking manner. The painter evidently does
not know that the eyelids are peculiarly transparent.
Seemingly, he has never seen a mother with a lamp in her
hand, looking during the night at her child in its cradle,
and fearing to awaken it.*"

Diderot is especially instructive, even to painters,
in the article where he lays stress on the necessity of
observing unity in the composition, and harmony as
well as effect in the *ensemble* of a painting ; in a word,
he insists on the *general conspiracy of movement.* He
instinctively understands the secret of this vast unity,
and incessantly reiterates his advice in this respect.
He dwells on the importance of attending to the con-
cordance of tones and expressions ; to an appropriate
union of the accessory portions with the *ensemble.*
Touching Deshay's painting, which represents Saint-

Benoit dying, and receiving the Holy Communion, Diderot proves that if the artist had depicted the saint a little nearer his last moments, "his arms slightly stretched out, his head thrown back, with death on his lips, and ecstasy on his countenance," he would, by reason of this alteration, have been obliged to change the expression of every face, and stamp each with the impress of a greater commiseration and tenderer piety. "Here we see a picture," he adds, "which demonstrates to young beginners that in altering one part, one must necessarily alter all the other portions of a painting; if not, the truth disappears. In these remarks is afforded a disquisition on *strength and unity.*" In all such questions as now treated upon, Diderot is an able critic. No art, under the pretext of technique, could escape his general criticism. "It appears to me," he remarks, "that when we take up our brush, we should be imbued with some strong, ingenious, delicate, or striking idea, and propose to ourselves the execution of a certain effect, or the portrayal of a certain impression. . . . Few artists have ideas, and yet there is scarcely a single painter who can afford to do without them. . . . They possess no resources, nor interesting ideas; they display no original subjects, nor any astounding mechanical skill in their pictures."

When Diderot meets with this *astounding mechanical skill,* without which the idea cannot after all subsist, this superior power of execution, characteristic of every great artist, he is the first to feel it, and describe it to us in astounding and singular words, such words emanating from an entirely new vocabulary, of which he is, so to speak, the inventor. His style is replete with flashes of inspiration. All Diderot's precious qualities have full play in these *flying leaves;* they which are his surest claim to posterity. They reveal his power of invention, his picturesque and lively imagination, his profound, ingenious, and daring ideas, and his love of nature and family life. In these *flying leaves*, he exhibits also his innate materialism, his marked taste in treating of and describing form, his conception of colour, of *flesh*, of life and blood—a quality for which the colourists often seek in vain, but which seemed to come to Diderot as he wrote.

He surpasses himself every time he mentions Vernet and Greuze. Greuze is Diderot's ideal as an artist. This painter is a sincere and congenial delineator of family life and dramatic scenes; pathetic and honest, he is withal slightly material, though moral. When Diderot discusses him, he interprets and explains him, adding also much from his own imagination—in fact, he sympathetically lingers over his works. " I am perhaps somewhat tedious," he remarks, " but if you only knew how much I amuse myself in wearying you ! I am like all the other bores in the world." The analyses, or rather the presentments that Diderot has given us of " The Village Bride," " The Maiden weeping over her Dead Bird," and " The Beloved Mother," etc., are master-pieces ; they are little poems written on the subject of the pictures. Diderot is fond, in speaking of his painters, of remarking, " He *paints boldly*, he *draws boldly;* " we might say the same of him in his criticisms, he launches out boldly. He is effusive in his criticisms. Even in describing with delight every family idyl by Greuze, he finds means of tincturing his description with his own tone of thought. In his analysis of the "Weeping Maiden," he goes further ; he introduces an elegy of his own invention. This young child, who appears to be shedding tears over the death of her bird, has her secret grief, and is crying for something else as well. "Oh, what a beautiful hand !" exclaims, in contem-

plating it, the excited critic,—"what a beautiful hand !
what lovely arms ! See the truth in the details of these
fingers, the dimples, the softness, and the slight tinge of
red with which the pressure of her head has coloured
their delicate tips. Look at the charm of all this. We
should approach this hand to kiss it, had we not too
great a deference for this child and her grief." Though
professing to respect her sorrow, he nevertheless draws
near to her ; he commences speaking to her, and
raises the veil of mystery as gently as possible. "But,
little one, your grief is very deep, and you seem to be
wrapped in profound meditation. What betokens this
dreamy and sad look ? What ? for a bird ! You are
not weeping, but you are inwardly grieving, and you
are thoughtful as well as sorrowful. Open your heart
to me, my little one ; tell me truthfully, is it really the
death of this bird which makes you muse so deeply and
so sadly ?" The picture itself is merely to him a pretext for *rêverie* and poetry. Diderot is the king and
the god of those half-poets, who, merely requiring an
exoteric stimulus to attain the highest form of poetry,
reveal themselves as entire poets in their criticism. In
analyzing this work, and also the other paintings of
Greuze, Diderot, let us remember, delights in inter-
weaving with the moral of the pictures a slight vein
of sensuality—a vein that may perhaps already exist
there, but which he certainly likes to explore and point
out, a vein which he would rather dwell upon in a spirit
of exaggeration than leave unnoticed. For instance, he
continually alludes to the roundness of the breast, the
softness of the outlines, even in the scenes of family
life where there figure mothers and wives. He
describes all this animal beauty with evident satisfaction, not as a critic nor artist, nor even as a subtle
libertine (Diderot was not in the least corrupt), but as a

natural, material, and sometimes somewhat coarse man. His inclination to animalism was his weak—in fact, vulgar, and somewhat low characteristic. This excellent, cordial, noble, and effusive man, this critic so animated, ingenious, and subtle, and who above all else advocates *morality*, is not content, in the presence of an *objet-d'art*, with elevating our idea of the beautiful, or even with satisfying our emotions; he goes further, he slightly troubles our senses. If at times you perceive on his brow a ray of platonic light, mistrust it, for on closer inspection you are certain to discover the foot of the Satyr.

Whosoever reads Diderot will not fail to recognise what we wish to point out, and of which it is difficult to give a perspicuous illustration. Here, however, is an example among a thousand, and one of those that can be quoted. Diderot speaks of the young landscape-painter Loutherbourg, who begins by painting pastoral scenes, replete with freshness. "Courage, young man!" he exclaims; "you have been further than it is permitted at your age. . . . You have a charming companion, who should keep you at home. Only leave your studies to go and consult nature." We wonder whence proceeds this young *companion* of young Loutherbourg. But Diderot enjoys the idea, and returns to it. "Inhabit the fields with her," he continues; "wander out together to see the rising and setting of the sun. . . . Arise from your couch in the early morn, in spite of the fascinations of the young and charming woman at whose side you repose." The description which then follows, of the beautiful landscape, is overflowing with ravishing purity, and is, so to speak, moist with dew and glistening with light. But nevertheless we feel how inappropriate and nearly indecent is the insertion and repetition of this idea in relation to the marital alcove. In the midst of all his charming, delicious, and suave qualities, Diderot hardly ever fails to display a certain indelicate and sensual habit of mind—a certain *bourgeois* looseness of ideas, by which he proves his inferiority to that other great art critic, Lessing.

But it would be unjust to dwell on this point, for he excels in so many other ways. What he remarked about sketches in general can also be applied to himself and his leaflets. "Sketches are usually characterized by a dash that pictures do not possess. The artist creates them in the heat of the moment ; they are the expression of an unalloyed ardour, without that appearance of artifice which reflection lends to everything ; it is the soul of the painter diffused on the canvas. The pen of the poet, the pencil of the skilful sketcher, seem to run and disport themselves. Rapid thought expresses itself in a single stroke. The vaguer the expression of art, the more it pleases the imagination." Here is Diderot, in his capacity of critic and painter, taken in the act of dashing off his rapid sketches. Touching the pastels of La Tour, he has somewhere remarked, "that one stroke from the wing of Time would suffice to raise the dust with which they are encrusted," and reduce the artist to a mere name. Many years have passed, and La Tour's pastels still live ; Diderot's sketches live also.

Diderot composed on Vernet and the seven pictures this painter exhibited at the *Salon* of 1767, a poem—I can find no apter term than poem. The critic pretends that at the moment he is about to commence the analysis of Vernet's views and seascapes, he is obliged to leave for a place near the ocean, and that there he makes himself amends for what he has missed seeing at the *Salon*, by contemplating several real views. He describes these scenes, giving us also the details of his excursions, of the

conversations and discussions of every kind that arise
between various interlocutors. The delicate relations
between art and nature are discussed, and there are
lengthy conversations touching the world, universal
order, and the point of view in relation to humanity in
its entirety. Diderot profusely scatters these thousand
germs of thought—germs in which his mind abounds.
Then suddenly, at the end of this article, his secret,
which two or three times has been at the tip of his pen,
at last escapes him, and these landscapes in reality, to
which he has led us, are, we discover, simply Vernet's
pictures, that he had taken a pleasure in thus describing,
imagining himself in the position of the artist who had
painted them ; imagining himself surrounded by the
same views of nature which had inspired the wielder of
the brush. There is quite a creation in this mode of
criticism.

In his *Salons*, Diderot has found that the only
true way of speaking to the French people in regard to
the fine arts, was to initiate them in this new feeling,
by wit and conversation, and to make them understand
the subtleties of colour through the medium of ideas.
How many individuals, before reading Diderot, might
have said with Mme. Necker : " I had never been able
to see in paintings aught but flat and inanimate colours ;
his imagination has enabled me to discover life and
relievo in them ; I owe to his genius the acquirement
of nearly a new sense." This newly acquired sense has
greatly developed in us since then ; let us hope that
to-day it has become quite an ordinary sense.* Diderot

---

* Diderot's *Salons* were not published during his lifetime ;
they appeared for the first time in the collection of his works
compiled by Naigeon (1798) ; but they were already known in
society, and copies were in circulation, as we see according to
Madame Necker's letter.

was quite as helpful to artists as he was to the public. I have been told that David, the great painter, or rather the great master of painting, spoke of him only in terms of gratitude. David's early ventures had been discouraging; he had failed two or three times in his first struggles. Diderot, who was in the habit of haunting the studios, happened one day to visit that of the great painter. He there sees a picture on the eve of its being finished. He admires, he interprets it, he discovers in it grand thoughts and intentions. David listens attentively to him, and avows he had never possessed all these beautiful ideas. "What!" exclaims the writer, "is it then unconsciously, instinctively, that you have thus proceeded; that is even better still!" And he explains the reason of his admiration. This cordial welcome on the part of a celebrated man encouraged the artist, an encouragement which did much to stimulate his talent.

Diderot has bequeathed to us several hastily written leaflets, short tales and fanciful sketches, which we have been in the habit of calling masterpieces. A masterpiece! We must be somewhat indulgent in using the word in relation to this writer. The properly so-called masterpiece—that is to say, a complete work, where good taste proportions all the movement and feeling, is certainly not his strong point. He dissipates his superior quality of mind; it is concentrated nowhere —nowhere do we find it radiant and disciplined within distinct limitations. He is rather, as we have already seen, a literary *sketcher*. In his intentionally short pieces, such as "The Eulogy on Richardson," or the "Regrets on my old Dressing-gown," we find great grace, many felicitous thoughts, invested with apt expression; but in several places he grows too emphatic, indulging in gusts of emphasis, and thereby spoiling the natural effect. In this he is slightly ridiculous—a fact which has deservedly induced many caricatures of his peculiar literary methods. Diderot is the most successful when he is the most spontaneous, and not striving after effect— that is, when his thoughts escape him, and the printer is hurrying him, awaiting the fruits of his pen. Or, again, he is at his best when, on expecting the arrival of the postman, he hastily writes a letter to his friend on the table of an inn. It is in his "Correspondence" with this friend, Mdlle. Voland, and it is in his *Salons*, written for Grimm, that his most delightful pages are to be found ; they are the frank and rapid sketches in which he relies. You must not, however, believe that in writing rapidly he writes in a careless manner. The style in his most rapid passages is correct and full of harmonious effects—effects which correspond with the most secret shades of feeling and thought. His pen mirrors nature with all its verdure ; his style suggests infinitely more in relation to her than either that of Buffon or Jean-Jacques. Diderot has imported into our language colours from the palette and the rainbow ; he sees nature with the eyes of a painter. I would bestow even greater praise on him in respect to the possession of this brilliant quality relating to colour, had not other writers since his day abused this manner of delineation.

His work entitled *Rameau's Nephew*, met with great praise. Goethe, whose conceptions and method were always of a superior order, endeavoured to discover in this book a plot or a moral. I must admit I find it difficult to grasp either one or the other. I find in this work a thousand daring, profound, probably true, and often libertine and reckless ideas, and a contradiction so feeble between the *dramatis personæ* of the story, that it appears as if there were rather a complicity between the two characters than otherwise. Then, again, there is no satisfactory outcome of the perpetual vicissitudes and hazards encountered in the work, and, what is still worse, the book concludes in doubts, ending without a definite impression. In this case we might appropriately apply what Chevalier de Chastellux remarked touching another of Diderot's productions—a remark which could be repeated in relation to nearly all his works : "They are intoxicated ideas, that are running one after the other." As Diderot was approaching old age, he asked himself whether he had well employed his life ; whether his had not been a wasted existence. After reading the third chapter of Seneca's treatise, " On the Brevity of Life,"— a chapter in which the reader is so severely admonished,—Diderot, whose conscience was touched, wrote this simple commentary : " I have never read this chapter without blushing ; *it is my own life.*" Seneca's words run thus : "Look over your past days and years, make them render account of themselves ! Tell us how much of this time has been dissipated through your own fault by a creditor, a mistress, a patron, or a client. . . . What a number of people have plundered your life, while you yourself did not feel what you were losing." Many years previously, Diderot remarked to himself : " I am not conscious of having put half of my powers to account ; up to now I have only *trifled.*" He could have uttered the same regret when dying. But by way of an emollient to his overwhelming self-reproofs as a writer and artist, he answered as a philosopher and moralist : " My life has not been stolen, I have given it away ; and what could be better than conferring a portion of it on him who respects me sufficiently to solicit this present ?" Imbued with a similar sentiment, he has inscribed somewhere else the following admirable and humane words :—

K

" A pleasure that I enjoy alone affects me but slightly, and is of short duration. It is for my friends as well as myself that I read, that I reflect, that I write, that I meditate, that I listen, that I look, that I feel. In their absence I am still devoted to them, I am continually thinking of their happiness. If I am struck with a beautiful line, they must know it. If I meet with a fine passage, I promise myself to impart it to them. If I have before my eyes some enchanting spectacle, I unconsciously plan a description of it for their benefit. I have consecrated to them the use of all my senses and faculties ; and it is perhaps for this very reason that everything becomes somewhat enriched in my imagination and exaggerated in my discourse. Neverthless, the ungrateful creatures sometimes reproach me."

We who belong to the number of his friends—to those of whom he thought at a distance, and for whose benefit he has written—we will be in no wise ungrateful, but while regretting that there should exist in his works that touch of exaggeration of which he is himself fully aware, that lack of sobriety, that slight freedom of morals and language, and that occasional breach of good taste, we will not fail at the same time to render homage to his *bonhomie,* his sympathy, his cordiality of intellect, his subtlety, his wealth of descriptive power, his breadth of view, his suave treatment of subject, and to his delightful freshness, of which, in spite of his incessant labour, he preserved the secret to the last. For all of us it is consoling to study such a man as Diderot. He is the first great writer up to date who really belongs to democratic modern society. He is the example, and shows us the way. His maxim was, that either belonging or not belonging to the Academies, an author should write for the public, address himself to the masses, and improvise and hasten onwards incessantly ; that a writer should fathom reality, even if he adores *rêverie;* that he should give and give again, but never hoard his mental treasures. He remarked, " It is better to wear oneself out than grow rusty." This maxim he carried out to the end of his life with energy and devotedness, though sometimes with a feeling of grief at his continual deperdition. Yet, in defiance of all his shortcomings, and without really great effort, he has been able to gather a few tokens of fame from out these scattered fragments. He teaches us how we can reach posterity, be it only by means of the shreds gleaned from the shipwrecks of every day.

LA BRUYÈRE.

1836.

————

AFTER much groping about in the dark, it has now been positively ascertained that La Bruyère was born in Paris, and baptized there on the 17th of August 1645. This has been proved from the parish registry of Saint-Christopher-en-Cité. . . .

From a note written about the year 1720, by Father Bougerel or Father Le Long, in one of the private memoirs which happened to be discovered in the library of the Oratoire, it is supposed that La Bruyère belonged to that brotherhood; but we do not know whether this means that he was simply a pupil, or that he at some time held an appointment there. His first acquaintance with Bossuet is probably connected with this circumstance.

Be that as it may, he had just bought a place in the Treasury of France at Caen, when Bossuet, whom he knew, we know not how, offered him the post of historical tutor to M. le Duc. La Bruyère spent the rest of his life in the Hôtel de Condé at Versailles, attached to the prince's household in the capacity of a scholar, with a pension of a thousand crowns. D'Olivet, who unfortunately is too concise on the subject of this celebrated author, but whose words possess authority, describes him worthily as "a philosopher who thought only of a quiet life among his friends and his books, making a good choice of both ; neither seeking nor evading pleasure ; disposed to simple enjoyments, and ingenuously creating them ; polished in his manners and wise in his discourse ; eschewing every kind of ambition, even that of displaying his talents." This testimony of the academician is strikingly confirmed by that of Saint-Simon, who, with the authority of one whose evidence would not certainly be suspected of indulgence, lays stress on those very same qualities, namely, good taste and wisdom. "The public," he says, "lost soon after (1696) a man illustrious for his wit, his style, and his knowledge of human nature ; I mean La Bruyère, who died of apoplexy at Versailles, after having surpassed Theophrastus, whose style he imitated. In his new *Caractères* he has depicted the world of our day in an inimitable manner. He was, besides, a simple honest man, with nothing of the pedant or the self-seeker in his nature. I knew him well enough to regret him, and the work which from his comparative youth and vigour might have been expected of him."

Boileau appears to have been a little more difficult to please than the Duke of Saint-Simon, when he wrote to Racine on the 19th of May 1687 : "Maximilien (why this sobriquet of Maximilien ?) came to see me at Auteuil, and read to me part of his *Theophrastus.* He is a very honest man, and in no sense deficient, if nature had only made him as pleasing as he would like to be. However, he is possessed of wit, wisdom, and worth." We question this judgment of Boileau's. La Bruyère was still in his eyes a man of a new generation, one of those who show more openly than is necessary that their intelligence is second to none, if not indeed superior.

This same Saint-Simon, who regretted La Bruyère, and who had on more than one occasion talked with him, describes to us the Prince of Condé's household, and more particularly M. le Duc, the philosopher's pupil, in terms which gravely reflect on the private life of this latter. *Apropos* of the death of M. le Duc (1710), he tells us, in the graphic way in which he handles every subject: "his complexion was bright yellow, his temper almost always outrageous, but at all times so haughty and imperious that it was difficult to get accustomed to him. He had some talent, was well read, and thoroughly educated (which I can believe), could be polite and even gracious when it pleased him, which it very rarely did. . . . The ferocity of his nature was extreme, and displayed itself in all his actions. He was like a millstone, always in motion, and making everything fly before him,—one of whom even his friends were never sure that he would not either insult them or make them the victims of some cruel practical joke."

In the year 1697, he relates how this young duke gave a grand example of the friendship of princes, and a good lesson to those who court them. He had inherited the Burgundy estates from his father, the prince, and one evening at Dijon, in drinking wine with Santeul, he actually thought it a good joke to empty the contents of his snuff-box into a large glass of champagne before offering it to him to drink. Poor *Theodas,* so simple and artless, a boon companion, full of wit and animation, was seized with terrible sickness, and died in frightful agony. Such was the grandson of the great Condé, the pupil of La Bruyère. In former times the poet Sarasin had been beaten to death by a Condé to whom he acted as secretary.

From the energetic way in which Saint-Simon speaks

of that race of Condés, we discover how by degrees the heroic spirit of the race came to be something no nobler than the excitement of the hunter or of the wild boar itself.

In La Bruyère's time, however, learning found favour in their eyes, for, as Saint-Simon further tells us of Santeul, "M. le Prince nearly always had him at Chantilly when he went there : M. le Duc brought him to all his parties ; he preferred him to any other member of the household, and liked to vie with him in wit, making rhymes and all kinds of amusing jests and playful witticisms."

As an observer, La Bruyère enjoyed an inestimable advantage, in being thus closely associated with a family so remarkable at the time for the rare mixture of such qualities as charming courtesy, ferocity, and debauchery. All his remarks on *heroes* and *the children of princes* originated there, and a certain bitterness, skilfully disguised, is always distinct.

"The children of the gods, so to speak, are exempt from nature's rules. They have nothing to learn from age or experience. Their merit is beyond their years, knowledge comes with their birth, and they arrive at perfect manhood before ordinary beings are out of childhood."

In his chapter on *The Great* he allows himself to utter what he must often have thought. "Great men have an immense advantage over others in one thing. I do not envy them their good living, their furniture, their dogs and horses, monkeys, dwarfs, fools, and flatteries ; but I envy them the happiness of having in their service men who equal them in heart and intellect, nay, who sometimes surpass them."

The princely morals were scandalous, and his inevitable reflections on them have not been lost. This is indirectly demonstrated in the following subterfuge: "There are miseries in this world which strike cowardice to the heart: some are denied even necessary food; they dread the winter, and fear to live. Others eat the earliest fruits; the seasons are forced forwards, and the earth is made to yield its riches in advance to furnish them with delicacies; obscure citizens, simply because they are rich, have the audacity to swallow in one morsel the living of a hundred families: I am not pleased with such extremes, and would not choose to be either so poor or so rich, but would find refuge in moderation."

The private citizens come in very appropriately to saddle with the reproach, but I am pretty certain the thought was written down one night on returning from one of those princely suppers at which M. le Duc drank champagne with Santeul.

La Bruyère was descended from an ancient leaguer who was famous in the memoirs of his time, having been one of the municipal councillors of Paris in the anti-Bourbon faction; it is a striking fact that the grandson, the tutor of a Bourbon, was able to study the race so intimately. Our moralist must often have smiled to himself, and probably thought oftener of that ancestor whom he does not name, than of that "Geoffroy de la Bruyère of the Crusades" to whom he jestingly alludes.

La Bruyère, who loved to read ancient authors, one day took it into his head to translate *Theophrastus;* he then thought of introducing at the end, and, as it were, under the patronage of his translation, some of his own reflections upon modern manners. Was this translation of *Theophrastus* simply a pretext he made, or was it really the deciding cause, and the first and principal design? We rather incline to this latter supposition, when we look at the form in which the first edition of the *Caractères* appeared, and see what a prominent place *Theophrastus* held in it. La Bruyère was entirely imbued with the idea with which he opens his first chapter, that "*everything has already been written,*" and that "*as men have lived and thought for more than seven thousand years, we have been born too late.*" He declares his own inclination to have been (and it has been shared in our own day by Courier), to read and re-read ancient authors continually, translate them if we can, and sometimes imitate them : " In writing we cannot always find the perfect expression, nor can we surpass the ancients but by imitating them." To the ancients La Bruyère adds *the learned among modern authors,* as having culled for their successors all that is the best and most beautiful. It is in this disposition that he begins to *glean,* and each seed, each grain which he considers worthy, he sets before us. Ideas of pain, of maturity, and of perfection visibly occupy his mind, and each word of his gravely testifies to us the solemn time of that century in which he writes. It was no longer a time for first attempts. Nearly all those who had produced great works were alive. Molière was dead, long after Pascal ; La Rochefoucauld had disappeared ; but nearly all the others remained. What names ! what a profound and accomplished auditory, men august and venerable, and rather silent ! In his discourse before the Academy, La Bruyère himself in their presence has enumerated them ; and in his studious vigils many times before he had reviewed them. These great minds, " quick interpreters of wit," Chantilly, " the rock of destruction for indifferent talent," and the king " sheltered in his majesty," who sways them all ! What judges, of whom as at the end of a great tournament to come and ask for glory ! La Bruyère had foreseen all, and he dares.

He knows the bounds of propriety and the point to strike. Modest and sure he proceeds; not a single vain effort, not a word too much ! At once his place, which is never yielded to another, is gained. Those who, from a certain inclination of heart and mind, an inclination only too rare, are *in a condition,* as he says, to *give themselves up to the pleasure which perfection in literary art can give,*—those alone experienced an emotion, conceivable to themselves only, on opening the little edition (in 12mo), a single volume, dated 1688, of 360 pages large type, in which *Theophrastus* and the preliminary discourse occupies 149 pages, when they think that, excepting the numerous and important improvements which finish and complete the following editions, the whole of La Bruyère is in that little volume.

Later, after the third edition, La Bruyère added much and successively to each of his sixteen chapters. Many thoughts which he had probably retained in his portfolio in his first heedful circumspection, witty or sarcastic remarks which the publication of his book suggested to him, eccentricities which might readily be applied, enriched and completed in diverse ways his *chef d'œuvre.* It is to be noted that the first edition contained incomparably fewer portraits than the following ones. The excitement and irritation following publication drew them from the pen of the author, who had at first thought chiefly of a collection of reflections and moral remarks, even supporting this idea by the title given to the book, of Solomon-Proverbs. The *Caractères* were made infinitely more attractive by the additions ; but the original and simple design of the book, its happy accident, if I may so call it, may be more readily observed in its first and shorter form.

M. Walckenaer, in his *Étude* on *La Bruyère*, recalls an agreeable anecdote extracted from the Memoirs of the

Academy of Berlin; the incident had been preserved by tradition : " M. de la Bruyère," says Formey, who had it from Maupertuis, " used to go nearly every day to the shop of a bookseller named Michallet, where he would sit down and turn over all the new books, amusing himself at the same time with the pretty little daughter of the bookseller, to whom he had taken a liking. One day he drew a manuscript from his pocket, saying to Michallet, ' Will you publish this (it was the *Caractères*) ; I don't know if it will pay you, but if it is a success, the profit will be for my little sweetheart here.' The bookseller, more uncertain of the result than the author, undertook to publish an edition, and no sooner was it issued than it was sold, and he had to print it over and over again, and made two or three hundred thousand francs by it ; and in this unexpected way the bookseller's daughter was dowered. And long afterwards she married a man in a very good position, a man known to M. de Maupertuis, indeed his name is known, M. Edouard Fournier having discovered it in the course of his researches on La Bruyère. She married, he says, an honest financier, who became Farmer-General of Taxes, and whose reputation was spotless. When he married the little Michallet girl, he received more than a hundred thousand *livres* with her. This book, with its bitter, almost misanthropical experiences, became the dower of a young girl ; a singular contrast, is it not ? "

Supposing La Bruyère to have been born in 1644, he was forty-three in 1687. His habits were formed, his manner of life determined and fixed, and he made no change in it. The sudden fame which came to him did not dazzle him ; he had dreamt of it long before, had turned it all over in his mind, knew the value of his work, and was perfectly well aware that even if fame had not come, his book would not have been less

valuable because of that.   Since his first edition he had
written, " How many admirable men of great talent
have died without ever being heard of ; and how many
are living now of whom no one talks, or ever will talk."
Praised, blamed, sought after, he probably was only a
little less happy after than before his success, and no
doubt some days he regretted that he had published so
much of his hidden life and thought.   Imitators at
once appeared on all sides, Abbé de Villiers, Abbé de
Bellegarde (besides Brillon, Alléaume, and others whom
he did not know, and whom the Dutch were never able
to distinguish from him).   We are told that after the
Caractères were published, there appeared thirty
different volumes, besides the translations of La
Bruyère's own work, and the ten editions of it.   In
fact, the whole literary world was inundated by
Caractères with various titles, and all more or less
copies of the original.   These authors, " born copyists,"
who fasten themselves on to every successful enterprise
like flies on a plate of sweetmeats, these *Trublets* of
his time, must often have annoyed him ; it has been
thought that his advice to an author " born a copyist "
(in the chapter *Works of Intellect and Learning*), which
is not found in the early editions, was directed to that
honest Abbé de Villiers.

Admitted a member of the Academy on the 15th
June 1693, at which time there were already in France
seven editions of his *Caractères*, La Bruyère died
suddenly of apoplexy in 1696, and thus disappeared in
the very height of his fame, before biographers had
dragged him from his modest retirement in attempts to
interview him.   It appears that once before, in 1691,
without any solicitation on his part, La Bruyère had
seven votes for his admission to the Academy, obtained
through the good offices of Bussy, who, with discreet

delicacy (we are allowed to suppose), laid the matter before the author of the *Caractères*. Among the *Nouvelles Lettres* of Bussy-Rabutin we find the few words of thanks addressed to him by La Bruyère. This is the only letter of his which has been preserved, except a pleasant little half-chiding note to Santeul, carelessly printed in the *Santoliana.*

We read in a manuscript note in the library of the Oratoire, and quoted by Audry, that "Mme. la Marquise de Belleforière, of whom he was an intimate friend, could have furnished some particulars of his life and character." This Mme. de Belleforière, however, has given no information, and was probably never interrogated. An aged lady in 1720 (the date of the manuscript), she was one of the persons of whom La Bruyère, in his chapter on *The Heart*, must have been thinking when he said, "It sometimes happens in the course of life that our most ardent pleasures, most tender attachments, are forbidden us ; it is natural we should regret them, they cannot be surpassed ; our only compensation is in the knowledge that we have had the moral strength to renounce them." Was it she, perhaps, who inspired this expression, the delicacy of which is almost sublime : "There are some women of such radiant loveliness and such perfect goodness, that to see them is to love them, even if we can never hope to converse with them" ?

By the exercise of a little imagination we are enabled to build and rebuild more than one kind of hidden life for La Bruyère, for some of his thoughts contain a whole life's story, and, as it appears, a buried romance. From the way in which he speaks of friendship, of its *relish,* which *no common nature can reach,* we may suppose that he renounced it for love ; and from the way in which he treats certain very delicately charming questions, we may be sure his experience of love was quite sufficient to cause him to neglect friendship.

The variety of faultlessly finished ideas, from which we may in turn collect various modes of existence, charming, delightful, profound, and scholarly, and which one person could never have formed direct from his own experience, is explained in one sentence. Molière, without being Alceste, nor Philinte, nor Orgon, nor Argan, is all of them in succession. La Bruyère, in his sphere of moralizer, has the similar gift of being each mind in succession ; he is one of the few men who have known everything.

If we study Molière closely, we shall find that he does not practise what he preaches. He represents unseemly things, ridiculous things, love and passion, and falls into the same mistakes himself ; La Bruyère, never. He has caught the little inconsistencies of *Tartufe*, and his *Onuphre* is irreproachable ; the same in his own conduct, he ponders everything, and conforms his life to his maxims and experiences. Molière is a poet, impulsive, irregular, a mixture of fire and simplicity, and probably greater and more loveable by his very contradictions ; La Bruyère is wise. He never married. " A single man," he has observed, " can, if he has wit, raise himself above his station, and mix in the world on a footing of equality ; which is less easy if he be married, for marriage seems to settle people into their proper rank."

Those to whom this bachelor calculation of his is displeasing, can suppose that he loved in some impossible quarter, and remained faithful to a memory in his renunciation. It has frequently been remarked how the human beauty of his mind forcibly declares itself through his deep learning. " I admit that there must of necessity be seizures, executions, prisons, and punishments; but apart from justice, law, and necessity, it is ever new to me to consider with what violence men act towards each other." How many reforms have been carried through, how many still unfinished, since this suggestive observation! The accents are more moderate, more self-restrained, but under them throbs the heart of a Fénelon. La Bruyère is surprised, as at something *ever new*, at that which Mme. de Sévigné finds quite simple, or merely rather amusing : the eighteenth century, which startles in so many ways, progresses.

I cannot omit to recall that grand passage on peasants in the chapter on *Men:*—" We see certain sullen animals scattered over the country ; they are male and female, dark and leaden-hued, tanned by the sun, and bound to the earth, which they are always digging and turning over with unconquerable obstinacy; they have voices almost articulate, and when they raise themselves on their feet they show human faces, and in truth they are men. They retire at night into their dens, where they live on black bread, water, and roots ; they save other men the trouble of sowing, labouring, and reaping for their livelihood, and thus do not deserve to lack the bread which they themselves have sown." And it also accords with what we know of La Bruyère, to recognise him in the portrait of that philosopher, always accessible, even in his deepest studies, who tells you to come in, for you bring him something more precious than gold or silver, *if it is the opportunity of obliging you.*

He was religious, and his spiritual belief is founded on sound reasoning, as his chapter on *Unbelievers* testifies. Coming last, the hidden beauty of its composition is in accordance with the cautious prescience with which he prepares for expected attacks, while at the same time it asserts his own deep conviction. The logic of this chapter is vigorous and sincere ; but the author had need to write it, to make up for more than one sentence which denotes the rather free and bold philosophy of the time in which he lived, and especially to support and cover his attacks on the false devotion then prevalent. On this point La Bruyère has not abandoned the heritage left by Molière ; he has continued his war on a much more exclusive stage (the former one would not have been tolerated), but with no less vengeful weapons. He has done more than merely point his finger att he courtier who, *instead of wearing his own hair as formerly, now wears a wig, long stockings, and a closely buttoned coat, because he is devout;* he has done more than denounce, in a spirit of prediction, the impious indemnities of the Regency in one indelible flash of wisdom : *A dévot is one who under an atheist king would be an atheist;* he even addressed to the *Grand Monarque* himself the direct counsel scarcely veiled in tactful eulogy : "It is a delicate thing for a religious prince to reform his court and make it pious ; aware how much the courtier desires to please him, and what sacrifices he has to make in order to advance his fortune, the prince treats him with prudence, and humours and tolerates him, even if he dislikes him, for fear of plunging him into hypocrisy or sacrilege ; he expects more from God and time than from his own zeal and industry."

Notwithstanding his dialogues on Quietism, and a few expressions we regret to read on the subject of the revocation of the Edict of Nantes, and a few passages in favour of witchcraft and magic, I would rather be tempted to suspect La Bruyère of liberal-mindedness than the contrary. "*Born a Christian and a Frenchman,*" he finds himself more than once, as he says, *constrained in his satire;* for if he specially thinks of Boileau in speaking thus, he must as a natural consequence think a little of himself and of these "great subjects" which were "forbidden" him. He probes them with one word, but immediately shrinks from them. His is one of those minds which would have had little, if any, difficulty in extricating itself without apparent effort or exertion from any accidental situation which might limit his design. It is less from certain detached expressions than from the general turn of his opinions that he allows himself to be understood thus; and in many of his ideas, as in his style, he readily concurs with Montaigne.

There are three important articles about La Bruyère which ought to be read, and nothing I here say about him is meant in any way to supersede them. The first in point of date is an article by the Abbé d'Olivet in his *History* of the Academy. We find in it traces of a kind of literal judgment of the illustrious author, a judgment which ought to be imbued with more of the classical spirit which prevailed at the end of the seventeenth and the beginning of the eighteenth centuries, the development, and in my opinion the elucidation, of Boileau's rather obscure expression to Racine, D'Olivet finds in La Bruyère too much *art*, too much *wit*, and some abuse of *metaphor*. As to style, exactly speaking, M. de la Bruyère ought not to be read with perfect confidence, because he has, although with a certain moderation, imparted to his style an affected, strained, perplexing, etc. Nicole, of whom La Bruyère seems to speak in one place when he says that he *does not think enough*, must have discovered in his turn that the new moralist thought too much, and was keenly annoyed by La Bruyère's criticism. We shall consider this again immediately. It is to be regretted that

L

besides such opinions, which coming from a man of taste and authority are valuable, D'Olivet did not procure more details, that is to say, academical details, about La Bruyère. The reception of La Bruyère at the Academy gave rise to quarrels, with which he himself entertains us in the preface to his *Discourse*, and of which we would like to have some explanations. He was admitted the same day as M. Cherpentier, who in his character of partisan of the ancients placed La Bruyère much before Theophrastus. His words, said in his presence, were sufficiently disagreeable: " Your portraits resemble certain persons, and can frequently be guessed at ; his only resemble mankind, and for this reason his portraits will always be likenesses ; while it is to be feared yours will lose something of the wit and brilliancy which we remark in them at present, when they can no longer be compared with those from whom you have drawn them."

However fortunate La Bruyère may have been at first, he had, we find, to strive with obstacles in his turn, as Corneille and as Molière had also to strive in their time, as indeed all have to do who are truly great. He had to bring forward his chapter on *Unbelievers*, and to advance a subtle religious design in his argument to render his faith a little ambiguous. He was also obliged to deny the reality of his portraits, to throw " these insolent keys," as he calls them, in the faces of their fabricators. Martial had already said well : *Improbe facit qui in alieno libro ingeniosus est.* " Of a truth I do not doubt," exclaims La Bruyère, with an accent of pride forced from his modesty by the outrage, " that the public is at last heedless and tired of hearing for so many years old crows croaking round them, and by liberal thefts with their light-feathered pens raising themselves to some notoriety by their writings." Who is this croaking crow, this *Théobalde* who yawns so loudly at the harangue of La Bruyère, and who, with some treacherous fellow-members of the Assembly, instigated the adverse criticisms in *Le Mercure Galant*, which it is easy to see revenged itself for having been put " *immediately below nothing* " ?   Bensarade, whom the description of Théobalde would suit, was dead ; was it Boursault, who, although he did not belong to the Academy, might have combined with some one in it ; or was it Boyer, or some one of equal power ?   D'Olivet is too discreet on the subject.

The other two articles on La Bruyère which it is essential to read, are an exquisite notice of Suard's, written in 1782, and a very sifting eulogy by Victorin Fabre (1810).   We learn from a paragraph which appeared in the *Esprit des Journaux* (February 1782), in which the anonymous writer shows a delicate appreciation of Suard's short notice, that La Bruyère, who was not highly appreciated in D'Olivet's time, had not been awarded his proper place in the eighteenth century, and Voltaire in his *Siècle de Louis XIV.* had spoken cursorily of him.   " The Marquis de Vauvenargues," says the anonymous writer (who is quite worthy of being Fontanes or Garat), " is almost the sole person, of all those who have spoken of La Bruyère, who has really thoroughly understood his great and original talent. But Vauvenargues himself has not the weight and authority which should belong to a writer who, with the great mind of a Locke, the originality of a Montesquieu, and the fervent style of a Pascal, mingles the flavour of Voltaire's prose ; he could neither have made La Bruyère's reputation nor his own."   Fifty years more, besides crowning La Bruyère with the glory of genius, have given to Vauvenargues himself the gloss of the master's hand.   La Bruyère,

whom the eighteenth century was so slow to appreciate, has more than one point in common with this
century.

In the various clever and charming studies of La
Bruyère, such as those of Suard and Fabre, in the midst
of every kind of praise, we find an expression which
astonishes us as applied to such an eminent writer of
the seventeenth century. Suard uses these words: " La
Bruyère had more imagination than taste." Fabre, after
a complete analysis of his merits, concludes by placing
him among the few who may be considered perfect
models of the art of writing: *if he had given as many
proofs of good taste as of wit and talent.* It is the first
time that, *apropos* of one of the great masters of the
great century, such a delicate point has been mooted ;
and it means that, coming late, and being really the
inventor of his own style, he had more in common
with the age which followed him. He has given us a
short history of French prose in these words : " During
the last twenty years the style of composition has been
careful and accurate ; construction has been properly
attended to ; the language has been enriched by many
new words ; we have thrown off the yoke of Latinism,
and confined ourselves to a phraseology purely French.
We have almost recovered that harmony which Malherbe
and Balzac first revealed to us, but which their numerous
successors suffered to be lost. Our language has now
all the method and distinction it is capable of, and this
will in the end add imagination to it." This imaginative
style did not exist before his time ; the only examples
of it La Bruyère found are in some of the writings
of Bussy, Pellisson, Flechier, Bonhours, who did
not display sufficient originality, continuity, or consistency, and La Bruyère determined to introduce it into
literature. After Pascal and La Rochefoucauld, and

without resembling them, he was destined to exercise a great and delicate influence.

Boileau as a moralist and critic had with a certain amount of perfection expressed many truths in verse. La Bruyère aimed at expressing in prose something similar; or, as he possibly thought to himself, something better, and still more refined. In Boileau's writings there are numerous thoughts, sound judgments, correct reflections, ·proverbial ideas, but so ordinary, that La Bruyère would never have admitted them into his choice diction. He must have felt in his heart that he wrote with a little more meaning, and (except for the verses which enhance Boileau's style) with more originality than is to be found in many of Nicole's (Boileau's) lines. With him everything assumes a more novel and indirect form, having a deeper meaning than can at first be understood. For example, instead of this kind of sentence used by the author of the *Art poétique*, "*what is well conceived is clearly expressed,*" etc., La Bruyère tells us, in that admirable chapter, *Works of Intellect and Learning*, which is to him his *Art poétique*, his classic rhetoric, "among all the different modes in which a single thought may be expressed, only one is correct ; it does not always occur to us in speaking or in writing ; nevertheless it exists, and any other is weak, and will not satisfy a man of talent who wishes to be understood." We feel how much this second criticism by its truthfulness and wisdom surpasses even the calm judgment of the first. In support of the opinion, not a recent one, on the character of innovator attributed to La Bruyère, I could make use of the judgment of Vigneul Merville and the quarrel he had with Coste de Brillon on this subject ; but the sentiments of these men as regards style is of no consequence, I keep to the expression already quoted of D'Olivet. Taste was

changing then, and La Bruyère unconsciously guided
the change. It was quite time for the century to end ;
a different, more varied, rejuvenized form of language
has sprung into existence, emanating from a great mind ;
left to others, it would soon have degenerated into a
storm of sparkling witticisms. *Les Lettres Persanes*,
for which La Bruyère so well paved the way, were not
long in marking the second epoch. La Bruyère does
not break out into any storm of words, but he is
already in quest of a new and eloquent attraction, and
here he borders on the eighteenth century more than
any other great writer of his age. Vauvenargues in
some respects belongs more to the seventeenth century
than he does. Yet no . . . ; La Bruyère does entirely
belong to his own century in this, that in the midst of
all his labour, containing so much that was new and
original, he never failed in simplicity of heart.

Although it was mankind and society which he
specially described, La Bruyère adapts the idea of the
picturesque to the things of nature more than was
usual in his time, as when he displays to our mind's
eye one "*clear day*" the little village which seemed to
him "*like a beautiful picture on the hillside ;*" and how
gracious and graceful is his comparison of the prince
and the pastor, the flock "*scattered over the meadow,
browsing on the young and tender grass.*" And it was
distinctive of him to have thought of. inserting in the
chapter on *The Heart* the two following ideas : "*There
are some places we admire and others we love.*" "*It
seems to me that wit, humour, passion, taste, and
sentiment depend on the place we live in.*"

Jean Jacques and Bernardin de Saint-Pierre, with
their strong love for places, would undertake one day
to develop all the beauty which lies dormant, so to
speak, in these charming thoughts. Lamartine only

translates poetically La Bruyère's idea when he exclaims:

> "Objets inanimés, avez-vous donc une âme
> Qui s'attache à notre âme et la force d'aimer ?"

La Bruyère is full of such brilliant germs.

He possessed the art of compiling a book without
seeming to make any effort, continuity being maintained
by a sort of hidden thread which appears and reappears
from place to place. At first sight it seems a collection
of fragments arranged in order, and we discover it
to be a labyrinth of unending wisdom. Each idea
corrected, developed, enlightened by surrounding ones,
then all at once the unexpected mingles with it, and
in an ever-moving play of wit and intellect we are
more than once raised to such lofty conceptions as no
continued discourse would admit. "*Neither the troubles,
Zénobie, which disturb your empire,*" etc. A fragment of
a letter it may be, or of a conversation, either imagined
or simply inserted in that chapter on *Judgments.* "*He
said that wit in that young woman was like a well-set
diamond,*" etc., is of itself a charming jewel, which all
the taste of an André Chénier could not have set more
worthily and artistically. I say André Chénier intentionally, in spite of their dissimilarity, because each
time I come to this passage in La Bruyère, the lovely air,
"Elle a vécu, Myrto, la jeune Tarentine," etc., comes
singing into my head.

If it surprises us now that, having so much in
common with the eighteenth century, La Bruyère was
not more often quoted, and more celebrated in it, the first
reply would be that he was too wise, too disinterested,
too unassuming for that ; attracted to, and interested in
mankind in general, in all sorts and conditions of men,
he must have seemed an inactive kinsman of the century,

with little fellow-feeling for its passions and hostilities ; and, moreover, the piquancy and applicability of certain personal portraits had disappeared ; fashion mingled with the form of the book, and some special fashions had gone by. Fontenelle (*Cydias*) opens the eighteenth century in discreet silence about La Bruyère, a silence justified by offended pride ; he indulged in many long last words over the enemies of his youth during the fifty years he remained a member of that illustrious Salon, after they had disappeared. At Sceaux Voltaire might have questioned Malezieu about La Bruyère ; he was one of the members of the Condé household, was associated with our philosopher in the education of the Duchesse du Maine and her brothers, and had read the manuscript of the *Caractères* before publication ; but Voltaire does not appear to have troubled himself. It was in harmony with a calm and delicate mind like Suard's to repair this unjust neglect before time gained it authority. Now La Bruyère's rank in literature is acknowledged. I admit that we may now and then experience a shock when we find the great repute of names both high and lowly reversed, overthrown with little apparent effort ; we feel inclined to shake off the yoke, but at each revolt we are again enraptured by that multitude of thoughts, admirable, concise, and eternally true, like so many imperishable links ; we are enthralled, bound, so to speak, in Vulcan's toils.

From La Bruyère we may easily choose many sentences which have much in common with similar ideas in our day. When he speaks of the heart and passions especially, we meet with passages which respond to our inner experiences. I remark one place where he speaks of young people, who, he says, can bear solitude better than old people, because of the passions *which amuse them*, and I compare this observation with one of *Leila's* on the solitary walks of *Stenio.* I also note his moan over the weakness of the human heart, too soon consoled, *containing no inexhaustible source of grief for certain losses*, and I compare this with a similar lament in *Atala.* Then we have that day-dream by the side of those we love, which comes with charming *naïveté* from the philosopher. But although, following the remark of Fabre, La Bruyère has said that " *a good choice of thoughts is a kind of invention*," we must acknowledge that this invention would be too facile and attractive in his work to indulge in freely.

In politics, we find some brilliant hits which pierce the centuries and come down to us like flashes. " Only to think of self and the present time is a great source of political error."

There is one important point of view on which the writers of our time could not too deeply meditate, and if they do not imitate him (La Bruyère), they may at least respect and envy him, for he thereby was so fortunate as to prove his great wisdom ; with immense talent he has written only to express what he thought : the most in the least, might be his motto.

Once, when speaking of Mme. Guizot, we pointed out the great number of memorable thoughts which she has sown in her numerous and obscure articles—thoughts which it required the hand of tender regard and the eye of love to discern and pick out. La Bruyère, born for perfection, in an age which favoured its development, was not obliged to sow his thoughts in this way ; in books of various kinds written at various times, he rather set each thought apart, left it to stand by itself, clear and apparent as a gorgeous butterfly posed on a beautiful white leaf. " The most talented man," he says, " is unequal . . . ; he begins with great

spirit, but it fails him ; then, if he is wise, he speaks
little and writes nothing. Does one sing with a cold ?
Do we not wait till the voice returns ? " It is from this
habit, this need to *sing* with any kind of voice, this idea
that the spirit is always present, that the greater part of
our literary defects arise.   Under so much that is lively,
pleasing, solemn, probe the groundwork, and you will
discover that the aim is to fill a page, a column, or a
volume.   An inordinate development is the consequence, out of keeping with the detail of the subject,
which is stretched, amplified, exaggerated, till nothing
is left for another occasion.   I might say how much of
this I find in works of eminent talent, in exquisite
poems, in beautiful pages of prose. Oh yes ! there is
much wisdom, facility of expression, learned workman-
ship if you like, but there is also a something which
ordinary readers may not perceive, which even a man
of taste may pass over if he be unheeding—the vain
shadow, the false semblance of talent, what in painting
is called *chique,* and which is probably only a knack
retained although talent is gone.   The amount of
chique to be found in the best productions of the day is
alarming, and I dare not mention it here, because,
speaking generally, the application might be laid on
some specially illustrious name.   There are passages in
the action of a poem or a romance which an experienced
author perceives to be shallow ; this shallowness will
find no echo in the vulgar mind.   But what have I
said ? This is one of the secrets of the method which
must remain sacred among artists in order that no
discredit may fall on the profession.   The wise and
facile La Bruyère was not of this kind ; he translated
Theophrastus at his leisure, and each thought he produced was essentially suited to his time.   It is true
that his thousand écus of pension as man of letters in

the Duke's household, and his lodgment in the Hôtel de Condé, procured for him a position of ease and security which has no analogy in our time; but granting this, and meaning no offence to our laboured merits, his first little book in 12mo ought to be found on the table of every modern writer; its far-reaching and original talent will help us to remember moderation, and teach us to proportion thought to language; it would even be a step gained to be able to regret our inability to do this.

L'ABBÉ DE CHOISY.

1851.

THE Abbé de Choisy was fond of disguising himself. During his childhood and early youth his mother accustomed him· to masquerade as a girl. Throughout his whole life he retained this peculiar taste for travesty. It has been said that even in very much later years—at an age when he should have blushed at this effeminate mania—he would still secretly don the silks and laces as worn by some ancient dowager, heartily regretting not to be any longer able to exhibit himself as a coquettish marchioness or charming shepherdess.

In the positions he successively held, he displayed the same spirit of frivolity, the same witty, odd, and graceful fancies. His life resembles a most varied and improbable comedy, and it is hard to tell at what point he ceases being a masquerader. From his earliest childhood he wore the tonsure of priesthood, but his mother appears to have principally dedicated him to female finery. As vain as a nun in *Vert Vert*, and as garrulous as a parrot, he alternately played the part of the Countess de Sancy in the parish· of Saint-Médard, and that of the Countess des Barres in the Province of Berry. After this he repented of his follies and went out to Siam, where he led the life of an apostle, converting his fellow-men, though never losing his peculiarly easy and happy temperament. After distinguishing himself as an agreeable and even subtle writer, he finally became an historian of the Church, and a senior member of the French Academy. His life, covering eighty years, was a complete masquerade. He entered fully into the various *rôles* he undertook, in each of which he acquitted himself with a playfulness and adaptability all his own. In his childhood he was engaging, and as an aged man he was still very interesting, and generally appreciated in spite of his years. Nevertheless, he could never make amends for his youthful escapades, nor conceal the innate frivolity of his character. Had he lived over a hundred years, he would have failed to acquire either consideration or authority; but, on the other hand, he was the object of affection and indulgence, and in these days his individuality is looked upon as a pretty freak of nature, and as one of the curiosities of a great century.

Francis-Timoléon de Choisy, Prior of Saint-Lo at Rouen, of Saint-Benoît-du-Sault, and of Saint-Gelais, and Dean of the Bayeux Cathedral, etc. etc., was born in Paris in 1644. He came of one of those fine middle-class families which had the privilege of providing the ancient monarchy with its leading State-Secretaries, and its most faithful and hardworking Ministers. His father had spent his life in occupying various stewardships and embassies, and last of all he became the counsellor of Gaston, brother to Louis XIII. His mother, a woman of great ability, a *précieuse* of her day (before the word was used as a term of ridicule), was handsome, active, and intriguing; she was the great - granddaughter of the illustrious and sapient

Chancelier de l'Hôpital. It is strange that from out this venerable stock there should thus proceed in the person of the Abbé de Choisy such a wild and wanton branch. In creating women, nature is sometimes mistaken, and produces *viragos*, who care for naught but manly games and warlike sports. Nature was, as regards the Abbé de Choisy, mistaken in the inverse sense, and had given him, with the addition of a pretty face, futile tastes and an innate love for the looking-glass. His mother did everything in her power to promote in him this weakness of nature. He received the most pernicious education that can be imagined ; in fact, one that only favoured the development of his effeminate and puerile character. Although this idolizing parent strove in her conversations with her son, and in the letters he wrote under her dictation, to initiate him in the principles of an elegant style while striving to endow him with well-bred manners, she was, at the same time, singularly successful in teaching him the worship of his own small person. " *My mother,*" he remarks, "*fostered such a weakness for me, that she was continually adorning me with fine apparel. She ardently desired to still appear young and beautiful. I was born after her fortieth year ; she imagined, however, that people seeing a child of eight or nine years old continually at her side, would consequently give her the credit of being still youthful ; for this reason I accompanied her everywhere. When the little Monsieur, brother of Louis XIV., visited our house, I was arrayed as a girl, and he was our guest at least two or three times a-week. My ears were pierced, I wore diamonds, and my cheeks were embellished with patches ; in a word, I was brought up in all those habits of affectation so easy to adopt and so hard to abandon.*"

While succeeding without any great effort in imbuing

her child's mind with all the futile ideas of a vain and affected woman, De Choisy's mother was withal careful in impressing on him all the principles pertaining to the art of the *sycophant.* This is the only kind of morality she appears to have taught him. "*Listen, my son,*" said this enervated granddaughter of the *Chancelier de l'Hôpital.* "*Do not be vain-glorious, and remember that you are merely a bourgeois. . . . Do not forget that in France the only nobility is that which is gained by the sword. . . . So as not to become vainglorious, my son, never cultivate any one except people of quality. Go and spend the afternoon with the little Lesdiguieres, the Marquis of Villeroy, the Count of Guiche and Louvigny : then you will early acquire a graciousness of manner, and throughout your whole life you will consequently retain an air of civility which will gain you the heart of every one.*"

Such were the precepts of this excellent mother, and by which her son ingenuously assures us he profited. "For it happens," he tells us, "that with the exception of my relations, I do not see a single gentleman of the long robe. I must therefore either spend my life *at Court with my friends,* or in my study with my books." Thus, on principle, he was only friendly with those who are at court. This method was on entirely new lines. Mme. de Choisy failed to encourage any friendship or real attachment that was not founded on purely interested motives. One day the little Abbé de Bouillon (he afterwards became cardinal), who was a nephew of Turenne, quarrelled at college with the Abbé d'Harcourt, and the fact became rumoured abroad. The following day Mme. de Choisy asked her son whether he had called on the Abbé de Bouillon. "I told her that I had not," writes De Choisy, "and that the Abbé d'Harcourt was a friend of mine. I thought she would have devoured me in her anger. '*What!*' she exclaimed, '*and he is the nephew of M. de Turenne! Hasten instantly to his house, or you quit mine for ever.*' She was a *maîtresse-femme* who insisted upon being obeyed, and she has been the means of making my fortune." Choisy, as we perceive, is unable to conceal his appreciation of his mother's great wisdom. In a similar manner she corrected him from his childhood upwards, instructing him in the code of *honour* as practised by an unworthy sycophant. This virtuous parent frequently counselled him not to definitely adhere to either the princes or any members of the royal family, but to the king alone. "Cling, my son, not to the branches, but to the *trunk of the tree.*" To her mind, apart from that tree there could be no salvation.

The Abbé de Choisy was always true to his mother's articles of faith, and to the very end of his days he worshipped the king, and was at times even indiscreet in his very eagerness to become a good courtier ; he was, moreover, a perfect model of complaisance and courtesy in his intercourse with all men. He was at heart a better man, and more faithful to his friends in disgrace, than might have been expected, considering the kind of discipline he had undergone.

This senseless mother kept her son at home until he was eighteen, and up to that age he was nearly always dressed as a girl. He had attained his twenty-third year at the time of her death (in 1666). In taking his share of the inheritance, divided between himself and his brothers, he chose by preference the family jewels ; and, like unto Achilles, who instinctively clutched the weapons of war, he instinctively seized them with avidity. "We were all three satisfied," he exclaims ; "I was delighted at having such beautiful stones ; I had never possessed anything beyond a few rings and earrings of no higher value than 200 pistoles ; and now I was in possession of pendants worth 10,000 francs, a diamond cross of the value of 5000 francs, and three beautiful rings. With such jewels as these I could adorn myself and *play the beautiful woman.*" Indeed, during the few following years, the Abbé de Choisy, left to his own devices, and free from all restraint, *played the beautiful woman* to his heart's content, and recklessly abandoned himself to all his mad caprices. We all know the charming scene in *The Marriage of Figaro*, that scene where Cherubin, seated at the feet of the Countess, is in the hands of the frolicsome Luzanne, who is arranging his collar : "Look at the child ; see how pretty he is as a girl ! I am perfectly jealous of him. How dare you be so pretty ?" During his early youth the Abbé de Choisy had often been the object of similar speeches, and the occasions on which they had been uttered were grafted in his memory as the most delightful he could imagine. He would have liked to perpetuate those blissful moments, and during his whole lifetime he endeavoured to revive this memory as frequently as possible.

One day Mme. de la Fayette happened to meet him wearing a garb which partook of the dress of both sexes. He had donned a male costume, while his ears were embellished with pendants, and his cheeks with patches. This woman of wit and sense, in order to shame him, remarked, undoubtedly in a tone of pleasantry, that he was not dressed in masculine fashion, and that he would be much better arrayed entirely as a woman. Latent passions require but a slight incentive. The Abbé de Choisy took the satirical Mme. de la Fayette at her word, and *on such a good authority* he

M

adopted the feminine style of dress in its completeness. It is highly amusing to hear him describe his *toilettes* down to the most minute details ; he revels, he excels in these particular descriptions. Here we perceive the most striking and original feature of this vain and fatuous nature, and can measure the extent of his innate feminine love of finery. People have often disguised themselves so as to give full scope to their licentiousness, and a change of apparel has frequently served to facilitate the indulgence of a passion or to further an intrigue. But the Abbé de Choisy, though not exempt from guilty irregularities, seemed to like falsifying his appearance for the sake of sporting himself in gaudy raiment. He loved the looking-glass for itself, finery because it was finery, and trinkets because they were trinkets. It was his ideal of supreme happiness to be seated before a mirror adorning himself, tricking his face up with a patch here and there, or adding a becoming curl, while a circle of friends surrounded him, incessantly exclaiming, " *You are as beautiful as an angel !* "

M. de la Mennais, in his work entitled *Affaires de Rome*, describes the journey he undertook in 1832. He has painted in a few satirical strokes, and far more subtlely than might have been expected, having regard to the pen of such an energetic writer, the character of the Cardinal de Rohan, who was in Rome at that time. "Being of an extremely frail and éffeminate constitution," says M. de la Mennais, "he never attained the age of virility ; nature had destined him to linger through a long childhood ; he possessed all the weakness, tastes, the little vanities, and innocence of a child. The Romans had given him the nickname of *il Bambino*. Such a man as he, is always led by others unworthier than himself." All those who have

known, or even only casually met the Cardinal de
Rohan, can judge of the veracity of this lightly-sketched
portrait. I have chosen this illustration, because it is,
as M. de la Mennais has remarked, an *innocent* illustration. There was no immorality intermingled with the
cardinal's effeminate vanity. But that innate love of
dress, which I have pointed out as one of the most
marked characteristics of the Abbé de Choisy, was
developed to a far higher degree in the person of the
Cardinal de Rohan. It was a satisfaction and a
triumph for him to be successful in gracefully draping
about his shoulders the folds of a rich lace shawl, and
he would stand for many minutes before the looking-
glass admiring the elegant reflection of his bedecked
person. Even at the steps of the altar his vanity did
not entirely forsake him. I can see him now, as he
appeared at Besançon on the occasion of a pontifical
ceremony. He was arrayed in all the splendour of his
sacerdotal robes, casting here and there smiling and
coquettish glances, for he had been told that several
people had arrived from Paris the preceding day to
attend this religious function.

But here ends all similitude between the abbé and
the cardinal. The Abbé de Choisy ventured far
beyond mere vanity, and I will refrain from following
him through the incredible episodes of his youth. In
those days the police must have been extremely badly
organized, and legal authority very indulgent, to have
permitted him to venture upon such escapades. We
cannot complain respecting the morals of the present
day, when we read the account of the immoralities that
were not absolutely prohibited to the Abbé de Choisy.
He was able for months, even years, to inhabit a house
in the Faubourg Saint-Marceau, keep his carriage, have
a seat in the parish church, join in the public worship

(he was even requested on one ceremonious occasion to enact the part of *quêteuse*, and hand round the poor-box). He was able to carry on this existence under the name of the *Countess de Sancy*, in spite of its being generally suspected who he really was. He was not reprimanded by the ecclesiastical authority until matters became aggravated. After quitting the Faubourg Saint-Marceau, the Abbé, though fully forewarned, still insisted on retaining his favourite dress, and displaying it before the public gaze, even in the theatre. One evening, at the opera, he happened to be seated in the box belonging to the youthful Dauphin, son of Louis XIV. Suddenly M. de Montausier entered the door. "I was at the very height of joy," he exclaims, "when suddenly that sullen-looking man appeared." The Chancelier de l'Hôpital himself, perceiving his unworthy descendant in this attitude, could not have experienced a greater feeling of contempt. "Madame or Mademoiselle, for I am at a loss what to call you," said M. de Montausier, while bowing ironically, "I will admit you are beautiful, but in truth are you not ashamed of wearing such habiliments, and of playing the part of a woman, because you are lucky enough not to be one ? Go—go, and hide yourself ; M. le Dauphin does not consider you are at all nice in this disguise." This last hit was not exactly in accordance with truth ; for, on the contrary, the little Dauphin was not at all scandalized by the Abbé's behaviour. De Choisy was greatly surprised at what he termed the "oddness" of M. de Montausier, but as nothing had a greater power of touching him than royal disapproval, or rather, any disapprobation that approached it, he deemed it wise, after this occasion, to disappear from Paris. He bought a castle in the province of Berry, and during two or three years he lived there *incognito*, under the name of the Countess des Barres. There he pursued a frivolous existence, enacting a perfect comedy, dressing, un-dressing, embellishing, and admiring himself the whole day, surrounded by all the nobility and gentry of the country, by the vicars, the intendants, the bishops, and the lieutenant-general's wife. These simple, unsuspecting individuals ardently admired him as an elegant Parisian. He took such underhand advantage of their credulity, that, had he lived during a more rigid period, he might have incurred the legal measures adopted by the attorney-general in cases of abduction of minors. When aged, and apparently con-verted, the Abbé de Choisy still experienced unutterable pleasure in relating these youthful adventures to his grave friends, such as D'Argenson, who would listen with astonishment, and even to philosophical ladies, such as Mme. de Lambert, who would question him indulgently.

He continued leading this unworthy existence as long as possible, and when he abandoned it he had already attained his thirty-third year. He was still beardless, for he had prevented the growth of any hair by applying to his face some particular kind of depilatory ; but the beauty of his countenance had vanished. He remarks that one passion drives out another. He journeyed through Italy, and became a gambler. He ruined himself, fell deeply into debt, and commenced seriously bemoaning the years of his initial irregularities ; for "ridicule," he thought, "is preferable to poverty." The unfortunate man, in spite of his wit and his many amiable qualities, was well on the way to rendering himself for ever ridiculous and despicable in the eyes of society, when, strange to say, his mind suddenly assumed a penitent gravity. He began to ponder seriously, and the advent of an unexpected

grave malady favoured his contrition. The 3rd of
August 1683, he fell ill at the Place-Royale, where he
was then living. He perceived the near approach of
death; he heard the doctors murmuring, "He can
hardly live two hours longer." The picture of his past
life appeared to him in its true, unvarnished colours;
the thought of God's judgment terrified him. He
recovered, but on quitting his dying bed he immediately entered the "College of Foreign Missions," and
from this college he went forth to the Indies as a kind
of missionary.

The Abbé de Choisy has noted the circumstances
and motives of his conversion in four *Dialogues* on *The
Immortality of the Soul*, *The Existence of God*, *Providence*,
and *Religion*, which he published the following year
(1684). He certainly lost no time. One of the
characteristics of the Abbé de Choisy was his perfect
lack of self-restraint, and in good as well as in evil he
was prompt, unconstrained, and essentially imprudent.
These *Dialogues* are not entirely original; they are the
result of serious discussions between himself and one of
his friends, the Abbé de Dangeau, an estimable man of
high distinction, who, besides being a most accurate
metaphysician, was both a grammarian and a philosopher. From the very commencement he exercised
a most beneficial influence on the Abbé de Choisy.
Dangeau even discovered, after a little time, that his
friend, who at the commencement seemed possessed of
a certain frivolous incredulity, was a subject easy to
convert; he found that, gifted with a lively imagination, De Choisy skipped the intermediate state, and
bounded from incredulity to thorough belief. Prove
to me that there is a God "*as clearly as I see that it is
daylight!*" exclaimed the Timoléon of the *Dialogues* to
Theophilus (that is, De Choisy to Dangeau). "The

moment I am convinced of the goodness of God, nothing will any longer be difficult for me to believe." "I have merely," replied Theophilus, "to prove to you that there exists a God, and that your soul is immortal, and straightway you are ready to become a Capuchin." When speaking of the Abbé de Choisy's easy and somewhat fragile conversion, in response to the complimentary remarks made to him regarding this successfully performed regeneration, Dangeau remarked: "Alas! I had hardly convinced this giddy creature of the existence of God, than he was forthwith prepared to believe in the baptism of the church-bells."

Nevertheless, we find many traits of sincere conversion in the Abbé de Choisy's *Diary*, which was published soon after his return from Siam. Towards the year 1684, a message was sent to Louis XIV. from Siam, to the effect that it would suffice to send out to the Siamese king, an ambassador and a few missionaries to convert him and his subjects to Christianity. The Abbé de Choisy, who was then at the Seminary, heard of this projected mission to Siam ; the palm of Saint Francis-Xavier immediately blossomed before his gaze, and, with all the zeal of a proselyte, he deemed it an excellent idea to strive to evangelize this far-off kingdom. It is true he merely bore the tonsure of a priest, and had not really been ordained as such. But no matter ! During his journey he would enter into *retreat*, and on landing he would go through the rites of ordination. He hastened to interview M. de Seignelay, the naval minister, in order to solicit the apostleship. But the mission had already been entrusted to a naval officer, the Chevalier de Chaumont, a man of religious and virtuous principles. De Choisy was only able to obtain the *coadjutorship* of the mission—an odd term, which appeared expressly made for him. This highly original coadjutor embarked at Brest on the 3rd of March 1685. Obeying the instincts of his curiosity, perhaps flying from his creditors, and withal believing that he was following a ray of Divine grace, he felt his heart bound with overwhelming joy. He has left us an account of his voyage and of his various daily impressions. He addressed this description of his travels to the same friend who had converted him the preceding year, the Abbé de Dangeau. The Abbé de Choisy was then forty-one years of age.

In this _Diary_ it is a little too frequently a question of the wind and tides ; but the letters in which the author speaks of himself are extremely natural and diverting. The Abbé de Choisy is the most sweet-tempered passenger imaginable ; never wearied, never for a single moment regretting having joined the enterprise, never failing to see the favourable side of everything. He is in the company of missionaries and Jesuits, some of whom are great mathematicians. He converses with them, with a view to gleaning knowledge. He has scarcely recovered from the throes of sea-sickness than he applies himself to the study of Portuguese and astronomy ; he expatiates on naval matters, and prattles on the subject of longitude and latitude. After the first few days he knows all the terms that are used on shipboard. " One cannot help becoming accustomed to nautical expressions ; I say to my valet, Anchor my collar." Sermons are given, and he finds all the preachers eloquent. " There is not a single cabin-boy on our vessel who does not wish to go to Paradise, thus proving that the sermons cannot be otherwise than good." " Oh, how easily everything leads us to thoughts of God ! " he exclaims, with strong and sincere feeling, " when we find ourselves on the ocean-wave, on five or six planks of wood, continually

between life and death ! How touching are our reflections when evil temptations are removed from our
path ! . . . I consider there can be no better Seminary
than a vessel." On calm days, when the sea appears
to him "like a vast pond ruffled by the zephyrs,"
dances are given on board ship by way of amusement,
and on these occasions there are wrestling matches
between the Brittany sailors and the Provincials.
The ambassador, with the help of the missionaries,
enacts the part of arbiter. There are shouts of *Long
live the King !* De Choisy has not failed to remember
that after God, and at the side of God, to the King is
due all honour. " His Majesty is highly respected on
land, but on the sea we love him," he adds, with a
certain heart-felt tenderness. Concerts are also given
on the vessel, and choruses are sung. The adaptable
De Choisy enjoys everything, admires everything. On
land he only found one Dangeau, one *Theophilus* (as he
designates him in his *Dialogues*) ; at sea he discovers
half-a-dozen *Theophiluses :*—

" *I discuss the Portuguese language with Father Visdelou;
M. Basset teaches me the meaning of Sacred Orders ; I peer
into the moon with Father de Fontenei ; I converse on the
question of pilotage with our ensign, who possesses considerable knowledge on this subject ; I converse on all these points
without any exertion whatever, while strolling upon deck.
When I wish to procure myself a great pleasure, I fetch
M. Manuel, one of our missionaries, who has an uncommonly beautiful voice, and who understands music as
well as Lully. You know my love of music; and the
exercise of this fine art is not forbidden at the Seminary.
What is Paradise but eternal music ?*"

In this short quotation we already discover the
vivacious, playful, inquiring, and elegant nature of the
Abbé's mind. On becoming more nearly acquainted

with the fascination of his intellect, we cannot refrain
from forgiving him many of his errors. The mode of
his career does not appear to have corrupted him so
greatly as might have been expected; it is evident
his actions were rather the outcome of mere frivolity
than of a deeply-rooted desire for debauchery. He
remained for ever extremely natural and capable of
receiving good impressions; his nature was eminently
plastic; it sufficed him to be surrounded by good
examples for him to imitate them. His was one of
those natures that are but the echoes, the faithful and
varied reflections, of their times and their surroundings.
The writings of such men form excellent testimonies
of the language current in their day.

The Abbé de Choisy's style is bright, light, and
invested with some of the graces of childhood. His
mind and his pen appear to have retained the youth of
Cherubin. He possessed all the facility of a child in
acquiring languages. After learning Portuguese with
such facility, he took up the study of Siamese. He
soon mastered this tongue, and was able to freely
converse in both languages. He acknowledges that the
principal defect of his mind consisted in a lack of
concentration and of the power of bringing his knowledge to a point of perfection. "I always wish to
write and never to read; I admit this is not the right
means of becoming well-informed. Every one has his
weakness. I can hardly help scribbling, for when I
hold a pen I am as joyous as the prince who wields his
sword. Oh, happy posterity! could these two weapons,
in their respective spheres, be as equally well employed!" The Abbé is a charming babbler, finding
pretty phrases that are sometimes precursory to a
felicitous thought, though oftener they are merely based
on some flying fancy. His mind was an admixture of

subtlety and credulity. He appears capable of fathom-
ing the truth concerning men and affairs, but at the
same time his natural mobility disposes him rather to
remain on the surface than to dive deeply into the
spirit of things. He is prepared on every occasion to
believe in appearances and to acknowledge the existence
of the miraculous. One day, M. Basset was preaching
on the vessel, and his eloquence struck De Choisy as
resembling that of Bourdaloue. " There is something
miraculous about this man," observed the Abbé ; " as
he approaches the land of his mission, God grants him
proportionately increased grace and fresh inspiration ;
for, indeed, we all know how differently he spoke in
the conferences at the Seminary ; he even experienced
some difficulty in giving expression to his ideas.
Here, on the other hand, he is a perfect torrent of
eloquence."

Had De Choisy and his fellow-workers been about to
perform a real apostolic mission, I should think twice
before contesting the fact of this sudden acquisition of
Divine eloquence by M. Basset ; but, in this particular
case, the voyage to Siam turned out to be nothing save
a sham affair, and we can clearly perceive that De
Choisy, in describing a miracle, draws largely on his
imagination.

The same man who is so credulous as regards M.
Basset, depicts, a little later on, with keen penetration
and in a charming manner, the cunning displayed by
the Jesuits. They had hardly landed at Batavia among
the Dutch Protestants, when they hastened to establish
their Observatory, in order to gain a good welcome by
placing their astronomical instruments at the disposal
of the inquiring inhabitants. " They are erecting their
apparatuses," says De Choisy, " in order to pay their
host with a little Jupiter and Mercury." He adds, by

way of a moral : "Cleverness is a grand thing in every country."

However, De Choisy, with his subtle and impression-able mind, caught at times the true spirit of apostolic inspiration. In speaking of a saintly priest whom he met at Batavia, he paints him by one simple and felicit-ous phrase : "He is a venerable man, who has been nearly thirty years in Cochinchina and Tonkin : *his past life has imprinted a perpetual brightness on his countenance.*"

De Choisy is modest ; he does not attempt to impress on others the importance of his own mind, and he is sufficiently gracious not to pretend to be greater than he really is. While the Jesuits on board ship were applying themselves to the study of astronomy, the other missionaries were holding debates ; De Choisy was merely a looker-on. "*As for myself, I tamper with nearly every subject,*" he observes in writing to Dangeau, "*and if I fail to become a savant—a condition it is now impossible for me to attain, considering I have not grown into a learned man even under your tuition—I shall at least possess a slight smattering of everything. I am an auditor at all the debates, and I often adopt your method— I assume a strictly modest demeanour, and refrain from talking much. When I am really conversant with the subject in question, then I allow myself to speak in an undertone, being as equally modest in the sound of my voice as in the words I utter. This makes an admirable effect, and often when I am perfectly silent, my confrères imagine I have no desire to speak, never suspecting that the true reason of my silence lies in my profound ignorance, which I deem it wise to conceal from the eyes of men.*"

At one moment the Abbé thought of studying Euclid. When the ship arrived at the Cape, the longitude had to be rectified. He describes this proceeding, and adds :

" I proved myself to be not utterly useless ; while Father de Fontenei was at his telescope, and the others attending to the clocks, I occasionally counted *One, two, three, four*, to mark the seconds." How could we bear any ill-will against so amiable a man, who in this way glories in his own acquirements ?

The whole tone of his *Diary* is bright. His style is sprightly, and overflowing with life and fun, but utterly devoid of anything like depth or gravity. He prattles gaily about the west wind, and even speaks triflingly regarding the storms. As the vessel approaches the Cape of Good Hope, we might fancy he were attempting to proportion his thoughts to the majesty of the horizon : "The sea begins to be extremely *hollow;* by that I mean we frequently discover ourselves in a valley between two mountains whitened with foam. At first this appears to be somewhat amusing ; but when, a moment later, we are hurled on the summit of the mountain, and the horizon fades into insignificance, we hold our peace, *mirabiles elationes maris.*" This description exhibits a certain attempt at profundity of thought ; but do not, my readers, for one moment expect that he will sustain this gravity of style. When, after having doubled the Cape, the crew are exposed to a violent tempest, and the vessel is wrapped in the fury of the elements, he finds no more apposite expression than that the sea now wears a different *phiz* to that of the preceding days. He who can employ the word *phiz* in the presence of so solemn a spectacle, may be fairly well judged by his very use of this term. The Abbé de Choisy contemplates the ocean through the wrong end of the telescope.

Those who have undertaken long sea voyages, assert that nothing can equal the weariness that in time they begin to feel in their own society and in that of their

companions. Every man becomes insupportable to the
other; little failings become magnified, and these individuals need divorcing for a long time before they are
able to meet again with any degree of pleasure. But
our Abbé was an exception to the rule; and in this
exception he demonstrated the adaptable, benevolent,
and essentially social qualities of his character. He
not only failed to find that the time lingered wearily
in its course, but he never once complained of his
companions; the longer he was in their society the
more enchanted he became. When they were discouraged, he was the first to inspire them with hope.
"Everything will succeed," he would remark; "we
have begun too well not to finish in the same way. If
we do not reach Siam, we will spend the winter at
Surat and at Bantam, in the midst of a beautiful
country. *We all like each other so much! We shall be
all the longer together!*" He uttered these words after
he had been on the sea for three months; he repeated
them after five months; he could not sufficiently con-
gratulate himself in having undertaken this journey.
He seemed to perceive in this undertaking the hand of
God, who had wished to remove him from the path of
danger. Happen what may, he thought to himself, "I
shall anyway have accomplished an interesting expedition; I shall have learned many little things. I shall
scarcely in any way have offended the Almighty during
two years. Alas! as regards this, they will be the
two best years of my life. Moreover, what could we do
on this vessel to offend God? We only speak of what
is good; there are none other than excellent examples.
Temptations are three or four thousand leagues from
here." He thus continues to see the beautiful side of
everything, and to demonstrate to his friend in France
how the days glide away like seconds, and how on board

ship he is the happiest of men. He says: "We have the prayers and debates; we read the Holy Scriptures; we converse in Portuguese and Siamese; we study the globe; we play chess; while, to crown everything, we have excellent living, and gaiety of heart—what more could we desire?"

We are commencing, are we not, to learn something of the character, the lightness, and the graceful wit of the Abbé de Choisy, and are, perhaps, also beginning to forgive him for his past errors. Duclos has aptly defined him as an agreeable writer, whose style has *the negligent graces of a woman.*

De Choisy possesses, moreover, that peculiarly daring wit which blends well with his lightness of style. Under his apostolic mien he has quite the nature of the old race of Frenchmen, who never hesitated, but who would wander forth to the end of the world, careless of harm, and ready for adventure, sustained in every vicissitude by their gaiety of heart, abandoning their welfare to the guidance of God, their Star, or the inspiration of the moment. "We are undertaking this journey *à la Française,*" he justly remarks in one portion of his *Diary,* implying thereby that he and his companions had, without forethought, entered upon this expedition.

In regard to the kingdom of Siam, where he had dreamt of gaining a wonderful conquest, and which other travellers have proved to be anything but a splendid country, De Choisy becomes an extremely superficial and inaccurate guide. He now merely considers the outside of men and things,—the *eidolons,* as Plato would say,—and is amused with the details of the various pageants, ceremonies, and orations. His only serious performance is his entry into the Seminary, where, in *four* days, he receives Holy Orders from the hands of

a bishop *in partibus.*   The King of Siam was governed
by a favourite adventurer,—a Greek by birth, of the
name of Constance.   He was a man of skill and cunning,
who, feeling he was hated by the natives, had, under
the pretext of religion, induced the Europeans to enter
Siam with a view of gaining their support.   After
speaking of this M. Constance, who used his utmost
efforts to attract and dazzle him, De Choisy sums him
up very prettily : "In short, he is a queer fellow, who
would be witty if he were at Versailles." There, again,
is a *trait à la Française.*   On his return to his own
country, De Choisy discovered he had only played a
sham part at Siam, and that Father Tachard, a Jesuit,
had been in league with Constance in this secret
negotiation.   De Choisy even found he had been dis-
honestly treated by this same Jesuit, who had robbed
him of a certain handsome present, which should, by
rights, have been handed over to the Abbé.   "I did
not know the exact details of the case," he remarks,
"till after I had returned to France ; but I was so
delighted on finding myself again in my own country,
that I bore no feeling of malice towards any single
human being."   De Choisy emphasizes more than once
the fact that he is devoid of spite, and that he has no
enemies.   "If I knew of any one who wished me evil,
I should instantly run to him, and display so much
politeness and such friendly attention, that he would
forthwith become my friend in spite of himself."
There, again, we notice his kind and complaisant disposition ; he might seek in vain for the power of hatred.
In everything he was exactly the reverse of Alceste
and M. de Montausier.

De Choisy's expedition to Siam rehabilitated him up
to a certain point in the public opinion, and conspired
to gain him the reputation for singularity—a notoriety

far less compromising than the one he had gained in his youth. On his return to court, however, he endured at first some degree of mortification, failing to receive the compliments he had anticipated. At the time he left France, his friend the Cardinal de Bouillon, the *grand-aumônier*, was in favour, and De Choisy deemed it appropriate to send him several presents as coming from the King of Siam. Unfortunately, during the Abbé's absence, the Cardinal had incurred the disgrace of Louis XIV., and these offerings arrived at Versailles addressed to an exile. This mishap caused a scandal. De Choisy was compelled to offer his excuses to the King, who thereupon merely remarked, "*That is sufficient*," and turned his back brusquely on him. "I thought it best to let the storm blow over," adds the unfortunate and mortified man, "so I hastened to Paris to seek seclusion in my Seminary, where half an hour spent in prayer before the Holy Sacrament enabled me soon to forget all that had occurred." Nothing less than this prayer before the Holy Sacrament could suffice to relieve the Abbé's sorrow in having for one instant displeased his terrestrial master.

A few months later, the Abbé de Choisy, in order to conciliate Louis XIV., dedicated and offered to him his *Life of David*, then his *Life of Solomon*,—works containing all kinds of flattering allusions to this monarch ; indeed, most of the histories he wrote at that time, be it that of the Church or that of the various kings of France, appeared invariably with dedications to Louis XIV., conceived in terms of the most idolatrous adulation. In 1687 the French Academy named De Choisy one of its members. M. Bergeret, who received him, ventured, after mentioning the Abbé's *great-great-grandfather*, the *Chancelier de l'Hôpital*, to compare Mme. de Choisy, who had

N

so strangely educated her son, with the illustrious
Cornelias of Rome. Where could there exist greater
dissimilitude than between Cornelia, mother of the
Gracchi, and the Abbe de Choisy's frivolous parent?

During the remaining thirty-seven years of his life
(1687–1724) the Abbé de Choisy incessantly wielded
his pen on every kind of subject. He wrote without
pretension, in a manner which savoured of no pedantry,
though it suggested a certain degree of research. His
four historical volumes on Saint Louis, Philip de
Valois, and Charles V., etc., met with great success at
.hat time. These works were chiefly to be found on
ladies' toilet-tables, being more particularly written for
the perusal of the fair sex. They were books that,
according to Madame de Sévigné, *were able to be very
well read.* De Choisy's talent consisted in his power
of introducing into every subject a certain familiar ease
and rapidity, which charmed and carried away the
reader. No matter whether it were sacred or profane
history, moral or saintly tales, his pen was ever ready
for the treatment of any subject. Had you proposed
to him that he should write on the question of moral
action, or on the Golden Legend, and told him to create
on this starting-point matter that would vie with the
fairy tales of Madame d'Aulnoi or Perrault, he would
have risen to the occasion. He relates the most serious
narratives with the same careless grace he would have
adopted in writing a story similar to the *Peau d'Ane*.
The last words in his *History of the Church* are singularly
characteristic of his mode of treatment: " Thank God,
my history is finished, I will now begin to learn it."

From among his numberless writings I should not
think of enumerating, there is only one that can commend itself to the reading public of to-day—that is,
the book containing his "Memoirs." They comprise

different sections, some of which are incomplete. The Abbé de Choisy writes as he speaks, and as he hears others speak. He likes to introduce parenthetical sentences ; and when a fresh idea suddenly suggests itself to his mind and arouses his interest, he interrupts the subject he has commenced. He announces that he is about to say many things in relation to the King, but speaks greatly about himself. "With my pen in hand I am somewhat of a chatter-box," he remarks ; "as you may well perceive, I am perfectly unceremonious, and hardly premeditating all that I tell you. I seriously promise you, however, to entertain you nearly all the time on the subject of the King ; he will constitute my sustained keynote. If from time to time you find *me* in some corner, pass over me." On the whole, these Memoirs are extremely lively and amusing, and, with the exception of certain inaccuracies in relation to facts and dates, they are a faithful record as regards the spirit of the people and things therein described. De Choisy possessed the art of extracting conversation from well-informed individuals—those men whom he named *old repertories.* He did not mention the fact of writing his Memoirs ; so, as he was only supposed to be confining his attention to the history of the Church and early French history, even cautious men did not hesitate in expressing their opinions before him. He would ask questions, he tells us, "without any appearance of eagerness, but with an air of ordinary curiosity. I make M. Roze talk of the time of Mazarin ; I converse with M. Brienne . . . ; I let that gossip, Du Plessis-Bellière chatter to his heart's content, for he never rants. . . . I sometimes extract a word from old Bontemps ; I extract twelve from Joyeuse, and twenty from Chamarante, who is delighted to have some one with whom he can converse, for there is nothing that loosens the

tongue so effectually as gout in the hands and feet."
Memoirs that are thus written, soon after the actual
conversations have taken place, are likely to be true
testimonies as regards the *ensemble*, although the details
may be inaccurate.

De Choisy's Journal abounds in anecdotes, witty
remarks, and amusing things that have been said in
society. Like the generality of writers of that period,
the Abbé excels in his portraits. Those of Fouquet, Le
Tellier, of Lyonne, and of Colbert—these four men who
rose to eminence after Mazarin's death—are admirably
sketched, and display a more than ordinary capacity.
De Choisy had conversed with these able speakers on
the days he painted them with such firmness of touch.
As soon as Mazarin was dead, these four men, who had
restrained themselves under his sway, and who had
disguised their pretensions and their weaknesses so as
to further their own interests, believed they need no
longer observe the same policy, and forthwith *each one*
revealed his real nature. "The ambitious man (Fouquet)
burst out into forming plans, and had the insolence to
remark, ' *To what height am I not able to climb ?* ' The
miser (Le T   .er) amassed piles of money ; the proud
man (Col' art) knit his brow ; while the sensualist
(Lyonne) hid his evil ways no longer in the darkness."
Then follow the detailed portraits of Fouquet, Le
Tellier, and Lyonne. Here is the beginning of Colbert's
picture : "*Jean Baptiste Colbert had a naturally sullen
expression of face. His deeply sunken eyes and his thick
black eyebrows conspired to give him an expression of
austerity, and at first sight an appearance of unsociability
and contrariness; but afterwards, on closer acquaintance,
one discovered he was fairly complaisant, obliging, and of
an unflinching reliability. He was convinced that fair
dealing is the only solid foundation in all transactions.*

*Great application and an unsatiable desire to learn, supplied
his lack of knowledge; the more ignorant he was, the more
he affected to be learned, sometimes quoting* mal-à-propos
*Latin phrases which he had learned by heart, and that his
salaried professors had expounded to him. He had not a
single passion since he had given up wine. He was faithful
in the execution of his duties, involved by the controllership
he occupied—an office which had hitherto been held by men
who failed to count and render account of the monies they
had received: he was rich solely through the donations of
the King, which he did not spend lavishly, foreseeing full
well, as he remarked to his intimate friends, the prodigality of
his eldest son. . . . .* His mind being solid and ponderous,
and more especially fitted for calculation, he was able
to unravel the complications that the controllers and
treasurers of the King had expressly brought about in
the affairs of the treasury, in order that they might fish
in troubled waters." . . . The rest of this description
must be read in the original. In this portrayal we see
that De Choisy was not altogether lacking in energy of
mind, or rather, that his essentially plastic brain was
capable of sometimes receiving strong impressions. If
the Abbé draws with so able a hand the portraits of
men, still more does he excel in his sketches of women.
He has drafted a delightful picture of Mme. de la
Valliere, which is worthy of being placed in face of the
one of Colbert, whom we have just quitted, with his
frowning brow :—

"*She had an admirable complexion, fair tresses, an
agreeable smile, blue eyes, and an expression so tender and
withal so modest, that it gained her at the same moment
both affection and esteem. As for the rest, she only possessed
a modicum of mind, which she daily strove to improve by
continual reading. She lacked ambition and strong opinions,
being more assiduous in thinking of the man she loved than*

in pleasing him. Wrapped up in herself and her passion, which had been the only one in her life, she preferred honour to all else, having courted death more than once, rather than allow her frailty to be suspected. She was liberal-minded, timid, and of a sweet and even temper. Never forgetting that she was acting wrongfully, she ever hoped she would return to the path of righteousness. These Christian feelings procured her all the blessings of God's mercy, and she spent a long life in steadfast and even great joy, withal in austere penitence. I speak of her with plea-sure, for I spent my childhood in her company."

This portrait has been taken from life ; here De Choisy had seen and felt for himself, and needed no one to inspire him. All the writers in the time of Louis XIV. wrote in a manner similar to that of the Abbé, though at that period they were hardly considered more than mediocre in their literary efforts. How agreeable, familiar, delicate, and light is their style, overflowing with those unfinished periods and graceful negligences that represent the genius of conversation, and which, so to speak, mirror more fully the various shades of thought.

De Choisy, as a writer of memoirs, can in many ways be compared to Mme. de Caylus, though perhaps of the two she wields the firmer and the more accurate pen, and possesses greater self-command. It is he' who betrays the more womanly qualities.

I might expatiate for ever if I mentioned all there is to mention in relation to this prolific writer. It suffices to have made him known in the principal phases of his talent. D'Alembert in his *Elogiums,* and the Marquis d'Argenson in his *Memoirs,* have both written perfect criticisms on De Choisy. As to-day is a general holiday,* do not let me evince too great a severity. De Choisy

* This article was written on the Shrove-Tuesday of 1851.

is entitled to some indulgence ; he was more frivolous than corrupt ; he was always natural in the midst of his strangest caprices ; he experienced at one time sincere feelings of pity—those feelings he endeavoured to cultivate ; he at least strove with might and main, during the last thirty years of his life, to become a serious man, though he never succeeded in being otherwise than amiable and amusing. In short, he spoke and wrote daily in excellent language, and from among the multitude of his works there is at least one which is deserving of posterity, and of ranking among the notable series of historical testimonies. His *Life* itself has its place in history as one of the most singular anecdotal Memoirs of the Great Century.

FONTENELLE.*

1851.

M. FLOURENS, one of the two permanent secretaries of the Academy of Sciences, has had the felicitous idea of writing a more or less detailed history of his predecessors,—not their biography, but rather the history of their works and opinions. During these last few years he has published on George Cuvier, Fontenelle, and Buffon, a succession of studies as remarkable for their clearness of exposition as for their elegant simplicity of style. The last-mentioned writer was not a permanent secretary, though he fully deserved to occupy that place of honour. M. Flourens promises to continue this series, devoted to the demonstration of the methods adopted by these celebrated *savants*. This work, taking us back to the most prominent names, affords an apt completion to the Eulogiums he has been accustomed to write yearly on the deceased contemporary members of the Academy. We shall have the pleasure on this occasion, of accepting him as a guide to the path we propose to pursue in relation to our remarks concerning Fontenelle.

In the one Fontenelle there are two distinct men, although, after an attentive study, we always find it

* *Fontenelle.* By M. Flourens.

easy to detect the one individuality in the other. There is Fontenelle the *bel-esprit*, the foppish, fastidious spark, who was the insipid writer of operas and pastoral poems, the editor of the *Mercure Galant*, and who was continually at war with Racine, Despréaux, and La Fontaine,—that Fontenelle appraised by De Vizé and scourged by La Bruyère. In the depths of this primitive Fontenelle, with his small mind and hateful taste, another Fontenelle early revealed himself, and slowly but surely blossomed forth into developed perfection. This other Fontenelle was the disciple of Descartes,—untrammelled in mind and broad of view,—a man utterly devoid of any prepossessed ideas or opinions. Fully understanding the modern world and its scientific methods,—in part new,—he commanded the accurate reasoning powers necessary for the expounding of science. His logic was characterized by subtlety and discretion; he introduced into his illustrations a certain charm, which conduced to soften the rigid outlines of science, and conciliate those readers who are the least severe. In short, here was the Fontenelle no longer of the Opera, but he of the Academy of Sciences, he who was the first and most worthy organ of this scientific body, a body he himself conceived in all its grandeur and universality when naming it the States-General of literature and intelligence. It is this last Fontenelle whom M. Flourens has exposed to our gaze, enlightened and cleansed from all his false taste. Our honoured contemporary has, so to speak, unveiled the statue of Fontenelle, and only dwelt upon the noble qualities of his mind. We will go back to the early career of this scientific man.

Fontenelle, who was born at Rouen, in February, 1657, was, as we know, nephew, on his mother's side, of the two celebrated Corneilles. At the first glance, it seems an irony on the part of nature to have made him nephew of the man who created the heroic souls of *Polyeuctus*, of the aged *Horace*, and so many other sublime and impetuous-hearted characters ; for Fontenelle's soul was singularly even and entirely exempt from passion and flame. Nevertheless, he greatly resembled his mother, the Corneilles' own sister. He remarked, with his characteristic indifference, which was not even influenced by feelings of filial delicacy : "My father was a fool, but my mother was clever ; she belonged to the sect of the Quietists ; she was a gentle, sweet woman, who would often say to me, *My son, you will be damned;* but the idea did not appear to cause her any sorrow."

In order to point out a certain existing degree of resemblance between Fontenelle and his illustrious uncle, I deem one remark essential, and I address it to those who find a pleasure in pondering over these subtle shades of similarity. The great Corneille possessed, with all his high qualities, one I should not exactly designate as wit in abundance, but rather explain it as copiousness of *bel-esprit*. When his *dramatis personæ* cease to be lofty and passionate, or rather, the moment they have uttered their sublime words, they continue to reason beyond measure ; they speak from their head, not from their heart ; in their case the brain takes the place of the heart ; they dissect ideas, and reduce them to the quintessence of thought. Let us for an instant picture to ourselves a Corneille stripped of his warmth, his inspiration of heart and soul, and then ask of ourselves what he would be if reduced to the mere cold and sapless condition of an accurate and astute reasoner. There existed in Thomas Corneille the secondary and purely mental qualities of his illustrious brother. In his case, however, they were more emphasized, so to speak, *in the first draft;* in him they were not held in check, or rather, as we might suggest, not gathered together under the shadow of genius. Thomas was, nevertheless, not quite lacking in fervour and poetical fire. In Fontenelle, however, this purely mental quality alone composed the whole man. He was all brain; Nature, who had doubly gifted his noble uncle, entirely forgot the heart in his case.

Already in early youth, Fontenelle evinced all the qualities of an exact and attentive mind. He first of all composed ingenious and subtle lines in Latin; then he wrote elegant French verses, merely displaying taste for that which pertains to intelligence and thought. He possessed a singular faculty of analysis, and was gifted with a rare and delicate power of expression.* He visited Paris when he was quite young, and after he was eighteen he frequently journeyed to the capital. He did not, however, take up his abode there until towards 1687, at the age of thirty years. The tone of his first literary efforts bore the unmistakeable stamp of the provinces. Since the time of Villon, Molière, Voltaire, and Beaumarchais, the Parisians have ceased to express themselves in a manner similar to his. Born in a romantic middle-class family, dating from a period prior to that of Louis XIV., Fontenelle remained somewhat backward as regards the literary style of the day, though later on he was singularly in advance of the times in relation to philosophy.

His uncle and god-father, Thomas Corneille, directed his first literary steps in the paper entitled *Le Mercure Galant,* and guided him in his early attempts in

---

* There are some new and accurate details to be found in the *Biography of Fontenelle* by M. Charma (1846), in relation to Fontenelle's family and his early literary ventures.

histrionic writing. Racine and Boileau ridiculed this
fledgling, this finical, backward Normandy provincial,
who arrived by coach in Paris in the nick of time to
find himself hissed in a musical tragedy, and applauded
in his sonnet on Orontes. However, in Fontenelle's
first work in prose (*The New Dialogues of the Dead*,
published in 1683), his philosophical tendency began
to make itself manifest, foreshadowing the heights
he might some day attain. This production contains,
under a somewhat cold but ingenious and elegant style,
liberal and unconstrained thoughts in relation to human
folly. With a cool sagacity, he discourses on the
foolishness of humanity, as exemplified throughout all
ages in the different beliefs and the diverse modes of
apparel. The famous discussion on the Superiority of
Ancient to Modern Times, was on the eve of breaking
out. Fontenelle, in his Dialogue between Socrates and
Montaigne, touched on this point with a few telling
strokes, worthy of the pen of a Saint-Evremond. But
Boileau was neither sufficiently patient nor philosophical to seek to enjoy a healthy thought if expressed
in a style essentially unhealthy ; and in his first works,
Fontenelle presented to his readers truth enclosed, so
to speak, in a *bonbonnière*, absolutely as if he were
offering them sugar-plums or pastils. Or, if another
illustration is preferred, his philosophy was arranged as
a minuet on the melodies of M. de Benserade.

The *Diverse Letters of M. the Chevalier d' Her*——
which Fontenelle published in 1683, at the same time
as his *Dialogues*, are all couched in an equally artificial language, and were written in such a way as to
give the vantage to his enemies. We cannot glean a
thorough knowledge of the primitive Fontenelle, of his
instinctive and early taste, until we have read these
Letters, bearing the impress of the most consummate

and nauseous affectation of wit. There we find the ideal of Fontenelle's imagination, the flowers of his spring; and what a spring! Everything appears to be decorated, painted, and perfumed with musk. They are letters in the style of Voiture, addressed to various people on chosen subjects, some of which have relation to sentiment, while others are written in a tone of raillery. Fontenelle has a singular way of discussing love-making, of dissecting it thread by thread, while he explains its economy and its *husbandry* (this is really the word he uses). "I will wait fifteen or twenty years, if you wish it," writes the Chevalier to the lovely ladies who correspond with him. "Time costs me nothing as regards such beautiful creatures as yourselves. Must it be years? Well, let it be years. I have nothing more agreeable to do. . . . *I will arouse you from your languor.*" Fontenelle feels that he has a long life before him, and he tells himself he can wait for the fruits of the conquests he undertakes. Against a few really pretty subtle passages to be found in these Letters, there are, on the other hand, dozens which are simply strokes of affectation; for instance: "*Love is the income of beauty,* and he who sees beauty without experiencing love, withholds *its income in a manner that cries out for vengeance.*"

After this expatiation on love, which he considers to be the *income* of beauty, Fontenelle enters, with the business-like air of an attorney, into all the details relating to *acquittance:* "You know that when any one has paid off a debt, he is anxious to secure a release, or rather, obtain a receipt to that effect. I *discharge the debt* of love I owe to you, but I declare at the same time the fact that I have *acquitted myself.*" We must bear in mind the fact that, throughout Fontenelle's love-making, it is again the Normandy element which

predominates—that essentially provincial element of
materialism and calculation.   In fact, in these Letters,
love is treated as a matter of addition and subtraction; he
introduces, as we have just seen, the question of *legal acts*
and *acquittances;* and in one place he also keeps account
of the *deficits*.   But wherefore take any heed of these
defects ?   One might perhaps remark : Wherefore ?
Fontenelle surely retrieved them through his later productions—those productions bearing the impress of a
vast and noble mind ;—but no.   Take him, for instance,
in his most lofty and majestic moments ; take him
writing the Eulogium on Newton—that splendid work,
the principal portions of which M. Flourens has so aptly
pointed out.   After a lucid illustration of scientific
systems, after manifold simple and affecting biographical
touches, how does Fontenelle conclude his criticism?
" He " (Newton) " left at his death," he observes, " about
thirty-two thousand pounds sterling in moveable goods,
being something like seven hundred thousand pounds
in our money. M. Leibniz, his rival, died rich also,
though considerably less so than Newton.   Leibniz left
a tolerably large sum of reserve funds.   These rare
examples deserve to be remembered."   This material
conclusion, which crowns in such a peculiar manner the
homage rendered to the greatest scientific genius of
modern times, will not astonish those who have already
noticed, in the *Letters from the Chevalier d'Her*——,
all the calculation and financial similes which Fontenelle,
even when young, brought into questions of sentiment
and love.

He frankly introduced this spirit of calculation into
every subject. In his little treatise *On Happiness*, he
advocates, before all else, the importance of looking to
the material things of this life ; and after we have justly
estimated the amount of pleasure or trouble they may

bring us, he further exhorts us to merely cling to those objects on which we can depend, and in which we find the greatest hope and the least uncertainty. "It is merely a question of calculation," he remarks, "and Wisdom should always hold *counters* in her hand." *Counters* for counting the points—that was his ideal of philosophy. We could never more appropriately quote the following words of Vauvenargues than after reading Fontenelle's early works : "We require soul in order to possess taste." Despite his abundant mental qualities, Fontenelle is lacking in taste, for in him the heart and soul are absent ; for the *pectus* and the *affectus* (as the ancient authors would say) never appeal to him. Taste—that is, a species of taste—only developed itself in him later on, after years of astute thought and reflection.

The three or four Letters of the Chevalier d'Her—— which revolve on the question of the *clandestine marriage* of a supposed cousin, offer another *trait* characteristic of Fontenelle's youth. He assumes that a cousin of the Chevalier's is compelled for some time to conceal the fact of her marriage with a certain gallant gentleman, so as not to vex an old aunt of the latter from whom he expects a large inheritance (it is again a question of money). One should see how the Chevalier (that is to say, Fontenelle) jokes about this clandestine marriage, which obliges this virtuous cousin to study the arts of dissimulation, and to hypocritically endeavour to preserve her maidenly appearance : "You will still belong to the amiable troop of girls who will appear as your equals, and who will perhaps be so." She will have to receive her husband in secret, and to treat him with ceremonious reserve before other people. "These are the *pleasures of virtue* that I propose to you," observes the Chevalier, in writing to his cousin. He persistently pursues a tone of pleasantry, and is occasionally even indelicate in discussing this equivocal position. A few light, malicious strokes of wit might be pardonable, but four letters overflowing with loose suggestions tend somewhat to exhaust our stock of indulgence. It has been aptly remarked that these Letters on the *clandestine marriage* are imbued with all the spirit of the Gallic *gaudriole* (obscene joke); but here the *gaudriole* is singularly devoid of anything like *verve.**

It were unjustly severe to dwell longer on the subject of his first works. Nevertheless, after reading these Letters, how well we can understand the epigrams of Racine, Boileau, and Jean-Baptiste Rousseau, written in relation to Fontenelle. We are bound to perceive the truth of the picture, in which La Bruyère has represented him in the flower of his youth.

"*Ascagne is a sculptor, Hegion a founder, Eschine a fuller, and Cydias (that is to say, Fontenelle) a bel-esprit; it is his profession. He has a sign, a workshop, bespoken work, and companions, who work under him. . . . No matter whether you require prose or verse, he is equally successful in the one as in the other. If you ask him to write letters of condolence, or letters on the occasion of an absence, he will undertake them without hesitation; if you require them ready-made, you have only to enter his shop and take your choice. He has a friend, whose only function on earth appears to have been that of extolling him for a long time to a certain set of friends into whose houses he has at last introduced him, as a man of rare and exquisite conversation; and there, similar to the vocalist who sings and the musician who plays his lute before those*

* In volume xx. p. 58, of the *Works of Frederick the Great* (1852), in the correspondence between Darget and the King, there exists a *gaudriole* in verse, written by Fontenelle at the age of ninety-five years.

to whom this performance has been promised, Cydias, after having coughed, raised his cuff, stretched out his hand, and opened his fingers, gravely gives utterance to his quintessential thoughts and sophisticated arguments."

Read the whole of this portrait, follow the conversation of *Cydias* — Fontenelle—whom La Bruyère so graphically depicts. Contemplate him as he appeared in society in the first flush of youth, with all the lustre of his natural ability, and already perfect as regards tact and tone. We see him exhibiting no undue haste to speak, waiting quietly till every one has uttered his word, then, with a half-smile, gracefully delivering his contradictions and his paradoxes, the which La Bruyère esteems impertinences. The latter fails to add that these impertinences might often have been truth in disguise, or at least a near approach to truth. La Bruyère's portrait of Fontenelle conveys to our mind a great lesson ; it shows us how an able painter, an astute critic, can sometimes be mistaken through telling the truth without mentioning everything, and by failing to remember that in our strange and complex human organism, the most strongly-marked faults and most ridiculous characteristics are never incompatible with some superior quality.

However, before pronouncing a verdict against La Bruyère, I would fain draw the attention of my readers to the first volume of the *Nouveaux Melanges,* by Mme. Necker, in which there exists the extract of a conversation of Mme. Geoffrin in reference to Fontenelle. Certainly nobody possessed a more thorough knowledge of the real Fontenelle than Mme. de Geoffrin, she who had spent her life with him, ultimately acting as his executrix. The principal peculiarities she accords to this exceptional character, are, in measure, exactly the same as

o

those we have seen engraved by La Bruyère. "He
never laughed," says Mme. Geoffrin. "One day I said
to him, 'Monsieur de Fontenelle, you have never
laughed.' 'No,' he replied, 'I have never emitted an
Ah ! ah! ah!' That is the idea he held in regard to
laughter : he merely smiled at anything witty ; but
he never experienced any strong feeling." Following
the tone of the subject, I will allow myself to add,
that if he had never emitted an *Ah! ah!* with far
greater reason had he never emitted an *Oh ! oh ! oh!*—
that is to say, he never admired anything. "He had
never wept," continues Mme. Geoffrin ; "he had never
been in a rage ; he had never run ; and, as he never
acted from motives of sentiment, he never received
impressions from other men. *He had never interrupted
any one ; he would listen to his interlocutor to the very
end, without losing anything ; he was never in a hurry
to speak ;* and if you had brought any accusation against
him, he would have listened the whole day to your
impeachments without uttering a single word." We
can hardly fail to perceive that this Fontenelle of
ninety years, and La Bruyère's Fontenelle of thirty,
the one painted by an enemy, the other by a friend,
are yet the very same man. I will not continue the
quotation of this striking description given on genuine
authority. In Mme. Geoffrin's portrayal, Fontenelle's
character is laid bare before us. His purely intellectual nature appeared to be deprived of the greater
portion of the feelings and impressions that have fallen
to the share of ordinary men, and from an early age
he governed his life on the principle that it is best to
avoid action as far as it lies in our power. "He who
wishes to be happy," he observed, "reduces and confines himself as much as possible. He has these **two**
characteristics : *he seldom changes his habitation, and*

does not care in particular for any habitation." Mme.
Geoffrin shows us Fontenelle according to his own
avowal : " When he took possession of any new quarters,
he let the things remain as he found them ; he would
never have thought of either removing or adding a
single nail." He remained unaffected by all that
pleases and amuses other men ; he neither cared for
beautiful music nor fine pictures. Everything, with
the exception of some new thought, a witty sally, or
epigram uttered in the course of conversation, failed to
interest him. In conversing, he always seemed to be
expecting another epigram in response to those he
uttered; no man has ever made wittier remarks than
he. His whole person seemed in harmony with the
tone of his mind. His very maladies bore the impress
of indolence and tranquillity : " He had the gout
without suffering any pain; his foot merely turned
into cotton; he would rest it on an arm-chair, and
that was all." Neither his body nor his soul had ever
felt a sting.

This portrait of Fontenelle by Mme. Geoffrin
might be appositely annexed to an excellent criticism
by Grimm ("Correspondence," February 1757), which,
severe as it may appear, is based on the precepts of
good taste. All these various estimates of Fontenelle
agree with each other, and in their entirety form a
harmonious whole. Even the religious historiographer,
the Abbé Trublet, confirms by his writings these
opinions, though he may in his own heart have believed
otherwise. The Abbé admits that his hero had never
loved *but once,* that his only kind of tenderness had
been the affection he fostered for his friend and companion in childhood, M. Brunel, who had been his
second self. Fontenelle was seen to shed tears of deep
sorrow at the death of his comrade. This loss occa-

sioned him the one grief of his long life, when his philosophy for the first and only time forsook him,—his friend's death humanized him for one day. This friendship had somehow found means of creeping into his heart from his tenderest childhood. Only this once were the counters of Wisdom found faulty.

La Bruyère's censorious sketch has led us far away, and we shall be compelled to retrace our footsteps, in order to extricate from its covering of insipidity and frivolity, Fontenelle's philosophic and more serious frame of mind. At an early age, Fontenelle displayed all the faults of a nature without an ideal and without passion ; but he had all the qualities compatible with these kind of purely intellectual organizations. He was a follower of the philosophy of Descartes, but no blind disciple, as he enjoyed the liberty of judging his master ; he believed there existed an intermediate *rôle* between that of the *savant* and that of the thorough man of the world ; that our intellect, which on the one hand serves us for the purpose of gleaning knowledge, might on the other be of use for the expression of this very knowledge. He therefore struck the golden mean, concluding it was quite feasible to combine his natural disposition for the exact sciences with his taste for an agreeable and elegant mode of expression. He solved this problem in his work entitled *Interviews on the Plurality of Worlds*, which, appearing in 1686, met with overwhelming success. In this singular book, which unites instruction with pleasure, he introduces the truths of Copernicus enveloped in a style *à la Scudery*. Despite this unclassical mode of treatment, truth gains the victory, and renders us oblivious to all defects. Let Boileau and La Bruyère ridicule as often as they please the finical Fontenelle, he nevertheless is more philosophical than they. In his *Interviews*,

Fontenelle, as we all know, pretends to be in the country, strolling after supper through the park in the company of a beautiful marquise. The conversation happens to turn on the subject of the stars ; the lady requesting a few explanations in astronomy, Fontenelle pretends that he wishes to discuss some other question. " No," he replied, " I will not allow myself to be reproached for having discoursed on philosophy in a wood at ten o'clock at night, with the most charming person I know. Seek your philosophers elsewhere." Nevertheless, he would have been vexed had he been taken at his word, for it is precisely in this admixture of philosophy, natural science, and gallantry, that he excels. In addressing his lovely marquise, he appeals to *the minds of all ignorant people*, at the same time taking a delight in picturing them under her coquettish form, and he thereby sustains a tone of elegant banter, which necessitates his putting into play all the subtleties of his plastic intellect. In thus concealing numerous truths under the cloak of frivolity, he failed to incur the wrath of the theologians of the period, who were still uninitiated in many things. Fontenelle frequently disguises truth in the garb of an amorous poem, thereby securing it a surer passport.

From the very first evening he endeavours to explain to the marquise the secret of the natural laws of evolution and compensation, and finds nothing easier than to compare the grand spectacle unfolded before his gaze, to the scenery of the opera. The philosopher who is in search of natural causes is similar to the *mechanic* seated in the pit of the Opera - house, who strives to discover the mainspring of certain scenic effects of *light and atmosphere*. With the help of this simple comparison, Fontenelle finds means to pass on to the principal physical systems that have alternately been suggested by the different philosophers. Nothing could be more keenly interesting. Nothing could be clearer. In following Fontenelle's provisionary illustrations, and his expositions in reference to the natural succession of errors that have been committed in the research of scientific truth, we begin to understand how easily men must, from the very first, have yielded to the belief in these erroneous theories. When he comes to the question whether it is the earth that is the centre round which the whole universe revolves, or whether, on the contrary, it is the earth that describes a revolution in the firmament, he draws those moral and tangible comparisons that enable the reader to grasp the pith of the argument :—" You must have noticed, if you please, that we are by nature all constructed like a certain Athenian madman of whom you have already heard. He believed all the ships that landed at the port of Piræus belonged to him. Our madness consists in believing that the whole of nature, without exception, is destined for our use ; and when our philosophers are asked the reason of the existence of such numberless fixed stars, of which a small quantity would suffice to perform the same function they all perform, they coolly reply that the stars serve to rejoice their sight." So as to avoid resembling this maniac of Piræus, we are already tempted to abandon the theory of Ptolemæus, and to embrace the doctrines of Copernicus. I can only convey a slight idea of Fontenelle's art of instilling science. He possesses this faculty to the highest degree. As regards astronomy and natural science, you have only to let him follow his own course, and, as it has been aptly remarked, he will *cajole you into truth.*

In what a different manner did Pascal study nature and the heavens ! We are unconsciously reminded of the glorious commencement of his *Thoughts:* "Let man contemplate Nature in its entirety, in its grand and lofty majesty. Let him cast from his sight the mean objects that surround him ; let him contemplate that dazzling light, placed like an eternal lamp to illuminate the universe ; let the earth appear to him as a mere speck as compared with the vast circle *that planet describes.* . . ." Instead of these noble and truly august expressions, Fontenelle, in referring to the celestial laws, purposely makes use of contracted similes. In speaking of the essential law of Nature,— Nature who performs all her operations at the least possible expense, and displays an extraordinary *economy* in her *great household,*—he will tell you it is only through these laws that we can *catch* the plan on which she has based her operations. Pascal felt, in trembling and in fear, the majesty and the infinity of Nature, while Fontenelle only appears to spy out her skill. This man is utterly devoid of the instinctive knowledge of celestial magnitude—that knowledge possessed by Pascal, Dante, Milton, and even Buffon. He is fully aware that he lacks this faculty ; he contracts the firmament in endeavouring to explain it. Yet, on one point, Fontenelle is even superior to Pascal himself ; for in his description of the vast spectacle, which he has so admirably gauged both in its moral and physical spirit, Pascal has, in one place, corrected his own phrase, contracted and altered his own words, in order to represent the sun as revolving round the earth, and not the earth as revolving round the sun. His great mind, fostering the remains of superstition, recoils before the truth of Copernicus, and lets himself remain in doubt. Incomparably inferior to Pascal in soul and imagination, Fontenelle, by right of his liberal, unprejudiced, accurate, and impartial mind, slowly gains the advantage, and at the close of that century of grandeur—a century of illusions and majestic reverence—he dares to perceive the reality, and express in pleasant words the natural truths such as they are. Therein lies his originality, therein lies his glory. In spite of his lightness and his amusing mannerisms, in spite of his affected familiarity of expression, which at times appears like a carping against the majesty of Nature, Fontenelle differs vastly from the frivolous writers who treat serious subjects without first seeking the truth itself. From the year 1686, he undoubtedly belonged to the family of strong, positive, and serious minds, whatever be the garb enveloping his thoughts. He was an enemy of ignorance, not an armed enemy, but one who was cool, patient, scornful in his gentleness, and, in his peculiar way, more irreconcilable than he himself believed. He is so given to believe that ignorance and stupidity are natural and universal, that nothing under these heads ever astonishes or irritates him. Nevertheless, he renders full justice to the progress of modern science, of which he was, in his way, an organ and an instrument. "In truth, I believe more and more," he observes, "that a certain kind of genius has never been away from Europe, or at least has never ventured very far beyond its limits." This European genius, which represents method, correctness, and analysis, and which, according to him, adapts itself to every kind of subject, owes, he believes, its discovery and its application to the illustrious Descartes ; but he also believes it could have been better applied than he (Descartes) ever applied it. According to M. Flourens, Fontenelle has, historically speaking, rendered the same service to Descartes as Voltaire has rendered to Newton. He has contributed to popularizing him, and his efforts have tended to the introduction of his works to the clubs and the salons. Fontenelle's book of the *Worlds,* offers, in a certain way, two different aspects. He appears to be writing under the influence of two perfectly dissimilar orders of mind. He has given us the first model of such works, a science adorned, embellished, and expounded in so lucid a manner that it can be easily comprehended by women ; he has bequeathed to us, so to speak, the prototype of those *hybrid* writings, such as have, on diverse subjects, proceeded from the pen of a Pougens and an Aimé-Martin—those rivals of Demoustier rather than of Fontenelle. But apart from this frivolous feature in Fontenelle's writings, we cannot fail to perceive in them the strong influence of utility and wisdom—an influence prelusive to that which the greatest minds have not since disdained to exercise. Employing a less agreeable and ornamental mode of treatment, though none the less bent upon adhering to a thorough clearness of exposition, Buffon, Cuvier, and even Humboldt himself in French, have not hesitated to write certain portions of their works for the perusal of the ignorant, and to publish them with a view to their being read by every class of reader. The first model of this style of lucid and agreeable illustration has been given by Fontenelle in his *Worlds* and elsewhere.

Even were we to criticise Fontenelle in the works he produced towards the age of thirty, at that period when La Bruyère both lashed him with all justice and misconstrued him with injustice, even then we should find him thoroughly formed as regards his ideas and his opinions. In his *History of the Oracles,* so highly appreciated by Bayle (1687), he wages war against the remains of that idea of the Middle Ages still anchored in many minds, which consisted in believing that the ancient heathen oracles were delivered by demons. He proves that this supernatural explanation is not at all necessary, and that before seeking the cause of an effect, we should first of all study the effect itself. "I am not so convinced of our ignorance," he observes, "through the things that exist, and the cause of which is unknown to us, but *through those that do not exist, and of which we find the cause.*" Then he relates the famous story of the golden tooth, which had grown, in the year 1593, in the mouth of a Silesian child. All the erudites commenced discussing this question of the golden tooth, and several tales were written in relation to it. "Nothing was lacking in such beautiful works," says Fontenelle, "except the fact of the tooth being really in gold. When a goldsmith tested it, he discovered it was merely a gold-leaf that had been applied to the tooth with considerable skill; but the erudites began by writing their books; only afterwards did they consult the goldsmith." In everything the operations of Fontenelle resemble those of this goldsmith; he endeavours to strip everything of its deceptive mantle.

In his *Digression on the Ancients and the Moderns* (1688), he is right on nearly every point excepting that of eloquence, and above all, on the question of poetry —poetry which, in fact, he utterly fails to be moved by, but whose spirit he believes he is animated by and possesses. Entirely denuded of the spirit of poetry and idealism, and that fertility of emotion which generally accompanies the poetical faculty, Fontenelle on every occasion speaks of poetry like his friend La Motte, that is to say, in the manner of a man who is colour-blind. He cannot imagine that in bygone days, at a certain period in the world's existence, under a particular climate, and under natural and social conditions that can never exist again, there could have lived a happy race, blooming in its fullest flower—a race that we modern people surpass in everything excepting in that early delicate development of mind, in that first Divine charm of poesy. Fontenelle is unable to fully appreciate ancient Greece ; he fails to realize it is pervaded by a spring-like, sacred breath. In all else he is at the fount of truth, and has an eye to the future. "Nature," he remarks, " holds in her hand a certain substance always of the same consistency, which she incessantly moulds and remoulds, creating from this substance men, animals, and plants." He concludes by observing, that as she has not broken her mould, there is no reason why she should not produce from the same form, illustrious modern men, as grand in their way as those of ancient times. The erudites were horrified at thus seeing a literary question reduced to a question of physics and natural history. Fontenelle grasps with his mind even those things he has never felt. We can hardly refrain from smiling, in seeing him arguing against the idolatrous admirers of the ancients, in favour of the powerful modern organizations, so perfectly dissimilar to his own ; he pleads for Molière, whom he knows, and for Shakespeare, whom he does not know. He calmly surmises the future occurrence of extraordinary events. "Some day we shall ourselves be considered as people of former times," he remarks, "and let us hope that, by virtue of the same superstition which we foster as regards the ancients, *we shall in our turn be admired to excess in centuries to come :* God only knows with what contempt the *beaux-esprits* of that future period will be treated in comparison to ourselves, though they may perhaps be *Americans.*" It is thus that Fontenelle, the man of the broadest mind, who heeds not time nor place, suggests the views and changes of the future, and amuses himself in thus coolly considering them. As he is purely indifferent to the feelings of others, he adheres to his own opinions not only in all good faith, but with a kind of audacity and deliberate wantonness. His marked tone of indifference appeared to the upholders of antiquity the height of insolence, and Boileau in his anger furiously denounced him. " It is a pity," he remarked one day in relation to La Motte, "that he should have become *contaminated* by that little Fontenelle ! "

Fontenelle was forty years of age when he was named permanent Secretary of the Academy of Sciences **(1697).** He had now published all the youthful productions of his pen, and during the sixty years of his secretaryship he continued to draw on the resources of his able mind in the writing of purer, more serious, and more powerful works. Henceforth his great mind held his *bel-esprit* in check. There are times when this second Fontenelle, so intellectual, so impartial, and so emotionless, appears to me like Goethe, but a Goethe contracted and somewhat less majestic. A French refugee from Berlin, of the name of Jordan, who visited Fontenelle in 1733, speaks of him in terms that give us a glimpse of him under his universally respected aspect : " M. de Fontenelle has a magnificent domicile ; he appears very well off, and to possess a rich share of the favours of Dame Fortune. Though he has already attained a considerable age, there is still great vivacity and penetration in the expression of his eye. We can see that Nature has taken a pleasure in shaping this man."

M. Flourens has delineated with great perspicuity this latter Fontenelle ; not only has he divested him of his peculiarities, but also of his pettiness. He has shown him on the threshold of the sanctuary, invested with the dignity of science, as its first exponent in the eyes of all men, withal devoid of solemnity, yet never lowering science except with a noble and decent familiarity. Fontenelle has worked up to perfection his succession of Eulogiums. They are ingenious, veridical, and concise. Everything that is obscure is therein elucidated, all technicalities are stated in general terms, while each *savant* is only appraised for the lasting and important services he has rendered at the shrine of scientific knowledge. M. Flourens has remarked that " *He praises by facts that depict character.*"

Fontenelle was the first man who, as permanent Secretary of the Academy of Sciences, ever wrote in French. His predecessor, Du Hamel, still wrote in Latin. Fontenelle was therefore the innovator of the elegant and worldly mode of expounding science. His work was divided into two sections ; he compiled the Extracts and wrote the analyses of the Academical works, and composed the Eulogiums of the members of the Academy. In the Extracts, he endeavours, before all else, to explain all he expounds. He bore in mind the principle that, in the teaching science, even the certainty of results should not allow the exponent to dispense with perspicuity, and that common reason has the right at any moment to intervene and require an explanation of the facts hidden from the uninitiated by technical methods. In the Eulogiums on the Academicians, he still retained his old ingenious and subtle manner of treatment ; but his love of accuracy induced him more and more to adopt a simplicity of style. The simplicity of Fontenelle possesses, as the reader may well imagine, a certain turn which prevents it resembling that of any other writer.

It has been justly remarked that his early writings were characterized by a kind of contradiction, or rather antithesis, between the tone, which was trivial and precise, and the substance of the thoughts, which was true and solid. This resulted in a disproportion and lack of harmony, that made his style appear like a continual epigram. At last, this affectation (for we can call it by no other name) became, by dint of his softening and curtailing it, his natural habit of thought. It has been said that, as a writer, Fontenelle *ambled* along where others ran, exerting all their strength and gravity. This easy pace is especially agreeable to women, and men of fastidious taste. His reasoning, too, is unaggressive, and adapted without weakness to the mundane mind. In the two prefaces of *The History of the Academy of Sciences* (the History of 1699, and that of 1666), his style has attained the height of perfection.

It is thus that his enlightened and healthy mind ended by triumphing over his own early unhealthy taste. Voltaire's behaviour may, in some way, have helped to correct Fontenelle's style. Grimm has aptly remarked, Voltaire had all the qualities of taste precisely opposed to the defects of Fontenelle—unaffectedness, sincerity, vivacity, frank and prompt repartee, and spontaneity. Fontenelle, in company with La Motte, was on the point of taking the sceptre under the Regency, and of giving the tone to the literature of the day, when Voltaire appeared, in the *nick of time*, to neutralize in the public mind the effect of this somewhat questionable influence, and, young as he was, he insensibly warned the ultra-refined Academician, by his example, that the time had come for him to court a greater simplicity. Fontenelle, physically worn out by old age, but as intellectual as ever, died on the 11th of January 1757, at the age of a hundred years minus a month. The century had already entered into the second and more tempestuous moiety of its course. But do you not admire the opposition of minds? The other day I spoke of Diderot. Fontenelle and Diderot—where could we find a more striking contrast? Fontenelle, who indicates better than any definition (as Fontanes has so ably remarked) the limits of intellect and genius, and Diderot, on the other hand, a kind of ebullient and extravasated genius, who could not restrict his powers within any confines ; the other, who opens discreetly the portals of the century, holding in his half-closed hand more truths than he allows to escape, and who seems to murmur *Hush* at every noise and every outbreak ; the other, who proclaims and preaches his doctrines in a loud voice, generously scattering the seeds to the wind while he apostrophizes the future ; Fontenelle, who yet clings to the theories of Descartes and to some of the correct minds of the preceding century ; and Diderot, who in the excess and vehemence of his speech seems already to appeal to the ardent generations, headed by Mirabeau and Danton. I bequeath to my readers the task of completing the parallel, which every added detail would render the more striking. As regards Fontenelle, my conclusion will be brief. He remains unequalled as regards his mental grasp, his longevity, his numberless aptitudes, and as regards his union of rare qualities with defects that ended by seasoning his very qualities. He is far beyond the pale of ordinary writers, and though not exactly a genius, he belongs to the order of infinitely distinguished minds. In the natural history of literature, he is entitled to be looked upon as a singular individual and unique of his kind.